AF601790

The Satisfaction Of Christ

The Satisfaction Of Christ

Arthur W. Pink

Sovereign Grace Publishers, Inc.
P.O. Box 4998
Lafayette, IN 47903

The Satisfaction Of Christ

ISBN 1-58960-190-4

Printed In the United States of America
By Lightning Source, Inc.

FOREWORD

The Death of Christ, the incarnate Son of God, is the most remarkable event in all history. It is a subject of never-failing interest to all who study prayerfully the Holy Scriptures. This is so, not only because the believer's all, both for time and eternity depends upon it, but also, because of its transcendent uniqueness.

The Atonement of Christ is the most important subject that can engage our minds. We do not believe a clearer, more lucid, helpful and scriptural setting forth of this glorious theme can be found anywhere. We are confident this work will prove a great benefit and blessing to every serious and careful reader.

The Publishers

CONTENTS

CHAPTER ONE

The Atonement — Introduction

The death of Christ, the incarnate Son of God, is the most remarkable event in all history. Its uniqueness was demonstrated in various ways. Centuries before it occurred it was foretold with an amazing fulness of detail, by those men whom God raised up in the midst of Israel to direct their thoughts and expectations to a fuller and more glorious revelation of Himself. The prophets of Jehovah described the promised Messiah, not only as a person of high dignity and as one who should perform wondrous and blessed miracles, but also as one who should be "despised and rejected of men," and whose labors and sorrows should be terminated by a death of shame and violence. In addition, they affirmed that He should die not only under human sentence of execution, but that "it pleased the Lord to bruise Him; HE hath put Him to grief" (Isa. 53:10), yea, that Jehovah should cry, "Awake, O sword, against My Shepherd, and against the man that is My Fellow, saith the Lord of hosts: smite the Shepherd" (Zech. 13:7).

The supernatural phenomena which attended Christ's death clearly distinguishes it from all other deaths. The obscuration of the sun at midday without any natural cause, the earthquake which clove asunder the rocks and laid open the graves, and the rending of the veil of the temple from top to bottom, proclaimed that He who was hanging on the Cross was no ordinary sufferer.

So too that which followed the death of Christ is equally noteworthy. Three days after His body had been placed in Joseph's tomb and the sepulchre securely sealed, He, by His own power (John 2:19; 10:18), burst asunder the bonds of death and rose in triumph from the grave, and is now alive forevermore; holding the keys of death and hades in His hands. Forty days later, after having appeared again and again, in tangible form before His friends, He ascended to heaven from the midst of His disciples. Ten days after, He poured out the Holy Spirit, by whom they were enabled to publish to men out of every nation in their respective languages, the wonders of His death and resurrection.

As another has said, "The effect was not less surprising than the means employed to accomplish it. The attention of Jews and Gentiles was excited; multitudes were prevailed upon to acknowledge Him as the Son of God, and the Messiah; and a church was formed, which, notwithstanding powerful opposition and cruel persecution, subsists at the present hour. The death of Christ was the great subject on which the apostles were commanded to preach, although it was known beforehand that it would be offensive to all classes of men; and they actually made it the chosen theme of their discourses. 'I determined,' Paul said, 'not to know anything among you, save Jesus Christ and Him crucified' (I Cor. 2:2) . . . In the New Testament, His death is represented as an event of the greatest importance, as a fact on which Christianity rests, as the only ground of hope to the guilty, as the only source of peace and consolation, as, of all motives, the most powerful to excite us to mortify sin and devote ourselves to the service of God" (Dr. John Dick).

Not only was the death and resurrection of Christ the central theme of apostolic preaching and the principal subject of their writings, but it is remembered and celebrated in heaven: the theme of the songs of the redeemed in glory is the person and blood of the Saviour: "Saying with a loud voice, Worthy is the Lamb that was slain to receive power, and riches, and wisdom, and strength, and honour, and glory, and blessing" (Rev. 5:12). "The Atonement made by the Son of God, is the beginning of the ransomed sinner's hope, and will be the theme of his exultation, when he shall cast his crown before the throne, singing the song of Moses and of the Lamb" (James Haldane).

Now it is evident from all these facts that there is something peculiar in the death of Christ, something which unmistakably separates it from all other deaths, and therefore renders it worthy of our most diligent, prayerful and reverent attention and study. It behooves us by all that is serious, solemn and salutary, to have just and right conceptions of it; by which is meant not merely that we should know when it happened, and with what circumstances it was attended, but that we should most earnestly endeavor to ascertain what was the Saviour's *design* in submitting to die upon the Cross, why it was that Jehovah smote Him, and exactly what has been accomplished thereby.

But as we attempt to approach a subject so important, so wonderful, yet so unspeakably solemn, let us remember that it calls for a heart filled with awe, as well as a sense of our utter unworthiness. To touch the very fringe of the holy things of God ought to inspire reverential fear, but to take up the innermost secrets of His covenant, to contemplate the eternal counsels of the blessed Trinity, to endeavor to enter into the meaning of that unique transaction at Calvary, which was veiled with darkness, calls for a special degree of grace, fear and humility, of heavenly teaching and the humble boldness of faith. Our prayerful hope is that He who is pleased to use ciphers (I Cor. 1:28) to promote His glory, may condescend to grant us now a special measure of the guidance of the Holy Spirit, and deign to bless this book to not a few of those whom God has loved with an everlasting love.

What has Christ done in order to secure the salvation of sinners? What is the import of that death of His on which salvation hinges? In the outset we may be fairly warned of what must be the consequences of submitting the question to human reason or of bringing the world's wisdom into the inquiry. "The preaching of the Cross is to them that perish *foolishness,* but unto us which are saved it is the power of God" (I Cor. 1:18). To which the apostle added, "But we preach Christ crucified, unto the Jews a stumblingblock, and unto the Greeks foolishness; but unto them which are called, both Jews and Greeks, Christ the power of God, and the wisdom of God." In view of these statements, it was an easy matter for bygone generations of the saints to anticipate what would be the inevitable result when the wisdom of the world, which was fully arrayed against the Gospel which Paul preached, should be constituted its interpreter, or should presume to accommodate it to worldly principles.

Sixty years ago Mr. James Inglis, writing in "The Waymarks of the Wilderness" on "The Atonement," said, "There is one question which underlies all theological controversy: and as we approach the crisis, it is coming more and more to the surface. The question in it all really is: whether God or man is to be the supreme; whether the glory of God or the supposed interest of man is the center around which all is to revolve; whether the will of God is to be supreme and unquestioned, or whether every expression of it is to be brought to the bar of human reason; and whether everything in theology, as in morals, is to be judged by its reasonableness and its apparent usefulness to man. Those who claim to be the most advanced theologians and moralists, exalt human nature to the place of the sovereign arbitrator of truth and right, and seek to apply their favorite maxim regarding earthly governments to the Divine government also: that it exists only for the sake — as yet they would scarcely have the hardihood to say by the *consent* — of the governed.

"This fundamental question of Divine or human supremacy underlies the views men adopt of the inspiration and authority of Scripture. On one side the question is simply, What is written? On the other side a right is claimed to decide what ought to be written — the very presumption which Satan taught our first parents regarding what God had said. When this claimed right is exercised, little of revelation is left unmodified. One of the first points on which proud reason comes into conflict with what is written, is the naturel condition of man. Nor need we be surprised if it should revolt against the Divine estimate of fallen man, and against the sentence under which he lies as by nature a child of wrath, dead in trespasses and sins, vile, polluted, helpless and hopeless in himself. It is only the Spirit of God that can convince a man of sin in the Scriptural sense; and so long as the appeal is to human reason, the Scriptural view of man's condition must be rejected. Though it cannot be denied that the facts in the case, whether in the history of an individual or of mankind, most painfully corroborate the Scriptural view, and though the most humbling descriptions of human depravity in the Word of God seem to be only history condensed, there is a wonderful facility in offsetting these sad realities by an ideal excellence, and in covering them up by glowing delineations of the possibilities of human progress. The power of self-deception and self-flattery in the human heart is amazing. The admirable sentiments which are elegantly expressed in the writings of men whose lives were very far from exemplifying them, serve to cover up the deep and general depravity of the age in which they lived. Their modern admirers estimate themselves rather by their admiration of these virtuous sentiments, than by what they know themselves to be in life and character. Never is this power of self-deception and self-flattery more signally illustrated than when it comes into the sphere of Christianity, substituting the Sermon on the Mount for the discourses of heathen moralists, and reckoning all the graces of the renewed man, if not the living perfections of the Word made flesh, among the possibilities of human cultivation. That man is fallen, may not be denied; but we are taught that the evil is incidental, not inherent, and may be traced to physical degeneracy, the influence of a disordered world, of bad example, and defective education. While undeveloped and dormant in the soul, there is inherent nobility, the germ of all excellence, which only needs to be aroused and cherished, until it expands into a perfection which renders it meet for inheritance of the saints in light.

"Such views of the natural condition of man lead to a corresponding modification of the Scriptural doctrine of *regeneration,* which, according to our liberal theologians, is but the awakening of the dormant excellence of man, giving a new turn to misdirected affections and powers, and is the first step in the development of his inherent nobility. The testimony of Scripture as to the utter ruin of man, and the necessity of being born again, in the singularly emphatic terms used with reference to the one as well as the other, might seem to present an insuperable objection to the self-exalting scheme; but an evasion of the objection has already been provided for in a theory of inspiration which permits everything in the Scriptures which is irreconcilable with their theology, to be explained away as the exaggeration of enthusiasts or the daring imagery of Eastern poets.

"In such a system of doctrine the mission of Christ can have no place, except as it provides for this moral development, or aids it. For, first of all, in the daring exaltation of man, the revealed character of God is tampered with; His perfections are rendered tributary to the supposed interest of His creatures; His righteousness, holiness and truth are resolved into benevolence; so that there are no claims of justice to be satisfied, no holiness and truth to be vindicated, and sin is only to be taken cognizance of in so far as it may interfere with the well-being of the creature. The humiliation, suffering and death of the Son of God furnished but an impressive spectacle, by which the evil effects of an unconditional pardon of sin might be averted, and by which the heart of the sinner might be melted and conciliated. The life and death of Christ, in short, are the moral influences by which the dormant excellence of the soul is aroused, love to God and man engendered, and by which the wanderer is to be won into the path of virtue. The 'influence' of the Holy Spirit, rather than His *personal agency,* now comes in to give effect to the truth and to aid the moral development, just as in the natural world the influence of the sun's rays change the desolation of winter into the verdure of spring."

When we remember that the Atonement is the most important subject which can engage the minds of either men or angels: that it not only secures the eternal happiness of all God's elect, but also gives to the universe the fullest view of the perfections of the Creator: that in it are hid all the treasures of wisdom and knowledge, while by it are revealed the unsearchable riches of Christ: that through the very Church which has been purchased thereby is being made known to principalities and powers in the heavenlies the manifold wisdom of God (Eph. 3:10)—then of what supreme moment must it be to understand it aright! But how is fallen man to apprehend these truths to which his depraved heart is so much opposed? All the force of intellect is less than nothing when it attempts, in its own strength, to comprehend the deep things of God. Since a man can receive *nothing* except it be given him from heaven (John 3:27), much more is a special enlightenment by the Holy Spirit needed if he is to enter at all into this highest mystery.

"Great is the mystery of godliness" (I Tim. 3:16). Amazing beyond all finite conception is that transaction which was consummated at Golgotha. There we behold the Prince of Life dying. There we gaze upon the Lord of Glory made a spectacle of unutterable shame. There we see the Holy One of God made sin for His people. There we witness the Author of all blessing made a curse for worms of the earth. It is the mystery of mysteries that He who is none other than Immanuel, should stoop so low as to join together the infinite majesty of Deity with the lowest degree of abasement that was possible to descend into. He could not have gone lower and be God. Well did the Puritan Sibbes say, "God, to show His love to us, showed Himself God in this: that He could be God and go so low as to die" (Vol. 5, p. 327).

To what source then can we appeal for light, for understanding, for an explanation and interpretation of the Cross? Human reasoning is futile, speculation is profane, the opinions of men are worthless. Thus, we are absolutely shut up to what God has been pleased to make known to us in His Word. If it be true that we can know nothing about the origin of the old creation save what the Holy Scriptures reveal — the wild and conflicting guesses of science "falsely so called" (I Tim. 6:20) only serving to make this the more evident — then much more are we entirely dependent upon the teaching of Holy Writ concerning the foundation on which the new creation rests. In his splendid work on "The Atonement" (1867) Dr. A. A. Hodge rightly affirmed, "I insist that, as the Gospel is wholly a matter of Divine revelation, the answer to the question, What did Christ do on earth in order to reconcile us to God? be sought *exclusively* in a full and fair induction from *all* the Scriptures that teach upon the subject. From a survey of all the matter revealed on the subject, what, in the judgment of a mind unprejudiced by theories, did the sacred writers intend us to believe? The result of such an examination, unmodified by philosophy or secular analogies, is alone, we insist, the true redemptive work of Christ."

Well did this deeply-taught servant of God say, "unmodified by secular analogies." The truth of God has been grossly perverted, the honor of Christ grievously sullied, and the people of God (who were too lazy to diligently study the Scriptures for themselves) have often been misled by the superficial efforts of irreverent preachers, who sought "Illustrations" from the imaginary analogies in human relations. For example: the case of a criminal is cited, in whose character there is no redeeming trait, who is condemned to death for his aggravated crimes. When he stands upon the scaffold, the Queen of England is supposed to send her son and heir to die in the villain's stead, that he may again be turned loose upon society. Yet this monstrous and revolting supposition was offered last century as an illustration of John 3:16 in the discourse of a popular preacher of wide reputation.

"The plan of redemption, the office of our Surety, and the satisfaction which He rendered to the claims of justice against us, have no parallel in the relations of men to one another. We are carried above the sphere of the highest relations of created beings into the august counsels of the eternal and independent God. Shall we bring our own line to measure them? We are in the presence of Father, Son and Holy Spirit; one in perfection, will and purpose. If the righteousness of the Father demands a sacrifice, the love of the Father provides it. But the love of the Son runs parallel with that of the Father; and not only in the general undertaking, but in every act of it, we see the Son's full and free consent. In the whole work we see the love of the Father as clearly displayed as the love of the Son: and again, we see the Son's love of righteousness and hatred of iniquity as clearly displayed as the Father's, in that work of which it were impossible to tell whether the manifestation of love or righteousness is most amazing. In setting out upon the undertaking we hear the Son say with loving delight, 'Lo, I come to do Thy will'; as He contemplates its conclusion, we hear Him say, 'Therefore doth My Father love Me, because I lay down My life, that I might take it again.' They are one in the glorious manifestation of common perfections, and in the joy of all the blessed results. The Son is glorified by all that is for the glory of the Father. And while, in the consummation of this plan, the wisdom of God — Father, Son and Holy Spirit — shall be displayed, as it could not otherwise have been, to the principalities and powers in heavenly places, ruined man will, in Christ, be exalted to heights of glory and bliss otherwise unattainable."

But while no parallel to the great transaction of the Atonement, or to the relations of the Father, Son and Holy Spirit as to its accomplishment, can be found in any of the relations of mere creatures to one another, God has graciously adopted a series of types, historical and ceremonial, to the illumination of His great plan, and especially to the illustration of the various aspects of the offices and work of Christ. In these, Divine wisdom is signally displayed. By means of the typical system God was educating men for the "good things to come," and preparing human language to be a fitting medium for the revelation of His grace in Christ. By introducing the Levitical system God has shown us the sense in which such words (in the New Testament) as sacrifice, priesthood, propitiation and redemption, are to be understood. We cannot here give an exposition of these types, our purpose in referring to them here simply being to call attention to the fact that *they* supply the needed key to unlock this New Testament mystery.

That which is outstandingly prominent in the typical sacrifices of the Old Testament is, first, that they were offered to God, having Him for their object and end, instead of being pageants for making impressions on men. Second, that they are expiatory, atoning for sin, blotting out iniquities. Third, that just as the sins of the offerer were imputed to the victim, so the excellency of the victim was ascribed to the offerer. Fourth, that something more was effected by these offerings than an atonement being made for sins — a *satisfaction* was offered to God's holiness and justice. This leads us to call attention to the title for this book, and here we cannot do better than give below a digest from Dr. Hodge's able comments on this point: —

During the latter part of the nineteenth century the word "Atonement" became commonly employed to express that which Christ wrought for the salvation of His people. But before then, the term used since the days of Anselm (1274), and habitually employed by all the Reformers, was "Satisfaction." The older term is much to be preferred, first, because the word "Atonement" is *ambiguous*. In the Old Testament it is used for an Hebrew word which signifies "to cover by making expiation." In the New Testament it occurs but once, Romans 5:11, and there it is given as the rendering for a Greek word meaning "reconciliation." But reconciliation is the *effect* of the sin-expiating and God-propitiating work of Christ. On the other hand, the word "Satisfaction" is not ambiguous. It always signifies that complete work which Christ did in order to secure the salvation of His people, as that work stands related to the will and nature of God.

Again: the word "Atonement" is *too limited* in its signification for the purpose assigned to it. It does not express *all* that Scripture declares Christ did in order to meet the complete demands of God's law. It properly signifies the expiation of sin, and nothing more. It points to that which Christ rendered to the justice of God, in vicariously bearing the *penalty* due the sins of His people; but it does not include that vicarious *obedience* which Christ rendered to the precepts of the law, which obedience is imputed to all of the elect. On the other hand, the term "Satisfaction" naturally includes both of these. "As the demands of the law upon sinful men are both preceptive and penal—the condition of life being 'do this and live,' while the penalty denounced upon disobedience is, 'the soul that sinneth it shall die'—it follows that any work which shall fully satisfy the demands of the Divine law in behalf of men must include (1) that *obedience* which the law demands as the condition of life, and (2) that *suffering* which it demands as the penalty of sin."

May the Lord graciously fit both writer and reader to contemplate and apprehend this wondrous theme in such a way that much fruit may issue to His glory and praise.

CHAPTER TWO

The Atonement — Its Source

"In approaching this solemn and sacred mystery we should do so with awe and reverence, remembering it is rather a subject of faith and adoration than of reasoning and arguing; a sanctuary open indeed to the meek and sorrowful, to the earnest and contrite, but always to be approached with solemnity and godly fear" (A. Saphir). It is written, "The meek will he guide in judgment; and the meek will he teach his way" (Psa. 25:9). The "meek" are they who have no confidence in the flesh, who lean not unto their own understanding, whose dependence is in and upon God alone.

The source of the Atonement or Satisfaction of Christ is *God.* This of necessity, for only God can produce that which satisfies Himself. Men can no more provide that which will meet the requirements of God's holiness and justice against their sins than they can create a universe: "None of them can by any means redeem his brother, nor give a ransom for him" (Psa. 49:7). A perfect law can only be kept by a perfect creature. One who has been rendered impotent by sin is "without strength" (Rom. 5:6) to do anything that is good; therefore deliverance must come from without himself: "For what the law could not do, in that it was weak through the flesh, God sending His own Son in the likeness of sinful flesh, and for sin, condemned sin in the flesh: that the righteousness of the law might be fulfilled in us" (Rom. 8:3, 4).

"In the beginning, God" (Gen. 1:1). Such words at the commencement of Holy Writ are worthy of their Divine Author. God is both the Alpha and Omega. He is the Beginning and the End of everything, for "of him, and through him, and to him, are all things" (Rom. 11:36). Nothing can exist apart from God. In creation, in providence, and in redemption, God is the Beginning. But for God, not a creature would have had being. But for God, not a creature could continue for a moment, for "in Him we live, and move, and have our being." But for God's direct permission, sin could not have entered the world; and but for His will in determining, His grace in providing, His power in securing, His Spirit in applying, there had been no satisfaction made for the failed responsibilities of His people.

Yes, God and God alone is the Source of the great and glorious Atonement. His will was the determining factor, His love the motive-spring, His righteousness the incentive, His manifested glory the end. In humbly attempting to amplify the several members of the preceding sentence, we earnestly cry with one of old, "That which I see not teach thou me" (Job 34:32). May it please the God of all grace to prepare the hearts of both writer and reader to contemplate the supernal glories of the Divine character.

1. The Will of God

Of necessity this must be the starting-point when considering the ultimate source of anything, for God "worketh all things after the counsel of his own *will*" (Eph. 1:11). It is nowhere said that He worketh all things according to "the requirements of His holiness," though God does not and cannot do that which is unholy. There is no conflict between the Divine will and the Divine nature, yet it needs to be insisted upon that God is a law unto Himself. God does what He does, not simply because righteousness requires Him so to act, but what God does *is* righteous simply because *He* does it. All the Divine works issue from mere sovereignty.

"Creation could be nothing else but a sovereign act. To deny sovereignty here, would be to deny sovereignty altogether: for, if the created universe came into being, and is what it is, as a necessary consequence of a 'First Cause,' that first cause could not be a person, could not be endowed with freedom of will, could not be God. Besides, if the existence of this first cause necessitated the existence of the universe, it must have done so from all eternity. There could have been no beginning of the created universe.

"Redemption, as well as creation, must also be a purely sovereign determination of the Divine will. This is required by the necessities of the case, as well as plainly declared in Scripture. No doctrine of Redemption that in any way casts the slightest shadow over the high mountain of Divine Sovereignty can be tolerated for a moment. All theologies that in any manner teach or imply that there was any obligation upon God to do this or that for fallen, rebellious subjects of law, are unscriptural, unreasonable, if not blasphemous. Divine sovereignty is to be recognized as determined to save any fallen ones, in determining who should be saved, in 'choosing,' raising up,' and 'delivering up' the Saviour, and in the Saviour's giving of Himself; but this Sovereign Redemption once determined, was wrought out under law, and in exact accordance with law" (Dr. J. Armour, "Atonement and Law," 1917).

What follows may be deemed to savor of metaphysics, yet do we feel it to be called for in view of modern slanderers of God. Even some who are regarded as quite orthodox have drawn a broad distinction, almost a gulf, between the nature of God and the will of God, failing to perceive that God's will is an *essential part of His nature.* Some have descended so low as to affirm there is in the very nature of things a standard of right which exists independently and apart from God, according to which He Himself acts, must act. Such a conception is not only degrading, but blasphemous. Others who have not adopted this insulting figment, have, nevertheless, been injuriously infected by it, and suppose that God's nature, as quite distinct from His will, is what determines His actions.

There is nothing determined by the nature of God which is not determined by the will of God. "When we affirm that God is holy, we do not mean that He makes right right, by simply willing it, but that He wills it because it is right. There must be, therefore, some absolute standard of righteousness"— is how a so-called Bible teacher has recently expressed himself. Even if it be said that the "absolute standard of righteousness" is the Divine nature, if by this be meant God's nature as separate from His determining will, the expression is, to say the least, faulty and misleading. The will of God is an essential part *of* His nature, and therefore His *will* is "the absolute standard of right." The will of God is not something related, dependent and determined; but is sovereign, imperial, regnant.

God Himself is the ultimate and absolute standard of righteousness. *Man* is commanded to recognize a standard of righteousness outside of and above himself, and his will and conduct must conform thereto. That standard of righteousness is the revealed will of God. But shall we reason from this that *God* also recognizes a standard of righteousness to which His will must be conformed, a standard which makes right right, and right being made right, He wills it *because* it is right? No, indeed. The truth is, that we best discover what the nature of God requires Him to do, by noting what He, by His will, *actually does*. When God says, "I will have mercy on whom I will have mercy" (Rom. 9:15), He assuredly sets before us His will, in its utmost freedom and sovereignty. But this supreme act of sovereign grace is the act of God Himself, an act into which the whole nature of God (His will being included in that nature) moved Him.

We fail to trace anything to its original source unless we track it right back to the sovereign will of God. This is true alike of creation, of providence, and of redemption. God was not obliged to have created this world; He did so simply because it so pleased Him (Rev. 4:10). Having created it, when Adam fell, He could have well left the whole race to perish in its sins, and *would* have done so, unless His sovereign will had, previously, determined otherwise. *Justice* did not require Him to intervene in mercy, for as the righteous Governor of the world, He might have proceeded to uphold the authority of His law by exacting its penalty upon all the disobedient, and thus have given to the unfallen angels a further example of His awful vengeance. Nor did His *goodness* require that He should rescue any of His rebellious subjects from the misery which they had brought upon themselves, for He had already given a complete display of *that* in creation. Nor did His *love,* abstractly considered, demand that a Saviour should be provided; had that been the case one must also have been given to the angels which fell.

It needs to be pointed out that the manifestative glory of

God does not depend upon the display of any particular attribute, but rather upon the exhibition of them all, in full harmony, and on proper occasions. He is glorified when He bestows blessings upon the righteous, and is equally glorified when He inflicts punishment on the wicked. God's manifestative glory consists in the *revelation* of His character to His creatures; yet this is purely *optional* on His part: it is quite voluntary, and contributes nothing to His happiness, and might have been withheld had He so pleased. Yet, as God always acts consistently with Himself, if He shows Himself at all to His creatures, the discovery will ever correspond to the greatness and excellency of His nature.

That the atoning death of Christ *had* its source in the will of God, is plainly declared in Acts 2:23, "Him being delivered by the determinate counsel and foreknowledge of God." Though accomplished in the fulness of time, it was resolved upon before time, decreed and enacted in heaven by the Eternal Three. Therefore do we read in Revelation 13:8 of "The Lamb slain from the foundation [or "founding"] of the earth." Christ was "the Lamb slain" *determinately,* in the counsel and decree of God (Acts 2:23); *promissorily,* in the word of God passed to Adam after the fall (Gen. 3:15); *typically,* in the sacrifices appointed immediately after the promise of redemption (Gen. 3:21; 4:4); *efficaciously,* in regard of the merit of it, applied by God to believers before the actual sufferings of Christ (Rom. 3:25; Heb. 9:15).

"He [God] made him [Christ, the Mediator] to be sin for us" (II Cor. 5:21): "made" or "constituted" by a Divine statute (i.e., He was ordained to enter the place of the penal condition of sinners). Had not God appointed it, the death of Christ had had no meritorious value. Once more in Hebrews 10 the efficacy of Christ's sacrifice unto the elect is traced back and directly ascribed to the eternal and sovereign will of God. In verse 7, we find Christ Himself saying, as He was about to become incarnate and enter this world, "Lo, I come to do *thy will,* O God"; while in verse 10 we are told, "*by* the *which will* we are sanctified [consecrated to God] through the offering of the body of Jesus Christ once for all." That which saves, or sanctifies, us is not simply the offering of Christ — for that had availed us nought if it had not been Divinely appointed—but the "will" and decree of the Eternal Three concerning that offering.

2. THE LOVE OF GOD

Love was, or better is, the motive-spring of all God's goodness and grace toward His people. He has for them an "everlasting love" (Jer. 31:3). It was "in love" that He "predestinated us unto the adoption of children by Jesus Christ to Himself" (Eph. 1:5). Proof of this is, that, from all eternity He, "accepted us in [not "in Christ," but] the Beloved" (Eph. 1:6)—note carefully that this declaration is given *before* reference is made to the forgiveness of our sins in verse 7. Had it so pleased God, He could have prevented the entrance of sin into this world, He could have restricted the progeny of Adam to the persons of His elect, and He could have taken them to heaven without their having been polluted by sin and redeemed from it, there to enjoy eternal bliss forever. *That* would have been an astonishing demonstration of His love for us. Yet it pleased God to grant unto His people still further, fuller, deeper, higher, manifestations of His love to and for them.

God loved His people in ordaining them to eternal life (Acts 13:48; Rom. 9:11-13), but He gave yet grander proof by suffering them to fall into a state of spiritual death, and then sending His own dear Son to redeem them out of it. Three hundred years ago Dr. Thomas Goodwin, in his incomparable exposition of Ephesians 1, pointed out that, "Had we at first been brought to that communion with Christ which we shall have in heaven after the day of judgment, without having known either sin or misery, it had been a good and blessed condition indeed; we should have infinitely rejoiced in it, and had reason to so have done. But certainly heaven will be sweeter to us by reason of our having once fallen into sin and misery, and then having a Redeemer that came and freed us from all, and then brought us to heaven. Oh, how sweet will this make heaven to be unto you! . . .

"I would have you observe this that it may mightily and wonderfully instance the love of God toward us. The last words of Ephesians 1:6 are that God hath accepted us in His

Beloved, while the first of verse 7 are 'In whom we have redemption through his blood.' What! Was He God's Beloved, and have you redemption in Him too? Shall God sacrifice His Beloved! God chose us to be holy in heaven with Himself (v. 4), to be sons with Him there (v. 5), to delight in us there (v. 6)! Let that purpose stand: let them never come to be sinful, let Me have them up in heaven presently with My Son. One would have thought God might have said this. No, God would *commend* His love yet further. He would let them fall into sin; to redeem them, He would sacrifice this Beloved. He had so much love in His heart that He could commend it to us no way but by sacrificing His Beloved. How wondrously has He displayed His love!"

That love *was* the motive-spring which caused God to provide for His people an atoning sacrifice for their sins, is clear from the well-known words of John 3:16, "For God so loved the world that he gave his only begotten Son." So too in I John 4:9, 10, "In this was manifested the love of God toward us, because that God sent his only begotten Son into the world, that we might live through him. Herein is love, not that we loved God, but that he loved us, and sent his Son to be the propitiation for our sins." Thus the sacred oracles celebrate the work of redemption as the highest and most remarkable instance and exhibition of Divine love, and direct us to behold it acted out in the highest degree and to the utmost advantage, to be seen and admired by all the elect as an exhaustless and endless source of gratitude and praise. The more unworthy and ill-deserving the objects of that love were in themselves — sinners, enemies (Rom. 5:7-10) — the more amazing that love. The greater the deliverance effected by it, and the costlier the sacrifice to procure that deliverance, the more is such love crowned. The greater the difficulties to be overcome — sin, death, the grave — the more was that love magnified. The greater the blessings bestowed — justification, sanctification, glorification — the more is that love to be adored.

"Herein was the *emphasis* of Divine love to us, that 'He sent His Son to be the propitiation for our sins' (I John 4:10). It was love that He would restore men after the Fall; there was no more necessity of doing this than of creating the world.

As it added nothing to the happiness of God, so the want of it had detracted nothing from it. There was no more absolute necessity of setting up man again after his breaking with God, than a new repair of the world after the destructive deluge. But that He might wind up His love to the highest pitch, He would not only restore man, but rather than let him lie in his deserved misery, would punish His own bowels to secure man from it. It was purely His grace [which is *love* bestowing *favours* on the hell-deserving—A. W. P.] which was the cause that His Son 'tasted death for every' son, Heb. 2:9" (S. Charnock, 1635).

3. THE RIGHTEOUSNESS OF GOD

The Atonement of Christ directs our thoughts toward God as One whose governmental holiness demanded satisfaction, whose inflexible justice insisted that its claim be fully met, and whose righteous law must be magnified and made honorable, before any resultant blessings could flow to His elect, considered as the guilty and depraved children of Adam. God can "by no means clear the guilty" (Ex. 34:7). Unlike so much that passes for it in the human realm, the love of God is not lawless; it is not exercised in defiance of righteousness. God is "light" (I John 1:5), as well as love; and because He is such, sin cannot be ignored, its heinousness minimized, nor its guilt cancelled. True it is that, where sin abounded, grace did much more abound. Yet grace did not abound at the expense of righteousness, rather does "grace reign *through* righteousness" (Rom. 5:21).

But could not God remit the sins of His people *without* an atoning satisfaction? This question is explicitly and authoritatively answered for us in Hebrews 9:22, "Without shedding of blood is *no* remission." Commenting on this in his remarkable book "The Atonement" (1871), the late Hugh Martin said, "No doubt, at first sight, this seems merely to allege a fact, without assigning a reason. It seems to intimate nothing more than the historical truth, that in point of fact God never has remitted the sins of men without shedding of blood. But if emphasis is placed on the word *remission,* and if a true idea is entertained of the transaction which that word represents, the proposition, 'without shedding of blood is no remission,' will be found not merely to allege the fact, but also assign a reason for that fact — to embody not only the historical verity, but the underlying principle which justifies it, and which only needs to be carefully investigated and apprehended to furnish a satisfactory answer to the question, Why should not God remit the sins of men without an Atonement?

"For, when the inspired writer affirms that without shedding of blood is no remission, it is as if he had said: You may imagine a forgiveness without shedding of blood, if you will; you may conjecture, or conjure up, some other scheme or principle of pardon; you may conceive of God as dealing with the sinner, and delivering him from the punishment due to his iniquities, without these iniquities being expiated, without the penalty incurred by them being exacted, without the law of which they are transgressors being relieved from the stain of dishonor which they had cast upon it, without any costly sacrifice, any solemn propitiation, any priceless ransom. But whatever this transaction might be, it would not be *remission.* Granting that it were quite possible for God to let the sinner off; to wipe out, by a mere arbitrary decree, and without any satisfaction to divine justice, the debt which the sinner had contracted; to cease from His anger toward His enemies and return to a state of friendship; to say, Your sins be forgiven you, you have nothing now to fear; all this, 'without shedding of blood,' without any sacrifice, or atonement, or expiation: still all this, whatever it might amount to, does not amount to *remission.* Call it what you please: be it what it may; it is not remission. It may be held up as an equivalent for it; it may be in room and lieu of it; it may be all that multitudes care to inquire after, or have ever felt the need of, or troubled themselves to seek. But, however possible it might be on God's part, however satisfactory it might be on their part, it is not *remission.* It may look like it. It may seem to carry with it all that the unenlightened have any thought of when thinking of remission; but real remission it is not. Without shedding of blood it is not remission.

"What the enlightened conscience of an anxious inquirer longs for *is* 'remission' — remission of sin. And what is that?

It is removal of guilt; removal of liability to the wrath of God; removal of criminality or ill-desert. It is a sentence of 'Not Guilty.' It is a recognition of blamelessness before the Holy One of Israel; a position and relation toward God, therefore, in which His wrath would be undue, unrighteous, impossible. That would be Remission."

We must not anticipate the ground which we hope to cover in later chapters, except to say here that, the great problem which confronted God, and which we make so bold as to say could never have been solved by either human or angelic intelligence, was, How mercy might act freely without justice being insulted, or how justice might exact its full due without mercy's hands being tied. A marvelous, perfect and completely satisfactory solution to this problem has been found and furnished in the Satisfaction made to God by the mediatorial Redeemer. It is in this satisfaction that "Mercy and truth are met together; righteousness and peace have kissed each other" (Psa. 85:10). It is this satisfaction which has enabled God to be "just, *and* the Justifier of him which believeth in Jesus" (Rom. 3:26).

4. THE GLORY OF GOD

Rightly has it been said that "The ultimate reason and motive of all God's actions are within Himself. Since God is infinite, eternal and unchanging, that which was His first motive in creating the universe must ever continue to be the ultimate motive or chief end in every act concerned in its preservation and government. But God's first motive must have been just the *exercise* of His own essential perfections, and in their exercise the *manifestation* of their excellence. This was the *only* end which could have been chosen by the Divine mind in the beginning, before the existence of any other object" (*The Atonement,* Dr. A. A. Hodge). The Scriptures are very explicit on this point, "The Lord hath made all things, *for himself*" (Prov. 16:4). "For of him, and through him, and *to him,* are all things" (Rom. 11:36). "Thou hast created all things, and for *thy pleasure* they are and were created" (Rev. 4:11).

The ultimate motive, therefore, which moved God to ordain Christ as Satisfaction for the failed responsibilities of His people must have been the Divine glory, and not the effects intended to be produced in the creature. But glory is manifested excellence, and moral excellence is manifested only by being exercised. The infinite justice and love of God both find their highest conceivable exercise in the sacrifice of His own Son as the Substitute of guilty men. God did ordain to have other sons beside Christ (Rom. 8:29). but it was in order that they might behold His glory (John 17:24), and that *He* might "be glorified in them" (John 17:10). To ordain Christ to come into this world as Man, *only* upon the occasion of man's sin and for the work of redemption, would be to subject Christ unto us, and to make *our* good the "end" of God's action. Such a conception is not only extremely absurd, but terribly impious. Adam was not made for Eve, but Eve for Adam; and as the woman is "the glory of the man" (I Cor. 11:7) so the saints are called "the glory of Christ" (II Cor. 8:23); and as the saints are Christ's, so is Christ, the Mediator, "God's" (I Cor. 3:23).

5. THE COVENANT OF GOD

Though we have made this a heading distinct from the preceding four, yet we would point out that it is in the Everlasting Covenant we find the will, the love, the righteousness, the glory of God, united, as the moving cause or causes of the perfect provision found in the Satisfaction of Christ.

As we have insisted in previous paragraphs, had God so pleased He might never have created a single being to admire His perfections. When creatures were admitted to that wondrous spectacle, and then became guilty of dishonoring Him, He might have further revealed Himself only in wrath, pouring out the vials of His indignation upon the spot which they inhabited, and turning it into a scene of desolation. What would be the loss of a world to Him in whose eyes it is as nothing, yea, less than nothing and vanity (Isa. 40:17)?

It follows from these premises, the truth of which cannot be gainsaid, that the plan which God designed for the salvation of His elect, who by nature also shared in the ruins of Adam's fall, originated not only in His sovereign grace, but was determined solely by His own imperial will. Therefore, in contemplating the work of redemption we need to ascend to its source, and begin with the consideration of that *eternal agreement* between the Persons of the Godhead, on which the whole dispensation of grace to fallen men is founded. That agreement is spoken of in the Scripture as "The everlasting covenant" (Heb. 13:20).

CHAPTER THREE

The Atonement—Its Necessity

In employing this term, the *necessity* of the Atonement, we are making use of an expression which calls for careful definition and explanation. Unfortunately, many writers have failed to perform this duty, with the consequence that loose and, oftentimes, most God-dishonoring views are entertained upon this aspect of our subject. To say that God must or must not do certain things is the language of fearful impiety, unless expressly warranted by the very words of Holy Writ. We are living in a day which is strongly marked by irreverence, and the most degrading views of the Almighty are now entertained by some who imagine their views of the Almighty are quite orthodox. It would be a simple matter for us to give illustrations and proofs of this, but we refrain from defiling our readers (I Cor. 15:33). Suffice it now to point out, once more, that never was there a time when God's people more earnestly needed to heed that word, "Prove all things" (I Thess. 5:21).

"The Lord of hosts is excellent in counsel and excellent in working" (Isa. 28:29). Infinite wisdom never acts aimlessly. God, who is perfect in knowledge, does nothing without good reason. All His works are proportioned according to His unerring designs. This is true alike in His acts of creation, providence and grace. At the close of the six days' work we read, "And God saw everything that He had made, and behold, it was *very good*" (Gen. 1:31). Concerning His government over us, "We know that all things work together *for good* to them that love God, to them who are the called according to his purpose" (Rom. 8:28). And as for the operation of His grace, faith unhesitatingly affirms "He hath done all things *well*" (Mark 7:37).

Now the most wondrous of all God's works is that which was performed by His Son here upon earth. When we attempt to contemplate what that Work involved, we are lost in amazement. When we seriously endeavor to gauge the depths of unutterable shame and humiliation into which the Beloved of the Father entered, we are awed and staggered. That the eternal Son of God should lay aside the robes of His ineffable glory and take upon Him the form of a servant, that the Ruler of heaven and earth should be "made *under* the law" (Gal. 4:4), that the Creator of the universe should tabernacle in this world and "have not where to lay His head" (Matt. 8:20), is something which no finite mind can comprehend; but where carnal reason fails us, a God-given faith believes and worships.

As we trace the path which was trod by Him who was rich yet for our sake became poor, we cannot but feel that we are entering the realm of mystery; the more so when we learn that every step in His path had been ordered in the eternal counsels of the Godhead. Yet, when we find that path entailing for the One in whom the Father was well pleased, immeasurable sorrow, unutterable anguish, ceaseless ignominy, bitterest hatred, relentless persecution, both from men and Satan, we are made to marvel. And, when we find that path leading to Calvary, and there behold the Holy One nailed to the Cross, our wonderment deepens. But, when Scripture itself declares that God not only delivered up Christ into the hands of earth's vilest wretches to be reviled and blasphemed, that God Himself was not merely a spectator of that awful scene, that He not only beheld the sufferings of Heaven's Darling, but that HE also smote Him, scourged Him with the rod of His indignation, and called upon the sword to smite His "Fellow" (Zech. 13:7), we are moved to reverently inquire into the needs-be for such an unparalleled event.

That the incarnation, humiliation and crucifixion of the Son of God were *necessary*, no one who (by grace) bows implicitly before the Word of Truth can doubt for a moment. The language of Christ Himself on this point is too plain to be misunderstood. To Nicodemus He said, "As Moses lifted up the serpent in the wilderness, even so *must* the Son of man be lifted up: that whosoever believeth in him should not perish, but have eternal life" (John 3:14, 15). To His disciples He declared, "how that He *must* go to Jerusalem, and suffer many things of the elders and chief priests and scribes, and be killed, and be raised again the third day" (Matt. 16:21). So too on the day of His resurrection, He asked, "*Ought not* Christ to have suffered these things, and to enter into his glory?" (Luke 24:26). Nevertheless, plain and positive as is the language of these verses, we need to be much upon our guard lest we draw from them a conclusion which will clash with other scriptures and lead us to a most dishonoring conception of God.

From the passages just quoted, and others of a similar character, not a few good men have drawn the inference that the sufferings of Christ were an *absolute* necessity, that the very nature of God rendered them so indispensable that apart from them the salvation of sinners was impossible; yea, that no other possible alternative presented itself to the omniscience of God. To such assertions we cannot assent, for they go beyond the express language of Holy Writ. However plausible the reasoning may be, however logical the deduction, we must, where Scripture is silent, resist a conclusion so momentous. To say that the all-wise God Himself could find no other way of saving sinners, consistently with His holiness and justice, than the one He has, is highly presumptuous. To declare that Omniscience was helpless, that God was obliged to adopt the means which He did, is perilously nigh unto blasphemy.

To affirm that God has selected the best possible way to magnify *all* His perfections in the redemption of His people, is to affirm that which is honoring to Deity, but to assert that this was the *only* way, is going beyond what Scripture declares. That supremest wisdom and supremest love would seek the noblest means to achieve the most glorious ends, we firmly believe; but to conclude that God was unable to contrive any other method is mere fatalism, and, we might add, semi-atheism. According to the theorizings of some theologians we ought to change Ephesians 1:11 so that it reads, "He worketh all things *after the necessities* of His own nature." Not so did Christ reason in Gethsemane: He did not accept the bitter cup because of the inexorableness of God's nature, but out of submission to His will.

From the words of our Saviour in the Garden, "If it be possible let this cup pass from me," it has been inferred that it was *impossible* it should do so. In one sense that is true: God had *ordained* that Christ should die, the terms of the everlasting covenant required it, the will of God demanded it; so die He *must.* But this is a very different thing from saying that when the Godhead held Their councils no other alternative could be devised, that the death of Christ was an absolute and unavoidable necessity. It is indeed most striking to note, and worthy of our most reverent attention, that at the very time our agonizing Saviour presented His petition, He said, "Abba, Father, *all things are possible* unto thee; take away this cup from me: nevertheless not what I will, but what thou wilt" (Mark 14:36).

In summing up this point, let us never forget that the Atonement originated in the mere good pleasure of God. He was not obliged to save any sinners; He was under *no* obligations to provide a Redeemer at all. That He did so, was purely a matter of grace, and, in the very nature of things, the bestower of "grace" is *free,* absolutely free, to bestow or withhold it, otherwise it would cease to be "grace," and become a debt owed to its recipient. As to the *method* by which God chose to manifest His grace, we can only say that the appointed Mediator has answered to every perfection of God and superlatively magnified all His attributes; and that this Saviour is both the gift of His *love,* and the appointment of His *will.*

Once again we would remind ourselves that we are within the realm of mystery, mystery deep and insolvable to finite intelligence. The entrance of *sin* into the world, God's infinite abhorrence of it, the moral requirements of His government concerning its punishment, the saving of His own people from it, the magnifying of His own name by it, are some of the principal elements entering into this mystery; and the relation which the whole mediatorial scheme of Divine grace has thereunto, is what is now to engage our attention. Conscious of our utter incapacity to even grapple with, much less solve, a problem so profound; conscious that reasoning thereon is worse than futile, we would prayerfully turn, in humble dependence upon the Spirit of Truth, to the Holy Scriptures, to ascertain what light God has been pleased to throw upon this mystery of mysteries.

1. The Atonement was Necessitated by the Will of God

Unless this be our starting point we are certain to err. God's Word implicitly declares that He "worketh *all* things after the counsel of his own will" (Eph. 1:11). The whole extent of this passage contains a revelation of God's eternal counsels concerning His own people. It takes us back before the foundation of the world to the time when He chose them in Christ. While it makes known that it was in *love* He predestinated them unto the adoption of children by Jesus Christ unto Himself, it at once adds, that this purpose was "according to the good pleasure of his *will*" (v. 5). It is in Christ that we have "redemption through His blood, the forgiveness of sins, according to the riches of His grace" (v. 7), yet right after we are told, "Having made known unto us the mystery of *his will, according* to his good pleasure which he hath purposed in himself" (v. 9).

The above passage ought to make it abundantly plain to every impartial mind that the Atonement or Redemption which God has so graciously provided for His elect, sprang from no obligation either in His own nature or from any claims which His creatures had upon Him. There have been not a few writers and preachers who have blasphemously asserted that the fall of man *obliged* God to provide a Redeemer. They have had the effrontery to affirm that since the Creator permitted Adam to bring ruin upon himself and his descendants, the least He could do was to raise up a Restorer. They say the exigencies of the situation which sin introduced into the world, *required* that some remedy be given that would neutralize its baneful effects. In short, these traducers of the Most High have argued that the Atonement was *imperative,* if God was to justify His creation of man and vindicate Himself for allowing him to lose his original uprightness. It is to such arrogant rebels that Jude 10 refers: "But these speak evil of those things which they know not."

Others, who gave vent to the enmity of the carnal mind against God in a more moderated form, have insisted that the *benevolence* of God required Him to provide a Saviour for sinners. While allowing that man himself is to shoulder the full blame for the condition in which he now finds himself, while granting that God has justly punished the disobedience of our first parents in ordaining that all their descendants shall taste the bitterness of sin's wages, yet they imagine that God's pity for Adam's fallen children *obliged* Him to provide a Saviour for sinners. A sufficient refutation of this widely-held error is found in the Creator's treatment of the angels that fell: no Saviour was provided for them! "God spared not the angels which sinned" (II Pet. 2:4). There is plain proof that the benevolence of God did not render the Atonement imperative.

Whatever claims an unfallen creature may have upon God, certainly a rebel against Him is entitled to nothing but summary judgment. Nor can offenders against His moral government by anything *they* perform, lay Him under obligation to furnish them with a legal ground of deliverance from sin. To say that they can, would be investing guilty sinners with the power to control the Divine Lawgiver, and would completely divest God's grace of its character of sovereign, free, and unmerited favor. No, there was nothing either in the perfections of God's character nor in the claims of His creatures, which rendered the Atonement an absolute necessity. God's purpose to save a remnant according to the election of grace arose solely out of His own free and sovereign will: the provision of a Saviour to save His people from their sins sprang from naught but God's own determination.

2. The Atonement was Necessitated by the Law of God

In saying that the Atonement was necessitated by the Law, we are not contradicting what has been said above, as will plainly appear if close attention be given to the sentences immediately following. The sovereign will of God was exercised in at least two things with respect to the Atonement: first, in His original *purpose to save* sinners, for that was solely His mere good pleasure; second, in the *process decreed* whereby they *should* be saved, namely, through the vicarious work of a Redeemer. Having purposed to save His people from the wrath to come, it pleased God to resolve that their sins should be remitted in a way whereby His Law should be honored and magnified. But let it be carefully remembered that in this too God acted quite freely, and not from any constraint. The Law itself is of His own appointment, and not something superior to Himself. Having *purposed to save,* the Everlasting Covenant was drawn up, and the Mediator having freely accepted its terms and having voluntarily placed Himself under the Law, thenceforward all was done in obedience to the Law. Thus, the Eternal Three having elected that redemption should be effected under the Law, all was wrought out in perfect accordance with the Law.

It is in the light of these facts that the passages quoted in an earlier paragraph, respecting the relative necessity of the Atonement, are to be interpreted. "As Moses lifted up the serpent . . . so must the Son of man be lifted up." There was no *absolute* necessity in either case. It was sovereign grace, pure and simple, which provided a way of life for the guilty Israelites who were dying in the wilderness. It was by Divine *appointment* that both the brazen serpent and the Antitype were "lifted up." So of Matthew 16:21: Christ "must" go up to Jerusalem and be killed. Why? Because God had so ordained, because the terms of the Everlasting Covenant so required. So it was not possible for the "cup" to pass from the agonizing Saviour. Why? Because God had willed that salvation should come to His people via His drinking it; thus it had been unalterably determined. "Without shedding of blood there could have been no remission" is what Scripture nowhere affirms. But under the regime God has instituted, "without shedding of blood is no remission" (Heb. 9:22).

It has been well said that "The work of redemption as well as the course of Nature proceeds in accordance with a predetermined plan, and under absolute and invariable law, law quite as exact as that which governs the material universe. Every end contemplated by the divine mind in the realm of the spiritual, and all means for its attainment under the reign of absolute law, were determined, with infinite exactness, from the beginning" (Dr. J. Armour).

The analogies between the reign of law in the natural and in the moral spheres are both close and numerous, the former serving to adumbrate the latter. For example, first, every law in the natural world, such as that of the recurring seasons or of gravitation, has been ordained and imposed by the Creator according to His own sovereign will. So too has every law in the moral realm, as that of sowing and reaping, sin and its punishment, been appointed by God. Second, the reign of law, as such, is invariable and inexorable: it knows of no exceptions. If the dearest child on earth drinks poison by mistake, it produces precisely the same effects as though the vilest wretch had deliberately taken it to end his earthly existence. Third, yet, though law and its demands cannot be defied with impunity, a *higher* law may be set in motion reversing the action of an inferior. Poisons have their antidotes. The law of gravity may be overcome by lifting an object from the ground. Law is never suspended, but higher power may intervene and deliver from the effects of a lower by magnifying a superior law. This was the case with the Atonement.

Law requires conformity to its precepts. The more perfect a law, the greater the obligations to respect it. Given a law which is "holy and just and good" (Rom. 7:12), and obedience to it becomes imperative. For God to repeal or even suspend it would be tantamount to acknowledging there was some defect in it. This could never be. Therefore, creatures made under that law must, of necessity, render obedience to it. In case of their failure, then, before it were possible to justify them, that is, pronounce them righteous, up to the required standard, another must fulfill that law on their behalf, and his righteousness or obedience be imputed to their account. This has actually been done. Christ was "made under the law" (Gal. 4:4), "fulfilled" it (Matt. 5:17), and His obedience has been placed to the legal credit of all His people (Rom. 5:19), so that they are now made "the righteousness of God in him" (II Cor. 5:21).

The law not only requires obedience to its precepts, but demands the punishment of its transgressors. Its invariable sentence is "The soul that sinneth, it shall die" (Ezek. 18:4). Inasmuch as God Himself declared this, and He "cannot lie," it inevitably ensues that wherever sin is found, death with all that it includes, must certainly follow. The Lord has expressly affirmed that He "will by no means clear the guilty" (Ex. 34:7). The only way of escape for law's transgressors is for Another to suffer the penalty in their stead. Under the regime which God has instituted, were He to pardon without satisfaction made to His broken law by a Substitute being paid sin's wages, then, God would not only trample upon His own law, but disregard His solemn threatening, and Scripture says "He cannot deny himself" (II Tim. 2:13). Therefore did God Himself provide that wondrous sacrifice upon which the righteous penalty of the law fell.

To understand aright the work of Redemption, it is all-important that we should hold correct views of the law of God under which man has transgressed, and the state into which he, by rebellion, has fallen. The law of God points out the duty of man, requiring from him that which is right and just. It cannot be altered in the least degree to exact more or less. It is therefore an unalterable rule of righteousness. This law necessarily implies, as essential to it, a sanction and a penalty — a penalty exactly fitted to the magnitude of the crime in transgressing it. Every creature who is under this law is bound by infinite obligations to obey it, without the slightest deviation from it throughout the whole of his existence. But by transgressing it, man has righteously incurred its penalty and fallen under its curse: "Cursed is every one that continueth not in all things which are written in the book of the law to do them" (Gal. 3:10).

Now the curse under which sinners have fallen, cannot be removed nor the transgressor released until full satisfaction has been made to it. Such satisfaction the sinner himself is utterly unable to render: "By the deeds of the law there shall *no* flesh be justified in his sight" (Rom. 3:20). Because the law of God is an unalterable expression of His will and moral character, neither its demands nor threatenings can be abated. The authority of the law must be maintained. To pardon without a satisfaction would be acting contrary to law. This insuperable barrier in the way of the sinner's deliverance is what underlies the relative necessity for the Mediator and Deliverer.

In order for the curse of the law to be removed from him who had incurred its anathema, it must fall upon another who is made a curse in his stead. It is at this point the amazing riches of Divine grace have been displayed. Not only was the Christ of God "made under the law," not only did He render perfect obedience to its precepts, but in addition — O wonder of wonders — He was "made a curse for us" (Gal. 3:13). Him did God Himself foreordain to be "a propitiation through faith in His blood to declare His righteousness . . . that He might be [not merely "merciful," but] *just*, and the Justifier of him which believeth in Jesus" (Rom. 3:25, 26).

3. THE ATONEMENT WAS NECESSITATED BY SIN

In asserting that the Atonement was necessitated by sin, let it not be supposed for a moment that the entrance of sin into this world was a calamity unanticipated by the Creator, and that the Atonement is His means of remedying a defect in His handiwork. Far, far from it. So far from man's fall being unforseen by God, the Lamb was "foreordained before the foundation of the world" (I Pet. 1:19, 20). The tragedy of Eden was no unlooked-for catastrophe, but foreknown and permitted by God for His own wise reasons. No, we employ the term used in this third heading in the sense of a *conditional* necessity. As we sought to show in the previous chapter, the ultimate reason and motive of all God's acts are found within Himself, and that reason and motive is ever His own glory. But "glory" is manifested excellency, therefore God magnifies His manifestative glory by the exercise and exhibition of His manifold perfections.

Wondrously has God used sin as an occasion for displaying His own attributes. He has employed it as a dark background from which has shone forth the more resplendently the beauties of His wisdom, His holiness, His faithfulness, His grace. Thus He *has* made the very wrath of man to "praise him" (Psa. 76:10). God is ineffably holy. As such, He is absolutely free from every vestige of moral pollution. He delights in whatever is pure, and therefore He hates whatever is impure: "Thou art of purer eyes than to behold evil, and canst not look on iniquity" (Hab. 1:13). Now sin is directly opposed to the holiness of God, for it is essentially impure, filthy, abominable; therefore is it the object of His unceasing detestation. How then shall God's abhorrence of sin be manifested but by His punishment of it?

The Atonement relatively necessitated by sin is obvious from other considerations. Had the creature never fallen, he had never merited sin's wages. Had he never transgressed against God's law, no satisfaction had been required for its outraged honor. Sin being obnoxious to both the nature and the law of God renders those who have committed it subject to His displeasure. Again; sin is a grievous dishonor to the manifested glory of God (Rom, 3:22), a direct insult offered to the high Majesty of Heaven, and were sin pardoned without an adequate satisfaction, it would be tantamount to saying that God may be insulted with impunity. But if the holiness of God requires that sin shall be punished, if the law of God requires a satisfaction should be rendered its honor, how can its transgressors possibly escape? Sin has imposed a gulf between the thrice holy One and those who have rebelled against Him (Isa. 59:2). Man is utterly incapable of filling up that gulf or of passing over it.

Well might Job exclaim, "For He is not a man, as I am, that I should answer Him, and we should come together in judgment. Neither is there any Daysman betwixt us, that might lay his hand upon us both" (9:32, 33). Ah, a "Daysman," a *Mediator,* one able to come "betwixt," is what was so urgently required. And what the terrible condition of fallen sinners needed, the matchless grace of God freely provided. Christ is the Divine answer to the Devil's overthrow of our first parents. And in Christ, and by Christ, every attribute of God has been glorified and every requirement of His law satisfied. Through the incarnation, life and death, of His blessed Son, God has shown to all created intelligences what a terrible thing sin is, what a dreadful breach it had made between Himself and His creatures, how impartial is His justice, what an ocean of love is in His heart to promote the happiness of His people, and above all, He has secured and advanced His own manifestative glory by the honoring of all His attributes. Through the Atonement God has been vindicated.

But let the final thought of our chapter be this: it was *sin* which required the Atonement. Let each truly Christian reader make it individual: it was *my* sins that brought down the eternal Son of God to this world of darkness and death. Had there been no other sinner on earth but me, Christ had certainly come here. Yes, it was *my* dreadful and excuseless sins which caused the Lord of glory to become "the Man of Sorrows." It was *my* sins which required the Beloved of the Father to descend into such unfathomable depth of shame and suffering. It was for *me* the ineffably Holy One was "made a curse." It was for *me* He endured the Cross, suffered separation from God, and tasted the bitterness of death. O may the realization of this make me *hate sin,* and cry daily to God for complete deliverance from it. May the realization of grace so amazing constrain me to *live only* for Him "who loved me and gave Himself for me" (Gal. 2:20).

CHAPTER FOUR

The Atonement — Its Pre-requisites

Before we are in the position to discern what was required in order for an atonement to be made for the sins of believers, or more specifically, what were the *qualifications* which must be possessed by him who should render an acceptable satisfaction to God, it is essential that we should know something of the actual *nature* of the Atonement itself. This we shall endeavor to define at length in the chapters which are to immediately follow; but, to pave the way for a more intelligent consideration of the perfections of the Mediator, let us briefly state *what it was* that Christ came here to do. The Son of God became the Son of man in order that sons of men might become sons of God. But these sons of men were not merely creatures, they were fallen and sinful creatures, and, as such, hateful to God, and under the condemnation of His inexorable law.

Sin has produced a tremendous gulf between the thrice holy God and the rebellious children of Adam. Man has no ability whatever to fill in or pass over that gulf. Not only is he alienated from his Maker (Eph. 4:18), but that law which he has broken insists upon full reparation, and this, man is incompetent to render. Thus, his case is desperate indeed. His only hope, as we sought to show near the close of our last chapter, lies in a mediator espousing his cause, a mediator acceptable to that God whom man has so grossly and grievously offended, a mediator both willing and qualified to undertake for him. But where was such an one to be found? where was one who could bridge the awful gulf sin had made, who was fitted to be entrusted with the interests of the Godhead, and who was capable of representing those who were, in the scale of being, so far, far below Him?

"Although man had remained immaculately innocent, yet his condition would have been too mean for him to approach to God without a Mediator. What, then, can he do, after having been plunged by his fatal fall into death and hell, defiled with so many blasphemies, putrefying in his own corruptions; in a word, overwhelmed by every curse? Since our iniquities, like a cloud, intervene between us and God, entirely alienating us from heaven, no one that could not approach to God could be a mediator for the restoration of peace. But who could have approached Him? Could any of the children of Adam? No; they, with their first parent, dreaded the Divine presence. What, then, could be done? Our situation was truly deplorable, unless the Divine majesty itself would descend to us; for we could not ascend to it. Thus it was necessary (as arising from the heavenly decree) that the Son of God should become Immanuel, that is, God with us" (Calvin's Institutes, Book 2, Chap. 12).

Yet instead of removing, this only seems to increase, the difficulty. As we have pointed out above, atonement could only be effected by a full satisfaction rendered to the Law; and this involved two things: first, a perfect obedience given to all its precepts; second, a full endurance of its unrelenting punishment. But how could a Divine Person enter the place of subserviency and become subject to the Law's demands? And again, how could a Divine Person suffer and die? This seems an insolvable problem, yet Divine wisdom provided a glorious solution. One of the Eternal Three, without in anywise ceasing to be God, took upon Him the form of a Servant and became Man. The Divine incarnation was undertaken in order to accomplish sin's expiation. The eternal Word's becoming flesh was a gracious means to a glorious end: it was that He might mediate between God and His people.

A mediator is one who intervenes between two parties at variance and makes peace. He must of necessity be a different person from each of the parties whom it is his design to reconcile; he can neither be the party which is offended, nor the party which has given offence. The party offended may forgive the offender; but in such a case, a mediator is not wanted. The party offending may be sorry for his conduct, and earnestly desire that peace be made; but he may have no access to the party offended, or the latter may reject his advances, because he does not deem the proffered satisfaction to be adequate. In this case a third party may interpose to adjust the difference, by the proposal of terms in which both will acquiesce.

What has just been pointed out raises a further difficulty: was not God the Son the party offended by the sinner, equally with the Father and the Spirit? Assuredly, for in His essential being, He is one with Them. But the Scriptures not only reveal the absolute unity of nature and essence in the three Persons of the Godhead, they also make known an economy or arrangement among those Persons, by which different characters and offices were assigned to each, and new *relations* are sustained by Them toward one another and toward us. In the economy of Redemption and its connection with the world, the Father appears in the character of the Supreme Governor of heaven and earth, the Son as Mediator, and the Spirit as the Applier of Redemption. In His office of Mediator, Christ does not press the claims of justice against sinners, but stands forth as their Friend, rescuing them from their perilous situation by rendering satisfaction for them to their offended Sovereign.

"The necessity of the mediation of Christ arises from the existence of sin; which being contrary to the nature and revealed will of God, renders those who have committed it obnoxious to His displeasure. As they had no means of appeasing His anger, the interposition of another person was requisite to atone for their guilt, and lay the foundation of peace. This is the great design of His office; but it extends to all the acts, by which sinners are actually brought into a state of reconciliation, are fitted for holding communion with God, and are raised to perfection and immutable felicity in the world to come. It comprehends the particular offices which our Saviour is represented as sustaining, the prophetical, the sacerdotal, and the regal; and it is by executing these that He completely performs the duties, and realizes the character of a Mediator" (Dr. J. Dick). Let us now particularize by endeavoring to point out what was required in the one who should make atonement for sinners to God.

1. THE MEDIATOR MUST BE MAN

"The mediator between God and men cannot be God only, or man only. This is taught in Galatians 3:20: 'A mediator is not of one, but God is one.' A mediator supposes two parties between whom he intervenes; but God is only one party. Consequently, the Mediator between God and men must be related to both, and be the equal of either. He cannot be simply God, who is only one of the parties, and has only one nature. Therefore the eternal Word must take man's nature into union with Himself if He would be a mediator between God and men. The same truth is taught in I Samuel 2:25, 'For if one man sin against another, the judge shall judge him; but if a man sin against the Lord, who shall intreat for him?' 'Therefore when He [the mediator] cometh into the world, He saith, A body hast Thou prepared me' (Heb. 10:5)" (Dr. J. Shedd).

Relationship of nature to those for whom Atonement was made is an essential element in its validity. Christ was required to be real and proper *man,* as well as true God. To qualify Him for the work of redemption, He needed to possess opposite attributes: a frail and mortal nature, combined with ineffable dignity of person. Humanity was requisite to fit the Messiah for suffering, to render Him susceptible of pain and death, to make it possible for Him to offer Himself as a sacrifice. Equally so was the possession of human nature required in order to impart validity to what He *did,* to give to His obedience and sufferings an essential value in the estimation of God's law. The work of our redemption being a moral satisfaction to the law of God for the sins of men, there existed a moral fitness that the satisfaction should be made by one in the nature of those who had sinned. It is striking to note in the types how that redemption had to be effected by a near kinsman (Lev. 25:25-27; Ruth 4:7).

Unless the Redeemer Himself possesses the nature of those to be redeemed the moral government of God had not been vindicated, nor the glory of the Divine Lawgiver been maintained, nor the principles of the law been upheld. The law in its precept was suited to man, and in its curse had a claim upon man. Its requirements were such as man only could fulfill; its penalty such as one possessing the nature of man only could bear. The penalty was *suffering unto death;* and no angel could die (Luke 20:36). The death only of a man could possess a moral and legal congruity to the cause of a law given to man and broken by man. Thus, it was not only to qualify Him for suffering that the Messiah took upon Him the nature of man, but to qualify Him for *such* sufferings as should possess validity in the eye of the Divine law. "For both He that sanctifieth and they who are sanctified, are all of one . . . Wherefore in all things it behooved Him to be made like unto His brethren . . . to make propitiation for the sins of the people" (Heb. 2:11, 17). "Since by man came death, by man came *also* the resurrection of the dead" (I Cor. 15:21).

The law required that its subject should love God with all his soul and serve Him with all the members of his body, seeing both are God's. Now none can do this but man, who consists of soul and body. Again; the law required the love of our neighbor, but none is our neighbor but man, who is of the same blood with us: hence the force of those words — "that thou hide not thyself from thine own flesh" (Isa. 58:7). Hence our Surety must cherish us, as one does his own flesh, and consequently we have to be "members of His body, of His flesh, and of His bones" (Eph. 4:30). Therefore has the Holy Spirit joined together these two things about Christ: "made of a woman, made under the law" (Gal. 4:4), intimating that the principal end of his incarnation was that He might be subject to the law.

"It is not without reason that Paul, when asked to exhibit Christ in the character of a Mediator, expressly speaks of Him as a man: 'There is one Mediator between God and men, the man Christ Jesus' (I Tim. 2:5). He might have called Him God, or might indeed have omitted the appellation of man, as well as that of God; but because the Spirit, who spake by him knew our infirmity, He has provided a very suitable remedy against it, by placing the Son of God familiarly amongst us (Christians, A.W.P.) as though He were one of us. Therefore, that no one may distress himself where he is to seek the Mediator or in what way he may approach Him, the apostle, by denominating Him a man, apprizes us that He is near, and even close to us, since He is our own flesh. He certainly intends the same in Hebrews 4:15" (J. Calvin).

2. The Mediator Must be Sinless

He who makes atonement for others must himself be entirely free from that which renders the atonement necessary. That which made atonement necessary was sin. The redeemer must be sinless, otherwise he would require redeeming. A sinner cannot expiate his own sins, still less can he be a saviour of others. Thus it was a prime prerequisite that the substitutionary victim should himself be undefiled, pure. This was plainly foreshadowed in the types. The lamb used in sacrifice must be "without blemish." The red heifer must not only be flawless, but also one "upon which never came yoke" (Num. 19:2). The levitical high priest was required to possess a high degree of ceremonial purity.

"Legal obligation to the curse may arise from one or both of two things: either from being born under the curse, that is to say, from original sin; or from becoming exposed to the penalty in consequence of a personal breach of its requirements, that is by actual transgression. Infants of the human family are under it in the former way; adults in both; but Jesus was neither the one nor the other" (Dr. W. Symington on *The Atonement*, 1854). Jesus was never under the Adamic covenant, and therefore the sin of our first father was never imputed to Him. He was supernaturally conceived of a virgin, and therefore, the virus of sin never entered His veins.

3. The Mediator Must be Holy

More than a sinless nature was required by the Redeemer. Satan was, originally, created without sin; yet he fell. Adam had no impurity in his nature when he left His Maker's hands, yet he transgressed. But Jesus Christ was not merely negatively sinless, He was, in His very humanity, positively *holy*—"that holy thing, which shall be born of thee" (Luke 1:35) were the words of God to His mother. It is striking and blessed to note that when the Holy Spirit exhibits, from the human side, the personal perfections of our High Priest, He speaks of Him first as "holy," which refers to the intrinsic excellency of His nature;

then as "harmless" which speaks of His entire freedom from evil in respect to conduct; "undefiled," which denotes the absolute purity of His official qualification and administration (Heb. 7:26). The intrinsic and unsullied purity of the Mediator was necessary to the acceptance of His services.

Beautifully has Dr. Dick pointed out, "This primitive purity He retained during the course of His life, conversing and familiarly associating with sinners, but not learning their ways. He died, indeed, as a criminal, but He died for sins not His own: He 'suffered, the Just for the unjust, that He might bring us to God' (I Pet. 3:18). Nay, He was not only free from actual transgression, He was incapable of sin; so fortified against temptation, that He could not be seduced . . . He stood firm in the severest trial. No argument, however subtle, could perplex His reason; no solicitation, however powerful, could seduce His affections. Satan exhausted his arts against Him in vain." To which we may add: He touched the leper, but was uncontaminated. He came into contact with death, but remained undefiled. He bare our sins in His own body on the tree, yet it was the "Holy One," unsullied, that was laid in the grave (Psa. 16:10).

4. THE MEDIATOR MUST BE MASTER OF HIMSELF

The one whose work it is to reconcile two parties at variance must not be under personal obligations to either. None could offer a satisfaction to law if he himself owed a debt unto it. A mediator must be independent, having full power over himself, possessing complete right to act on the part of others. Those who are subject to the authority of another cannot dispose of themselves and their services without his consent. Now angels and men are the absolute property of their Creator, and must wait His command before they may venture to engage in any enterprise not comprehended in the original law of their nature. The life of man is God's gift, and must not be thrown away nor surrendered, no matter what good might be anticipated from the sacrifice, without the direct permission of the Giver. In a word, a Mediator between God and men must have full power over His own life, to lay it down and take it again.

"It is not enough that the substitute be innocent, is free

from the claims of the law for which he gives satisfaction to others. He may be under obligations to another law, the fulfillment of whose demand may render it impossible to occupy the place of surety. His whole time and energies may be thus, as it were, previously engaged, so as to put it out of his power to make a transfer of any part of them for the behoof of others. This is, indeed, the case with all creatures. Whatever service they are capable of performing, they owe originally and necessarily to God. They are, from their very nature, incapable of meriting for *themselves,* much less for *others.* The right of self-disposal belongs not to creatures. Themselves and all that pertains to them, are the property of Him who made and preserves the same. They are under law to God. They are not under the covenant which God made with man, to be sure; but the law under which they exist demands all their energies, it has a claim upon them for the full amount of the service which they are capable of performing, and thus denies them all right of giving satisfaction to another law, in behalf of a different order of creatures" (Dr. W. Symington).

5. The Mediator Must Act Voluntarily

This is so self-evident it should need no arguing. Without this qualification, all others would be worthless. Let an appointed mediator be ever so dignified in his person, let him be most intimately related to man, let him be entirely free from all moral contamination, let him be completely at his own disposal; yet, it is manifest that, unless he choose actually to dispose of himself for the good of others, no validity could attach to what he did. Vicarious satisfaction can never be compulsory: willingness enters into its very essence. To *compel* one to suffer for another would be the height of injustice. Moreover, God will not accept any sacrifice which is reluctantly offered to Him: the heart must be in it: "My son, give me thine heart" (Prov. 23:26) is His first request from His children, for when He has *that,* He has everything.

Inexpressibly blessed is it to observe how plainly and how frequently this very element is seen in the great Mediator. To the proposal in the eternal covenant He gave His cheerful consent: "Lo, I come: in the volume of the book it is written of me, I *delight to do* thy will, O my God" (Psa. 40:7, 8). In all that He did to make atonement for sin, the Lord Jesus manifested no degree of reluctance. His meat was to do the Father's will (John 4:34). He was "led [not "driven"] as a lamb to the slaughter" (Acts 8:32); He "*gave* His back to the smiters, and His cheeks to them that plucked off the hair" (Isa. 50:6). "He *poured out* His soul unto death" (Isa. 53:12); He "*gave up* the spirit" (John 19:30). Let the interested reader turn to the Song of Solomon and behold how blessedly He is there represented as "leaping" and "skipping" over the mountains of separation as He hastens to His people!

6. THE MEDIATOR MUST BE FEDERALLY UNITED TO HIS PEOPLE

In his defense of the Satisfaction of Christ, Turretin pointed out how that there are three kinds of union known to us in human relations which justifies the imputation of sin one to another; natural, as between a father and his child; moral and political, as between a king and his subjects; voluntary, as between friends, or between an arraigned criminal and his sponsor. But the union of Christ with His people rests on far stronger ground than any of these considered alone. It was voluntary on His part, for He spontaneously assumed all the obligations He bore. But it was also a *covenant* ordinance, decreed by the three Divine persons in counsel, whose behests are alone the foundation of all law, all rights, and of all obligations. "The Scriptures plainly teach that God has established between Christ and His people a union *sui-generis,* transcending all earthly analogies in its intimacy of fellowship and reciprocal co-partnership both federal and vital" (Dr. C. Hodge).

The mediatorial position assumed by Christ and the redemptive work which He performed cannot be rightly understood till they are viewed in connection with the Everlasting Covenant. It is not difficult to see that the death on the Cross was only made possible for the Son of God by His becoming Man. But we need to go farther back and ask, What was the relation between Christ and His people that made it meet for Him to become incarnate and die for them? It is not enough to say that He was their Surety, and Substitute. True, blessedly true, He wrought and suffered for them because He was their Surety to the offended Law-giver and Judge. But *what* rendered it proper that He should occupy such a place? No satisfactory answer can be given till we go right back to the counsels of the Godhead. *Covenant oneness* accounts for all, vindicates all, explains all.

Christ was substituted *for* His people because He was and is one *with* them—identified with us and we with Him; not merely as decreed by the sovereign authority of the Godhead, but as *covenanted* between the eternal Father and the eternal Son. Christ "bore the sins of many" because in His covenant identification with them, their sins became sinlessly but truly His sins; and unto the sons and daughters of the covenant, the Father imputes the righteousness of His Son, because, in their *covenant oneness* with Him, His righteousness is undeservedly but truly their own righteousness. This alone explains all Christ's history as the incarnate Son of God; all His interposition as the Saviour of His people; and it places the career of Christ on earth in its true relation to the eternal purpose of God. In its completeness, as bearing on the covenant-clients as well as the covenant-Head, it is the formal instrument by which faith comes into sure possession of Christ Himself and the benefits of redemption.

Christ is expressly denominated "the last Adam" (I Cor. 15: 45), and therefore are we told that the first Adam was "the figure of Him that was to come" (Rom. 5:14). Adam was a "figure" of Christ in quite a number of ways, but supremely in this, that he stood as the federal head of a race. God entered into a covenant with him (Hos. 6:6, margin), and therefore he stood and fell as the legal representative of all his family: when he sinned, they sinned; when he died, they died (Rom. 5:12-19). So was it with the "last Adam": He stood as the covenant Head and federal Representative of all His people, being legally one with them, so that He assumed and discharged all their responsibilities. The birth of Christ was the begun *manifestation* of the eternal union between Him and His people.

In the Covenant, Christ had said to the Father, "I will declare thy name unto my brethren, in the midst of the Church will I sing praise unto thee. And again, I will put my trust in him. And again, Behold I and the children which God hath given me" (Heb. 2:12, 13). Most blessedly is this explained in what immediately follows: "Forasmuch then as the children are partakers of flesh and blood, he also himself likewise took part of the same," and therefore "He is not ashamed to call them brethren." *Federation* is the root of this amazing mercy, covenant-identification is the key which explains it. Christ came not to strangers, but to "brethren"; He came here not to procure a people for Himself, but to secure a people already His (Eph. 1:4; Matt. 1:21).

Since such a union has existed between Christ and His people from all eternity, it inevitably followed that, when He came to earth, He *must* bear their sins, and now that He has gone to heaven they *must* be clothed (Isa. 61:10) with all the rewardableness of His perfect obedience. *This* is the strongest buttress of all in the walls of Truth, yet the one which has been most frequently assailed by its enemies. Men have argued that the punishment of the Innocent *as though He were guilty* was an outrage upon justice. In the human realm, to punish a man for something of which he is neither responsible nor guilty, is, beyond question, unjust. But this principle did not apply to Christ, for He had *voluntarily* identified Himself with His people in such an intimate way that it could be said, "For both He that sanctifieth, and they who are sanctified, are *all of one*" (Heb. 2:11).

When we say that the union between Christ and His people is a *federal* one, we mean that it is of such a nature as to involve an *identification* of legal relations and reciprocal obligations and rights: "By the obedience of One shall many be made [legally constituted] righteous" (Rom. 5:19). God's elect were "chosen *in* Christ" (Eph. 1:4). They are "created *in* Christ Jesus" (Eph. 2:10). They were circumcised *in Him* (Col. 2:11). They are "made the righteousness of God *in him*" (II Cor. 5: 21). In view of this ineffable union, Scripture does not hesitate to say, "We are members of his body, of his flesh, and of his bones" (Eph. 4:30).

7. THE MEDIATOR MUST BE DIVINE

Think of the *work* the Mediator had to perform. He was to restore to Divine favor those who were under the curse. He had to render unto the law an obedience which one created sinless (Adam) had failed to perform. He was required to present unto God a satisfaction possessing *infinite* merits, which procured infinite blessings for His people. This a finite creature could not do. He was to endure the full weight of God's outpoured wrath upon all the sins of His people, as they were concentrated upon the Surety. He was to vanquish the Devil, so as to deliver his captives. He was to overcome sin, so that its sting was destroyed. He was to swallow up death and bestow eternal life on all those the Father had given him. Finally, He was to give the Holy Spirit unto His people, who would apply to them the redemption purchased. Who but a Divine person was competent for *such* an undertaking?

Again; think of what has been *effected* by the Mediator's work. It has restored God's people to true liberty (Gal. 5:1). Now as Witsius rightly pointed out, if any mere *creature,* however exalted, had redeemed us, we should have become the personal property of that creature, for he who sets us free makes a purchase of us for his possession (I Cor. 6:19, 20). But it is a manifest contradiction to be freed and be free, and yet at the same time be the property of any creature, for true liberty consists in subjection alone. Thus, our Lord says, "If *the Son* therefore shall make you free, ye shall be free *indeed*" (John 8:36). Again; for the redeemed to glory in anyone as their Saviour, to say to Him, thou art our Lord, to render to Him adoring homage, is an honor to which no mere creature could have the slightest claim. Thus, the Mediator *must be* a Divine person.

"It is not possible that the blood of bulls and goats should take away sins" (Heb. 10:4). Why? In the first place, those typical sacrifices could not, in the nature of them, magnify the *precepts* of the law: they were totally incapable of rendering that perfect obedience which was required. Nor, secondly, could they endure the full *penalty* of the law: "Lebanon is not sufficient to burn, nor the beasts thereof for a burnt offering" (Isa. 40:16). The fires of God's wrath had utterly annihilated the cattle upon a thousand hills, and would still wait for something else to consume. Therefore did God "lay help upon one that is *mighty*" (Psa. 89:19). Christ *was able* not only to perfectly keep the law, but to suffer the full extent of its unbated curse.

It is "the altar that sanctifieth the gift" (Matt. 23:19), the reference being to the type of Exodus 29:37: "it shall be an altar most holy; whatsoever toucheth the altar shall be holy." Upon this Dr. T. Ridgley (1815) well said, "From whence it is inferred, that the altar was more holy than the gift which was laid upon it, and it signifies, that the altar on which Christ was offered, added an excellency to His offering. Now nothing could be said to do so, but His divine nature's being personally united to His humanity, which rendered it infinitely valuable." For this reason, the mercy seat was made not of wood, but of "pure gold" (Ex. 25:17).

How often does the Holy Spirit give supreme emphasis to *this* fact. Before He tells us in Hebrews 1 that Christ has "by himself purged our sins," He first presents this vicarious Sufferer as God's "Son," the "Heir of all things" the "brightness of God's glory," yea, the "express image of his person"! So in Philippians 2, the One who "humbled himself and became obedient unto death" is first set before us as Him who subsisted "in the form of God," and "thought it not robbery to be *equal* with God." So again in Colossians 1 He is described as the Creator of all things (v. 16), ere we read of the peace which He made by the blood of His Cross. It is because Christ was who He *was* which gave an infinite value to what He *did*.

We close this somewhat lengthy chapter with the concluding words of Dr. Symington on this enthralling subject: "From the perfection of His atonement, arising out of the circumstances specified above, does it proceed, that He makes intercession for us within the veil of the upper sanctuary, that He dispenses with a munificent hand the gifts of His purchase and causes the prey of a great spoil to be divided. And pardon and peace, redemption and holiness, eternal glory and bliss are, among the rich fruits of the royal and triumphal conquest He achieved, when by His infinitely meritorious death, He spoiled principalities and powers, and made a show of them openly. With the most entire confidence, then, may the needy sinner, smitten with the deepest sense of conscious unworthiness, rely for salvation on this all-sufficient atonement."

CHAPTER FIVE

The Atonement—Its Nature

An inadequate conception of the terrible enormity of sin necessarily results in a faulty view of the Atonement. In reading through scores of books which were written at varying intervals during the last four hundred years, we have been struck by the fact that side by side with the modifying of the immeasurable heinousness of sin there has been a whittling down of the most essential features comprised in the character of Christ's redemptive work. The more lightly sin be regarded, the less will appear the need for such a stupendous undertaking as that which the Son of God entered upon and triumphantly carried through. Sin is an evil of *infinite* magnitude, for it is committed against an *infinite* Person, unto whom every creature is under infinite obligations of rendering unceasing and joyful obedience. This is why God's punishment of sin unatoned for will be *eternal*: necessarily so, for nothing less will fit the case, nothing less will satisfy Divine justice. And this is why God could receive no satisfaction to His broken law save from one that possessed infinite merits.

Romans 3:22 defines sin as a "coming short of the glory of God," i.e., His manifestative or declarative glory. Sin is failing to render unto God that to which His high honor is entitled, namely, implicit, perfect, constant homage and service. God's *essential* blessedness cannot be affected by the creature: were He to so please, He has merely to utter the words and every rebel throughout the entire universe would immediately cease to exist. But His declarative glory can be affected, yea, *is* so, by our sins. Sin dishonors God, and fallen man is utterly unable to restore His honor, yet this inability so to do is criminal and increases his guilt. Not only does sin dishonor

God, but it cannot be remitted by Him and the transgressor pardoned, till every claim of His law has been met. This the creature cannot do. As we showed in our last chapter, none but a mediator who was Divine as well as human, was competent to render full satisfaction unto God. This is what Christ has done: His Atonement has brought back to God's declarative glory that revenue of honor and praise to which He is entitled.

Now the life and death of Christ are historical facts which are, practically, universally admitted, but the "*word* of the cross" (I Cor. 1:18, R.V.), i.e., the scriptural explanation of His atoning work is purely a matter of Divine revelation, and is to be received with uncavilling humility and rested upon with peaceful assurance, simply because it is made known to us on the authority of God. Reasoning thereon is utterly vain, and speculating thereabout is profane. Moreover, as we stated in the opening chapter, all attempts to *illustrate* from supposed analogies in human relations dishonor God and grossly pervert His Truth. The atoning work of Christ is unique. It stands alone in its solitary grandeur. There is nothing in all history which in anywise resembles it. When a preacher attempts to "simplify" the mystery of the three Persons of the Godhead by some illustration from "nature," he only exhibits his own foolishness, and helps no one. So too every effort to explain the Atonement with what is outside Scripture, is only turning from light to darkness. Divine mysteries cannot be understood by means of those things which come within the range of our physical senses.

It has been rightly said that "accuracy of terms clarifies thought," to which we may add, Accuracy of thought is essential to right views of any portion of the Truth, and right views of the Truth are honoring to God. Therefore, no effort should be spared in seeking to attain unto the utmost possible precision of language when seeking to set forth the things of God. Many a reader has obtained only a cloudy view of a subject because the writer confused *effects* with the nature of the thing he was dealing with. For example, *assurance* of salvation is one of the fruits of faith (as well as a gift of the Spirit), yet it has often been regarded as an essential element of faith itself. In consequence, because they lacked assurance, some real Christians have been plunged into what Bunyan termed the Slough of Despond, because they imagined they were not saved at all. In like manner, many writers on the Atonement have carelessly jumbled together some of its leading effects and fruits with the nature of it.

A pertinent example of what we have just said is seen in the now almost current idea that the Atonement of Christ signifies "at-one-ment," the bringing of God and the sinner together. But *that* is not the meaning of the term at all, either as used in Scripture or as employed in sound theology. Reconciliation is one of the many effects or fruits of Christ's Atonement, but was not part of the work He did. Many others have failed to distinguish between the Atonement of Christ and the Redemption which is one of its fruits. It is vitally important to distinguish between what Christ did and that which has resulted therefrom. To understand *what* He did, let us now attempt to define the *nature* of His Atonement.

1. IT WAS A FEDERAL WORK

By the term "federal" we mean that there was an official oneness existing between the Mediator and those for whom He mediated, or in simpler language, that there is a *legal union* between Christ and His people. "When, in the Old Testament, the elect are spoken of as the party with whom God makes a covenant, they are viewed as in Christ and one with Him. The covenant is not made with them as alone and apart from Christ. This is taught in Galatians 3:16: 'To Abraham and his seed were the promises made,' but this seed 'is Christ.' The elect are here (as also in I Cor. 12:12) called 'Christ,' because of the union between Christ and the elect. And in like manner, when Christ, as in Isaiah 42:1-6, is spoken of as the party with whom the Father covenants, the elect are to be viewed as in Him. As united and one with Him, His atoning suffering is looked upon as their atoning suffering: 'I am crucified with Christ' (Gal. 2:20)" (Wm. Shedd, 1889).

"Christ is not only the Substitute but the Surety of His people. The Gospel is founded on the fact Adam and Christ are covenant heads and representatives of their respective families. Hence they are termed 'the first man' and 'the second man' (I Cor. 15:47), as if there had been none other but themselves, for the children of each were entirely dependent on their head. In Adam all die; in Christ all are made alive (I Cor. 15:22). The first *all* includes every individual of mankind, the last *all* is explained by the apostle to mean 'they that are Christ's' (I Cor. 15:23)" (James Haldane, *Doctrine of the Atonement*).

It was as the Head of His elect that God covenanted with Christ, so that, in a very real sense, that covenant was made with them. This it is which explains all those passages that speak of the saints' oneness with Christ, as that, they were "crucified with Christ" (Gal. 2:20), "died with Him" (Rom. 6:8), were "buried with Him" as scriptural baptism symbolizes (Rom. 6:4), were "quickened" with Him (Col. 2:12), "raised with Him" (Eph. 2:6), and made to "sit together in the heavenlies in Christ Jesus" (Eph. 2:6). So they were legally one with Him, and He with them, in all that He did in rendering a full Satisfaction to God. On this vitally important point we cannot do better than give a synopsis of the last section from chapter two of H. Martin's invaluable work:

"How are we to formulate and establish the relation subsisting between Christ and His, as Redeemer and redeemed, unless we fall back upon the doctrine of the Covenant? *Some* relation, it is evident, must be acknowledged as subsisting between Christ and those on whose behalf He dies, else we do not even come within sight of the idea of a vicarious sacrifice. The possibility of real atonement absolutely postulates and demands a conjuncture between Him who atones and those for whom His atonement is available. This is beyond the need of proof. And as there is an absolute and obvious necessity for *some* conjuncture or relation, so in searching for *the* conjunction or relation which actually subsists, our search cannot terminate satisfactorily till we reach and recognize the covenant oneness. The same reason that demands a relation, remains unsatisfied till it meets with *this* relation."

It does not meet the necessities of the case to refer to the union between Christ and His people which is effected in their regeneration by the agency of the Holy Spirit and the instrumentality of that faith which is His gift. True, this is indispensable before any can enjoy any of the blessings of His purchase. But there must have been a relation between Christ and His people before He ransomed them. Nor are the necessities of the case met by a reference to the Incarnation. True, the Redeemer must take upon Him flesh and blood before He *could* redeem, yet there must be a bond of union more intimate than that which Christ holds alike to the saved and the unsaved. He took hold of "the seed of *Abraham*" (Heb. 2:16), not the "seed of Adam"! Nor is it sufficient to say that the relation is that of suretyship and substitution, for the question still calls for answer, *What* rendered it fit and righteous that the Son of God *should* suffer for others, the Holy One be made sin? It is to *this* point the inquiry must be narrowed.

Christ was the Surety of His people because He was their Substitute. He acted *on their behalf* because He stood *in their* room. The relation of a substitute justifies the suretyship; but *what* shall justify the substitution? There is the hinge upon which everything turns. We heartily concur with Dr. Martin when he says, "We can obtain no satisfaction on this point, no sufficient answer to this question, and therefore no satisfactory conclusion to our whole line of investigation, till the doctrine of the everlasting *covenant-oneness* comes into view. *That* is the grand underlying relation. That is the grand primary conjunction between the Redeemer and the redeemed, which alone bears up and accounts for all else in respect of relation which can be predicated as true concerning them. 'Both He that sanctifieth and they who are sanctified are *all of one*: for *which* cause He is not ashamed to call them brethren' (Heb. 2:11). He is substituted *for us,* because He is one *with us*—identified with us and we with Him."

Promoted by infinite love, Christ, as the God-man, freely accepted the terms of the Everlasting Covenant which had been proposed to Him, and voluntarily assumed all the legal responsibilities of His people. As their Head He came down to this earth, lived, wrought and died as their vicarious Representative. He obeyed and suffered as their Substitute. By

His obedience and sufferings He discharged all their obligations. His sufferings remitted the penalty of the law, and His obedience merited infinite blessings for them. Romans 5:12-19 explicitly affirms that the elect of God are, legally, "made righteous" on precisely the same principle by which they were first "made sinners." "Our union with Christ is of the same order, and involves the same class of effects, as our union with Adam. We call it a union both *federal and vital*. Others may call it what they please, but it will nevertheless remain certain that it is of such a nature as to involve *an identity* of legal relations and reciprocal obligations and rights" (A. A. Hodge). "For *as* by one man's disobedience many were made sinners, *so* by the obedience of one shall many be made righteous" (Rom. 5:19) — "made the righteousness of God *in* him" (II Cor. 5:21).

More than a thousand years ago, Augustine remarked, "Such is the ineffable closeness of this transcendental union, that we hear the voice of the members suffering, when they suffered in their Head, and cried through the Head on the cross, 'My God, my God, why hast thou forsaken me?' And, in like manner, we hear the voice of the Head suffering, when He suffered in His members, and cried to the persecutor on the way to Damascus 'Saul, Saul, why persecutest thou *me?*' (Acts 9:4)."

The *federal* relation of Christ to His people was a *real* one, upon which the infallible God deemed it just to punish Christ for the sins of His people, and to credit them with His righteousness, and thus completely satisfy all the demands of His law upon them. As the result of that union, Christ was in all things "made like unto his brethren" (Heb. 2:17), being "numbered (reckoned one) with transgressors" (Isa. 53:12); and they, in turn, are "members of His body, of His flesh, and of His bones" (Eph. 5:30). In consequence of this federal union, Christ is also made "a quickening Spirit" (I Cor. 15:45) so that, in due time, each of His people becomes a living and vital member of that spiritual body of which He is the Head (Eph. 1:19-23).

The relation between Christ and those who benefit from His Atonement was, therefore, no vague, indefinite, haphazard one, but consisted of an actual covenant oneness, legal identity, vital union. Suretyship presupposes it. Strict substitution demands it. Real imputation proceeds upon it. The penalty Christ endured could not otherwise have been inflicted. They for whom Satisfaction was made do, by inevitable necessity, share its benefits and receive what was purchased for them. This alone meets the objection of the injustice of the Innocent suffering for the guilty, as it alone explains the transfer of Christ's sufferings and merits to the redeemed.

2. IT WAS A SUBSTITUTIONARY WORK

The terms "substitutionary" and "vicarious" are often used very loosely. Many who have sought to gain a reputation for orthodoxy and thereby ingratiate themselves into the confidence of God's people have made use of the bare terms, yet intended by them nothing more than that Christ suffered on the behalf of others, for the benefit of others. But *that* is only a half truth, and therefore close akin to a lie. Vicarious suffering or punishment is more than suffering endured for the good of others. The suffering of martyrs for the good of their cause, of patriots for their country, of philanthropists for mankind, are *not* "vicarious," for they are not *substitutionary*. Vicarious suffering is suffering endured not only on behalf of others, but in the stead of others, in the actual *place of* others. It therefore carries with it the *exemption* of the party in whose place the suffering is endured. What a substitute does for the person whose place he fills, absolves that person from the need of himself doing or suffering the same thing. Thus, when we affirm that the sufferings of Christ were "vicarious" we mean that He substituted Himself in the room of sinners and satisfied the law in their behalf, and that, in such a way, the law can now make no claim whatever upon them. Christ's sufferings were "vicarious" in identically the same way that the death of animals in the Old Testament sacrifices was in lieu of the death of the transgressor offering them.

The Scriptures teach that Christ was in a strict and exact sense the Substitute of His people, i.e., that by Divine appointment and of His own free will, He assumed all their liabilities, took their law-place, and bound Himself to do in their stead all that the law demanded, rendering to it that obedience upon which their wellbeing depended, and suffering its penalty which their sins deserved. Christ became their vicarious Sponsor, assuming their obligations and undertaking to satisfy Divine justice on their behalf. So real was His substitution in their place, that what He did and suffered for them precluded all necessity of their meeting the demands of the law in their own persons. Thus, the Satisfaction which Christ made was far more than an expedient for "removing those obstacles" which prevented God from justifying the ungodly: it was that which *required* Justice *to* remit the sins of all for whom it was made. The Satisfaction of Christ was infinitely more than a means for "opening a way" whereby the grace of God could flow forth: it was that which *necessitated* all for whom it was made being vested with all its meritorious efficacy.

In becoming the Substitute of His people, in placing Himself under their liabilities, in engaging to discharge all their responsibilities, Christ was, necessarily, "made under the law" (Gal. 4:4), so that He might keep its statutes, fulfill its requirements, and thus "magnify" and render it "honourable" (Isa. 42:21). The Scriptures plainly teach that Christ's *obedience* was as truly "vicarious" as was His suffering, and that He reconciled the elect to God by the one as well as the other — that is why we insist on using the wider term "the *Satisfaction* of Christ," for "atonement," strictly speaking, covers only the expiation of our guilt by His vicarious suffering. The active obedience of Christ to the law was required as the meritorious condition upon which the Divine favor and the promised reward of the Covenant might come upon all whose Surety He was. We must never attempt to separate between the active obedience and the passive sufferings of Christ, either when contemplating His mediatorial work, or when considering the effect of that work upon the covenant-standing of His people. Christ's vicarious obedience is an intrinsic part of that "righteousness" which He wrought in our stead, and which is imputed to us as the ground of our justification. *All* that Christ did on earth He did *as Mediator*. He was acting in our stead just as truly when He was obeying God as when

He was enduring His wrath. It is in reference to both of these *conjointly* that He is designated "the Lord *our righteousness*" (Jer. 23:6).

It needs to be pointed out that the "obedience" of Christ is not to be restricted to what He wrought prior to the Cross, nor are His "sufferings" to be limited to what He endured during the crucifixion and immediately preceding it. No, He suffered all through His life, and obeyed throughout His dying. "The whole earth life of Christ, including His birth itself, was one continued self-emptying, even unto death. His birth, and every moment of His life, in the form of a servant, was of the nature of holy sufferings. Every experience of pain during the whole course of His life, and eminently in His death on the cross, was, on His part, a voluntary and meritorious act of obedience. He lived His whole life, from His birth to His death, as our Representative, obeying and suffering in our stead, and for our sakes; and during this whole course, all His suffering was obedience, and all His obedience was suffering. The righteousness which He wrought out for His people consisted precisely in this suffering and obedience. The righteousness of Christ, which is imputed severally to each believer, as the ground of his justification, consists precisely of this suffering and obedience. His earth life as *suffering* cancels the penalty, and as *obedience,* fulfills the precepts and secures the promised reward of the law; but the suffering and the obedience were not separated in fact, and are inseparable in principle, and equally necessary to satisfy the law of the covenant and to secure the salvation of the elect" (A. A. Hodge).

The law, as a covenant of life, was accompanied by two sanctions. First, the promise of "life" or Divine favor and eternal well-being, conditioned upon perfect obedience: see Leviticus 18:5; Matthew 19:17; Romans 10:5; Galatians 3:12. Second, the penalty of "death" suspended on disobedience. Now the object for which Christ became incarnate was "*that* the *righteousness* of the law might be fulfilled in us" (Rom. 8:4), and therefore is Christ declared to be "the end of the law for righteousness to every one that believeth" (Rom. 10:4). And this was only made possible by His fulfilling all the law's conditions. Had not Christ vicariously obeyed the law, had

He merely suffered its penalty, due our sins, then we should be destitute of any positive righteousness, and would be left just where Adam was before he fell. But the Scriptures emphatically affirm that Christ saved by His obedience as well as by His sufferings: "For as by one man's disobedience, many were made sinners, so by the obedience of One shall many be made righteous" (Rom. 5:19) — Christ's "obedience" is to be interpreted here in the same natural and obvious way as the "disobedience" of Adam. Thus our *twofold* obligation to God, as creatures and as sinners, was met and discharged by Christ.

"As our Representative, He bore in the union of His divine personality our nature impersonally, 'a true body and a reasonable soul,' in order that He might thus be *made vicariously under the law,* to the end that by His purely vicarious obedience He might 'redeem them that are under the law, *that* we might receive the adoption of sons' (Gal. 4:4, 5). This means necessarily (a) that Christ was *made* under the law, that He did not belong there naturally, but was transferred to that position by an act of divine sovereignty; (b) that He was placed there, not for Himself but in *our stead;* (c) that He was made under the law for the purpose of securing for us not only the remission of sins, but also the *adoption of sons,* whereby we become 'heirs of God *through Christ*' (Gal. 4:7); all of which is conditioned not upon suffering but upon obedience. All that Christ did on earth He did as our Mediator, and all that He did as Mediator, He did in the stead of those for whom He acted as Mediator. Therefore He said (Matt. 3:15), 'for thus it becometh us to fulfill all righteousness,' that is, all that God requires of His people" (A. A. Hodge).

In Romans 8:3 (the context should be carefully weighed) we read of "what the law could not do, in that it was weak through the flesh." That which the law was unable to do was *justify the ungodly*. The reason for this was that the law demands perfect obedience, and this the flesh, because of sin, makes it impossible for the sinner to render. In view of this, God sent His own Son in the likeness of sinful flesh and for sin. Sent Him into the law-place of His people and by His executing the penalty upon Him "condemned sin in the flesh," and by accepting His vicarious obedience the "righteousness of the law" is fulfilled in us. The phrase "the righteousness of the law" is used in the New Testament to express the totality of that which the law demands as the condition of favor. In Adam, before he fell, the righteousness of the law was perfect obedience. In the case of all his descendants, it is perfect obedience plus the suffering of its penalty; hence the impossibility of our achieving a legal righteousness by our own personal agency.

Now "the righteousness of the law" is placed in antithesis from "the righteousness of faith" (Rom. 10:5,6). That is to say (see context) the futile attempts of the sinner to satisfy the requirements of the law in his own person, is contrasted from the vicarious satisfaction of Christ which faith apprehends and appropriates. "To them that have obtained like precious faith with us through the *righteousness* of our God and Saviour Jesus Christ" (II Pet. 1:1). To the same effect our worthless righteousness is contrasted from God's perfect righteousness in Christ: see Romans 3:20-26. Obedience is therefore the essence of righteousness, and that obedience, the obedience *of Christ*. Therefore we read that He is "made unto us wisdom and righteousness" (I Cor. 1:30). And therefore Paul declares his desire to "be found in him, not having mine own righteousness, which is of the law, but that which is through the faith of Christ, the righteousness which is of God by faith" (Phil. 3:9). The endurance of penalty by Christ demanded that our sins should be remitted; the performing of obedience by Christ demanded that His righteousness be imputed to us and that we should be eternally established in God's favor.

In the above passage (Rom. 8:3) we are told that God sent His own Son "in the likeness of sinful [literally "sin's"] flesh." This remarkable expression needs to be carefully investigated, lest we err by overstatement, or come short of its meaning by defective statement. First, it affirms the *reality* of Christ's humanity. Second, inasmuch as that humanity was united to Godhead, it must be *sinless* humanity: generated by the Holy Spirit it was pure and holy. This was secured by the fact that though He took flesh from Adam through the Virgin, *He* was *not* in Adam's covenant. Third, its "likeness" or appearance was after the order of "sin's flesh": between Him and sinful men there was *no perceptible* difference that could be traced: in weariness and exhaustion, sorrow and heaviness, Christ was in all respects "made like unto his brethren." But toil and sorrow, weakness and pain, came not on Him as the inevitable consequence of the Incarnation, but resulted from His coming here as the Surety of His people.

Christ was *personally* exempt from all the consequences of Adam's sin, but *officially* He was subject to them. Personally, He was a Divine person assuming a sinless humanity, and had He not come here as the Head of God's elect (considered as fallen creatures), He had doubtless appeared in a humanity as glorious as that of unfallen Adam's. But officially He assumed "the likeness of *sin's* flesh," an expression referring to the effects of which sin was the cause: namely, subject to suffering and mortality and this from the moment of His birth. O infinite stoop! O marvel of condescensions! He bore in His body the weight of imputed sin, a body bearing the sad marks of sin, for "*His* visage was so marred more than any man, and *His* form more than the sons of men" (Isa. 52:14). There was no *perceptible* difference between His humanity and ours, *not* because precisely the same flesh had been transmitted to Him from Adam, but because as our Sin-bearer He voluntarily assumed the burden of imputed guilt, which carried with it abasement and degradation, suffering and death: it was officially assumed, not personally inherited.

Christ came in the likeness of sin's flesh "*for* sin" (Rom. 8:3), i.e., on account of sin: *that* is why God "sent" Him. "Condemned sin in the flesh": sin is still *personified,* as in Romans 5, 6, 7: see 5:21; 6:14, etc. — the potentate having men in bondage. God "condemned sin" speaks of sin as a person judged before the highest tribunal and righteously condemned. In consequence of God's judgment, sin has no further claim on those over whom he had tyrannized: they are set free. "Condemned sin in the flesh" means condemned it in *Christ's* humanity, as the sinless Sin-offering — cf. 2:1; 5:18 — a condemnation freeing His people from condemnation: 8:1. Christ was "condemned," visited with penal suffering, because He appeared before God only in the guise of our accursed sins. And, this, in order that "the righteousness of the law might be fulfilled *in us*," i.e., as if *we* personally had done it.

Rightly did Mr. J. Inglis point out, "The fact that God sent forth His Son in the likeness of sinful flesh and for sin, intimates that He entered into the condition of His people, which, with all its evils, is the consequence of sin. If we find Him poor and despised, hungry and thirsty, subject to toil and fatigue, a man of sorrows and acquainted with grief, not exempt from the fear of death nor from actual mortality, to say nothing of all else that He endured at the hands of Satan and of man; all these are indubitably the consequences of sin, and He could be exposed to them *only* as He *represented* sinners" (Waymarks, Vol. 10).

A fuller light shines forth from the four Gospels when we perceive that they are not the biography of a private individual, but the history of the Surety of God's people. Christ was the Representative Head of an elect company: from Bethlehem to Calvary He was their vicarious Victim. The appearing of the Son of God on earth was the direct consequence of sin. The Incarnation and the Cross are inseparable; both were a means to an end—the vindication of Divine justice, the expiation of sin, the rendering of meritorious obedience to the law. We cannot survey the meanness of His birth, made lower than the angels; the poverty of His condition, His manual occupation, earning His bread by the sweat of His brow, according to the curse upon His people; His temptation by Satan; His privations, the enduring of hunger and thirst and public execution; these, we say, cannot be contemplated without the firm conviction that they were all included in *our* guilt and related to *our* punishment.

CHAPTER SIX

The Atonement—Its Nature (continued)

The particular aspect of the Satisfaction of Christ which is now before us leads into the very heart of this wondrous theme. It is most important for the honoring of God and the establishing of our souls in the Truth that the nature of the Atonement should be scripturally and clearly defined. Mistake at this point is fatal. Until we apprehend aright *what* it was that Christ did, we are not prepared to contemplate the design, the efficacy, the extent, or the fruits and results of it, and still less are we equipped to proclaim and expound it. For these reasons we must proceed slowly and endeavor to make quite sure of our ground. The great majority of the errors of men upon the Atonement are the consequences of an unscriptural conception of the nature of it. We would therefore beg the reader to prayerfully and patiently read and re-read what we are writing on this vital phase of our subject, testing all by God's Word.

In our last chapter we pointed out that the atoning work of Christ was, first, a *federal* one: that there was an official union existing between the Mediator and those for whom He mediated, that there is a *legal oneness* between Christ and His people. Before the foundation of the world God's elect were "chosen in Christ" (Eph. 1:4), "promised" eternal life (Titus 1:2), and were "given" grace in Him (II Tim. 1:9). It was therefore as their covenant Head, and because of this, as their covenant Surety, that when the fulness of time was come God sent forth His Son to transact on their behalf. All that Christ did and all that He suffered was as their legal Representative. Unless this be firmly grasped as what lies at the very foundation of the redemptive sacrifice of Christ, we are certain to err when attempting to interpret its scope and application. Christ and His people together formed one mystical Person in the repute of God.

Second, the atoning work of Christ was a *substitutionary* one. What Christ did and suffered was not only on the behalf of others, but it was also expressly in the stead of others. True, blessedly true, that His obedience and His sufferings have benefited others, but it needs to be emphatically said and firmly held that His obedience was performed and His sufferings were endured in the actual room of others. Christ took the law-place of His people, assumed their liabilities, became their Sponsor, and undertook to satisfy Divine justice for them. This Christ *engaged* to do when He accepted the terms of the Everlasting Covenant. This Christ *came* to do when He became incarnate. From Bethlehem to Calvary He is to be regarded as having taken the place of His guilty people, suffering and doing, doing and suffering, what the righteous law of God required at their hands.

"When the fulness of the time was come, God sent forth his Son, made of a woman, made under the law" (Gal. 4:4). Christ's derivation of real humanity through His mother is no unimportant matter, concerning the Atonement, for His fraternity, as our kinsman Redeemer, absolutely depends upon the fact that He derived His humanity from the substance of His mother; for without this He would neither possess the natural nor legal union with His people, which must be at the foundation of His representative character. To be our Redeemer His humanity could neither be brought from heaven, nor immediately created by God, but derived as ours is, from a human mother; but with this difference, His humanity never existed in Adam's covenant, to entail either guilt or taint. He must be within the pale of mankind. Nevertheless, Christ was "made under the law" not by the condition of creaturehood, but for the ends of Suretyship: hence the imputative value of His obedience. (Condensed from George Smeaton.)

The words "made under the law" need to be carefully defined. "Christ became subject to the law by a special Divine constitution. He was not born under it as all men are; their subjection to the law follows upon their being the natural descendants of Adam, to whom the law was originally given, and his being to them a representative. But Christ was not a natural descendant of Adam, nor was the first Adam a representative of the second Adam, for He was the Lord from heaven. His obligation to the law ariseth not from His birth, but He was made under it by an *appointment* peculiar to Himself, to answer a specific end, viz., the redemption of sinful men. And therefore what the law required of them, either in a way of suffering or obedience, He became obliged by this Divine constitution to undergo and perform" (John Brine, 1743, *The Certain Efficacy of the Death of Christ*).

Christ was both "born" and "given" to the people of God (Isa. 9:6), and that with a view to their salvation: what He did and suffered was for the sake of and in the room of those on whose account He came into the world. Some have sought to evade the vicarious character of His obedience by arguing that as Man, Christ was *under obligation* to keep the law. But this is to deny, if not implicitly yet explicitly that He was the Son of God. Great care needs to be exercised at this point. The humanity of Christ, as such, was *impersonal,* and therefore owed no obedience to the law. The God-man is *not* two persons in one: He is one person with two natures. As the Son of God He was a person before He became incarnate. In becoming incarnate He took to Himself humanity, but not a second personality. Therefore the manhood of Christ being united to the Son of God, He was not and could not be *obligated* to obey the law. It was by a Divine constitution, by covenant agreement, that He was "made under the law," with a view to the redemption and justification of God's elect.

Now the moment Christ *was* "made under the law" He entered the place occupied by His people, considered as fallen creatures. This alone explains the experiences He encountered, the degradation He suffered, the injustice He met with at the hands of men, and the punishment He received from God Himself. We harbor the most dishonoring and degrading views of God if we imagine for a moment that He would allow an innocent person to suffer, still less so that He would permit His beloved Son to unrighteously suffer at the hands of human wretches. We shall never view aright the manger-cradle, the necessity for the flight into Egypt, the laboring at the carpenter's bench, the having not where to lay His head, the horrible indignities He endured from His enemies, and the wicked treatment He received from those who passed sentence of death upon Him, till we recognize that from Bethlehem to Calvary He was the vicarious Victim of His people, that He was bearing their sins, and suffering the due rewards of their inquities.

"No good thing will He withhold from them that walk uprightly" (Psa. 84:11). But as the descendants of fallen Adam, God's people, in their unregenerate days, did the very reverse from walking uprightly. They forsook the way of God's commandments and followed a course of self-will, and that, not occasionally, but constantly. In consequence, many good things were withheld from them. Though addressed directly to Israel, the words of Jeremiah 5:25 contain a principle of wide application: "Your iniquities have turned away these things, and your sins have withholden good things from you." Therefore, when Christ came here as the Sinbearer of His people, Divine justice required that He should be deprived of many "good things."

As a wanderer from the Father's house (Luke 15:13), man has forfeited all right to so much as an earthly abode, hence we find Christ taking the place of the homeless Stranger here. Inasmuch as fallen man prefers the "world" to anything that God sets before him, we find Christ carried down into Egypt (the outstanding symbol of "the world" in Scripture), and therefore did God say "Out of Egypt have I called my Son" (Matt. 2:15). In consequence of the Fall, God pronounced the following curse upon man, "In the sweat of thy face shalt thou eat bread" (Gen. 3:19), therefore do we find Christ toiling for His (Mark 6:3). Because the elect in their unregenerate days failed to love their neighbors, we find Christ experiencing the hatred of men. Because we have been guilty of gluttony, He was made to hunger. Because we have been intemperate in drinking, He thirsted. Because we have misused our money, He was penniless (Matt. 17:27). Because we have spoken ill of God, He was spoken against; because we have denied Him, He was denied. "Not one throb of pain did He feel, not one pang of sorrow did He experience, not one sigh of anguish did He heave, not one tear of grief did He shed, for Himself. All were for men; all were for us. If not one of His sufferings was personal, it follows that they were all substitutionary, that they were all, of course, included in the matter or substance of His atoning sacrifice. During the whole period of His mortal life the victim was a-slaying. At the moment of His birth, the sword of justice was unsheathed against the man who is Jehovah's fellow, and returned not to its scabbard till it had been bathed in the blood of Calvary.

"It may be deemed at variance with this view of the subject, that the redemption of man is sometimes in Scripture ascribed simply to the blood of Christ, or to His death alone. But such language is not to be understood as limiting the Atonement of Christ to the simple act of dying, or to those sufferings in which there was an effusion of literal blood. The bloody agony of the garden, and the accursed death of the Cross, were prominent and concluding parts of His sufferings, and, by a common figure, so to speak, the completion of His humiliation, without which all that went before must have been in vain; and may be regarded as having procured salvation, in the same way as that last instalment of a sum which is paid by degrees, may be supposed to cancel the debt and procure a discharge. But, as when Christ is said to have been 'obedient unto death,' we are to understand the phrase, not of a *single act,* but of the *duration* of His obedience throughout the whole period of His life, so may it be said that He *suffered unto death,* as expressive of the duration of His suffering throughout the whole of His earthly course" (W. Symington).

It is in the closing scenes of "the days of His flesh" that we may the more fully discover Christ occupying the place of His sinful people, and receiving from God that which was due them. Even where we behold Him before men, that which transpired is to be read and interpreted in the light of His vicarious position and His complete identification with His guilty people. What took place here on earth was but the visible adumbration of the trial and verdict of the Higher Court. Take His appearance before Caiaphas and Pilate. We venture to say that all the annals of human history will be searched in vain not only for a parallel but for anything approaching a resemblance. Nevertheless, the deeper meaning of the unprecedented treatment meted out to Christ has been perceived by but few. Here, as almost everywhere else, men have been occupied with the *human* instead of with the Divine side of things. Many a writer has marveled at the iniquitous conduct of Israel's high priest and Judea's Roman governor, and have scathingly condemned their unrighteous actions; but apparently it never occurred to them to ask, Why did *God* not only suffer, but ordain it all? (Acts 4:27, 28).

The Romans were renowned for their respect for the law, the equity of their dealings, the generosity with which they treated those whom they conquered. How then is Pilate's unjust treatment of Christ to be accounted for? True, from the human side, he feared that if he resisted the demands of the Jewish leaders, a complaint would be made to Caesar, and then he would probably lose his position. Nevertheless, this still leaves unsolved the deeper and more important question: Why should *God* require His Son to be mocked by submitting to a trial which appears to us worse than a farce, really, a travesty of justice? We submit that one consideration alone supplies the key to this mighty problem, and that, the two fold relation which Christ sustained: personally innocent, officially guilty; in Himself, without sin; by virtue of His identification with His people, "made sin." It was the Sinner who was arraigned for sentence. "He was [judicially] *reckoned* [by God] among the transgressors" (Luke 22:37): this applies equally to His trial, His buffetings in the judgment-hall, and His actual crucifixion. John 18:8 proves this: If the Representative be seized, then those whom He represented *must* go free.

As the Substitute of His sinful people, Christ had to be found innocent and yet pronounced guilty! Though personally spotless, Divine justice required that He should be dealt with as officially deserving of condemnation. What occurred in Jerusalem was but the *visible* expression of the great Assize which had been held in Heaven. The sentence pronounced by the human judges was but the intimation or announcement of the sentence which had been passed by the Divine Judge upon the Sin-bearer. Christ hid not His face from shame and spitting. Why? Because as guilty criminals, as convicted outlaws, as the vilest of wretches, *that* is what our sins deserved. When before His accusers He was "dumb," making no reply to the charges brought against Him (Matt. 26:60). Why? Because though *personally* innocent, He occupied the place of *guilty* sinners, therefore was there nothing which He could adduce in extenuation.

A marvelous flood of light does this throw upon the Gospel narratives. The charge which was laid against Christ as He stood before the Sanhedrin, as brought against *those whom He represented* was not false! Guilty of blasphemy against God each of us most certainly is. Therefore as the official Representative of His sinful people, the Lord Jesus stood silent, putting in no plea to arrest judgment. So true was the accusation *against us,* there was no need of witnesses (Matt. 26:65)! We say again, the earthly court, dealing with the charge of blasphemy, or dishonor done to the Name and Word of God, and in sentencing to death our Surety, was the pronouncement on *our* sins, much in the same way as the shadow on the sundial registers the movements which are taking place in another sphere! Christ's holy Person was there in the room of guilty persons, and the human judge but expressed the verdict of the Divine Judge! It was the Sinner who was arraigned for sentence. At the beginning, the Judge of all the earth had formally pronounced sentence, "Thou shalt surely die," and that sentence was now fully and finally executed, *vicariously,* on elect sinners.

It were an insult to His moral government to suppose for a moment that the inflexibly righteous and ineffably holy God would permit a perfectly innocent and pure Man to endure the indignities, the sufferings, and the sentence which Christ received. His own infallible Word assures us, "When a man's ways please the Lord, he maketh even his enemies to be at peace with him" (Prov. 16:7). Ah, it was *no* innocent person that stood before Caiaphas and Pilate; instead, it was *the sinner* who was on trial — there in the person of his sinless and immaculate Substitute. The earthly court of judgment was but the foreground; in reality it was the Bearer of sin making a *real* appearance before *the Bar of God!* Hence, there could only be one decision possible: though personally sinless He was officially guilty, and nothing remained but sentence of condemnation and the prompt execution of it. Thus may we, and thus should we *admire* the over-ruling providence of God, which caused the lower court on earth to shadow forth so clearly the action of the Supreme Court on High.

What we have attempted to bring out above is so little apprehended, yea is so completely unknown to almost all of our readers—so superficial to the last degree are the pulpit-ministrations of the best today!—that we trust they will bear with our repetitions, and even go to the trouble of re-reading what has been written. So we say again, that there is no possible explanation of that (seemingly) anomalous trial, which passed through the due forms of law and order, unless we recognize that it was a symbolical representation, yea, a Divinely-arranged tableau, of a spiritual mystery, setting forth the altogether unique, because *dual,* relation which Christ occupied. Thus was Pilate obliged to affirm to absolute innocence of that blessed One who stood before him: seven times over he declared "I find *no* fault in Him." Nevertheless, he sentenced Him to death! Christ was *personally* innocent, yet as the vicarious Victim, as the Representative of His criminal people, He was *officially* guilty. Thus, Christ was *righteously* pronounced personally spotless, but officially condemned to death. *That* is why God caused His beloved to endure such mockery, ignominy and suffering.

> "Bearing shame and scoffing rude,
> In *my* place condemned He stood;
> Sealed my pardon with His blood,
> Hallelujah! *what* a Saviour."

The passages of Scripture which expressly set forth the vicarious character of Christ's atoning work are so numerous that we can here but make a selection from them. It was predicted that, "After three score and two weeks shall Messiah be cut off, *but not for Himself*" (Dan. 9:26). Then for whom was He "cut off"? Hear the answer of God's Spirit-taught people, "He was wounded *for our* transgressions, bruised *for our* iniquities: the chastisement of *our* peace was upon Him; and with His stripes *we* are healed" (Isa. 53:5). From His own declarations we may cite the following. "The Son of man came not to be ministered unto, but to minister, and to give His life a ransom *for* many" (Matt. 20:28); "The Good Shepherd giveth His life *for* the sheep" (John 10:11). From the writings of the apostles, the following may be taken as samples: "Christ died *for* the ungodly" (Rom. 5:6); "Christ also hath once suffered for sins, the Just *for* the unjust" (I Pet. 3:18); "God . . . sent His Son to be the propitiation *for* our sins" (I John 4:10).

Enemies of the Truth, anxious to repudiate the substitutionary nature of Christ's obedience and death have pointed out the word "for" is not conclusive. It *may* signify "in the stead of," or it may also mean only "on the behalf of." Thus: the soldier dies "for," or on behalf of his country. The sufficient answer to this is that though in some passages the Greek preposition "huper" is used, which also has the same double meaning as our English "for," yet there are other passages where the Holy Spirit has employed the term "anti" and this cannot signify anything else than "in the stead of." *This* is the word used in Mark 10:41, "This is My body which is given *for* (anti) you."

In the Septuagint Greek translation of the Old Testament the word "anti" is used to express the setting of one thing or person over against another. This may be seen by a reference to the following passages, where "anti" is used for the words we place in italic type: "God hath appointed me another seed *instead* of Abel" (Gen. 4:25). "Joseph gave them bread *in exchange for* horses and flocks and cattle" (Gen. 47:17). "Aaron died, and Eli his son ministered in the priest's office *in his stead*" (Deut. 10:6). These passages are so clear and the scope of the preposition is so obvious that comment thereon would be superfluous.

This Greek preposition is also used in the New Testament in passages other than where Christ is in view, which define its meaning unequivocally. Take the following instances where "anti" is the Greek equivalent for the English words placed in italic type: "Archelaus reigned in Judea *in the room of* his father Herod" (Matt. 2:22). "Ye have heard that it hath been said, An eye *for* an eye and a tooth *for* a tooth" (Matt. 5:38). "If he ask for a fish, will he *for* a fish give him a serpent?" (Luke 11:11). "Recompense no man evil *for* evil" (Rom. 12:17). In none of these passages can "anti" possibly mean "on behalf of." No, it has—except in those cases where it is used in the sense of *against,* as in "anti-christ"—the uniform significance of "in the stead of."

Thus, after a minute examination of the passages where this Greek preposition is found, we are thoroughly satisfied that we are fully warranted in saying with A. A. Hodge, "If the Holy Spirit intended us to understand that Christ was strictly substituted in the Law-place of His people, He could have used no language more exactly adapted to express His meaning. If this were *not* His meaning, we may well despair of arriving at the understanding of His meaning on the subject through the study of His words in any department of Scripture."

Though the Greek preposition "huper" has the double meaning which our English "for" possesses, that is no reason for allowing the enemies of Truth to wrest from our hands those passages which treat of Christ's Atonement, where this particular term occurs. That "huper" sometimes has *the same* force as "anti" no honest scholar will deny. That we are obliged to understand it as signifying "in the stead of" in many places, may be clearly shown and definitely established by various considerations. Take just one passage: "For the love of Christ constraineth us; because we thus judge, that if One died *for* (huper) all, therefore all died" (II Cor. 5:14 R. V.). Here the fact of substitution is plain; since Christ died in the room and place of the "all," then the "all" are legally regarded as having died too. In other words, the vicarious atonement of Christ is reckoned as the personal atonement of the believer. It would be mere nonsense to say, "If one died for the benefit of all, then all died." Should it be asked, Why has the Holy Spirit used the somewhat ambiguous "huper" in some passages rather than the unequivocal "anti," the answer is, Because Christ not only died in His people's stead, but *also* for their benefit!

Summing up what has been before us under this second division of the *nature* of Christ's Satisfaction, we would say:

The sufferings to which the Lord Jesus was exposed, from the hour of His birth until He committed His spirit into the hands of the Father, were strictly and definitely vicarious, borne as the Substitute of His people — not only for their advantage, but *actually in their room and stead.* He came here as their Representative and federal Head, undertaking and discharging all their obligations, receiving in His spirit and soul and body, all that was due them. He was their Ransom, paying their debts. He was their Mediator, coming in between God and them, receiving from Him and rendering to Him, whatever was due to and from them. He was their High Priest offering for them. He was abased because of our pride. He was made poor to atone for our covetousness. He was an hungered because we, in Adam, eat of the forbidden fruit. He thirsted, because we have drunken from forbidden fountains. He died, because we were dead in sins.

Though it be an anticipation of what belongs, strictly speaking, to a later aspect of our theme, we cannot close this chapter without calling attention to the clear, unescapable, and inexpressibly blessed *implication* of what has been before us. Christ not only died in our stead, He died to secure our salvation. He not only died in our room, He died for our benefit. Because He became poor, we are enriched. Because He was forsaken of God, we are reconciled to God. Because He was stripped of His garments, we are clothed with the robe of His righteousness. He was abased that we might be exalted. He came to earth that we might go to heaven. He became servant that we might be "made free." He was troubled that we might be comforted. He was tempted that we might triumph. He was scourged that we might be healed. He was dishonored that we might be glorified. And there is no contingency or uncertainty about it. That His people should reap the benefits of Christ's satisfaction is not made dependent on their fulfilling any conditions. Repentance and faith were *purchased* by Christ for every one for whom He obeyed and suffered. Divine justice *requires* that Christ shall see of the travail of His soul and be satisfied. The law of God *demands* that its reward should be bestowed on all for whom Christ obeyed it. The very righteousness and faithfulness of God *insist* that, because the Captain of their salvation was made perfect through suffering, He *shall* bring the "many sons *to glory*."

"Payment God cannot twice demand,
First at my bleeding Surety's hand
And then again at mine.

"Complete atonement Thou hast made,
And to the utmost farthing paid
What e'er Thy people owed.

"How then can wrath on me take place
If sheltered in Thy righteousness
And sprinkled with Thy blood?

"Turn, then, my soul, unto thy rest,
The merits of thy Great High Priest
Speak peace and liberty.

"Trust in His efficacious blood,
Nor fear thy banishment from God
Since Jesus died for thee." (Toplady)

CHAPTER SEVEN

The Atonement — Its Nature (continued)

Rightly has it been said that, "The doctrine of the Atonement is put in its proper light only when it is regarded as the central truth of Christianity, the great theme of Scripture. The principal object of Revelation was to unfold this unique method of reconciliation by which men, once alienated from God, might be restored to a right relation, and even to a better than their previous standing. But the doctrine is simply *revealed,* or in other words, is taught us by Divine authority alone" (George Smeaton). If it be a fact that the great Atonement is the central luminary in the firmament of God's truth, it is equally true that the *nature* of the Atonement is the very heart of this vital subject. Therefore it behooves us to give it our most prayerful and careful consideration.

In seeking to set forth the nature of the Satisfaction which the Mediator rendered to God on behalf of His people, we have seen, first, that His work was a *federal* one: that Christ entered this world not as a private individual, but in an official character, as the covenant-Head of God's elect, as their legal Representative. Remarkably does this appear in His first ministerial utterance. In Luke 2:49 we have the first *personal* word which Scripture records as proceeding from those lips into which *grace* had been "poured" (Psa. 45:2), viz., "Wist ye not that I must be about my Father's business?" There He expressed His relation to *God,* to the One who had sent Him: He had come here to do that business or work the Father had assigned Him. Those words were uttered by Him as a Boy of twelve. An interval of eighteen years pass before we hear another utterance from Him who spake as never man did, viz., "Suffer it to be so now: for thus it becometh *us* to fulfill all righteousness" (Matt. 3:15). Here He expresses His relation to His *people*, to those on whose behalf He was sent.

The Saviour had now come forth from the seclusion of Nazareth and presented Himself for baptism at the hands of His forerunner. John is to be regarded as the living expression and culminating point of the law and the Prophets (Luke 16:16). who had for long centuries witnessed to the coming of Messiah, and which now, by their great representative (Matt. 11:11), was to induct Christ into His office (John 1:31). As Christ recognized *them* (by coming to John), so *they* (in Him, their representative) were to authenticate Him as the *truth* of the Prophets and the *substance* of the law's types. At first John demurred, and Christ said "suffer it to be so *now*." In the Greek the "now" is emphatic: suffer it in My *present* state of humiliation, as an act suited to My office *as Substitute*. The reason given was: "for thus it becometh *US*" not "Me" personally, but "us"—Christ *one with* those whom He had come to save! There is the federal relationship seen from the beginning!

"*Thus* it becometh us to fulfill all righteousness." Those words are not to be limited to the act of baptism: the language is more general in its scope, though particular in its terms. The words "becometh" signified, It is not unworthy of the Son of God to stoop so low, for "righteousness" requires it. His language intimated, It is suitable that I should appear in the "likeness of sin's flesh," identifying Myself with them in "confessing their sins" (Mark 1:5). It was becoming that He should be immersed in that river which spoke of death (Jer. 12:5) at the very outset of His public ministry, for it symbolized that "baptism" of *suffering* which He would undergo (Luke 12:50). and showed His *willingness* to endure it. Passing beneath the waters of Jordan was a fitting emblem of all those "waves and billows" (Psa. 42:7) of God's wrath which would shortly break over Him. It was meet that He *should* "fulfill all righteousness," submit to all that the law had foreshadowed and the prophets predicted, and thus meet all the demands of God upon His people.

Second, we have seen that the Satisfaction which Christ rendered unto God was a *vicarious* one. Now as the Substitute of His people the law exacted two things from Christ: first, that He should render that obedience which was required from them as creatures; second, that He should endure that penalty which they merited as sinners. Thus, the mediatorial work which was given to Christ to perform involved two things, which though inseparably connected, yet are clearly separable in thought, namely a work of obedience distinguished from the sufferings He bore. In all His obedience He suffered; in all His sufferings He obeyed. Hence, it is of first importance to recognize that throughout His earthly course Christ sustained a twofold relation to the law: personally sinless, officially under its curse. The very fact of His putting on "the likeness of sin's flesh" (Rom. 8:3) evidences that sin had been transferred to Him from the moment He was conceived in the Virgin's womb. Nevertheless, He who "bore sin" all through the days of His flesh, was also the sinless Doer of a Divine work.

The very sinlessness of Christ was the necessary basis of His work of sin-bearing (II Cor. 5:21). He must be innocent to stand for the guilty; He must be holy to take the place of the unholy, otherwise He too had needed a Saviour. It was the Just who suffered for the unjust (I Pet. 3:18). Thus the wondrous life of Christ is far more than a spectacle to be gazed at in admiration, and more than an example for His people to follow (I Pet. 2:21); it must be regarded as the work of *one for the many.* Unique, glorious, perfect, was His lovely life. "I seek not mine own will, but the will of the Father which hath sent me" (John 5:30), sets forth the guiding principle which ever regulated Him: cf. John 4:34. "I do always those things that please Him" (John 8:29). His was a life of constant service to God: uninterrupted in duration, perfect in degree, flawless in its balance. One grace neither excluded nor marred another: all was there, all was perfectly blended. Such a life, such obedience, such service, *merited reward,* and is actually bestowed on all He represented, on all whose substitute He was. We are now ready to contemplate:

3. It was a Penal Work

Scripture plainly teaches that God is both holy and righteous, and that "justice and judgment" (*not* "love and pity") are the establishment of God's "throne" (Psa. 89:14). Thus there is that in the Divine Essence which abhors sin for its intrinsic sinfulness, both in its respect of pollution and in its aspect of guilt. The perfections of God are therefore displayed both by forbidding and punishing the same. He has pledged Himself that "the soul that sinneth, it shall die" (Ezek. 18:4). Therefore, in order for a full Satisfaction to be rendered unto God, sin must be punished, the penalty of the law must be enforced. Consequently, as Saviour of His Church, Christ had to vicariously suffer the infliction of the law's curse.

What we shall now seek to show is that the sufferings and death of Christ were a satisfaction to Divine justice on behalf of the sins of His people. In case any should object against our use of the term "satisfaction," let us point out that this very word is found in our English Bibles, being given by the translators as the equivalent for the Hebrew word which is ordinarily rendered "Atonement": "Moreover ye shall take no *satisfaction* for the life of a murderer, which is guilty of death: but he shall surely be put to death. And ye shall take no *satisfaction* for him that is fled to the city of his refuge, that he should come again to dwell in the land, until the death of the priest" (Num. 35:31, 32).

The deep humiliation to which the Son of God was subjected in taking upon Him the form of a servant, and being made "in the likeness of sin's flesh," was a judicial infliction imposed upon Him by the Father, yet voluntarily submitted to by Himself. The very *purpose* of His humiliation, His obedience, His sufferings, makes them *penal,* for they were unto the satisfying of the claims of God's law upon His people. In being "made under the law" (Gal. 4:4) Christ became *subject to* all that the law enjoins: "Now we know that what things soever the law saith, it saith to them who are under the law" (Rom. 3:19), which means the law calls for the fulfillment of its terms. "Christ in our room and stead, did both by doing and suffering, *satisfy Divine justice,* both the legislatory, the retributive, and the vindictive, in the most perfect manner, fulfilling all the righteousness of the law, which the law otherwise required of us, in order to impugnity, and to our having a right to eternal life" (H. Witsius, 1693).

"For Christ also hath once suffered for sins, the Just for the unjust" (I Pet. 3:18). The reference here must not be restricted to what Christ endured at the hands of God while He hung upon the Cross, nor to all He passed through during that day and preceding night. Beware of *limiting* the Word of God! No; the entirety of His humiliation is here included. The whole life of Christ was one of sufferings, therefore was He designated "the Man of sorrows," not simply, "sorrow". From His birth to His death, suffering and sorrow marked Him as their legitimate Victim. While yet an infant He was driven into exile, to escape the fury of those who sought His life. That was but the prophetic fore-runner of His whole earthly course. The cup of woe, put to His lips at Bethlehem, was never removed till He drained its bitter dregs at Calvary.

Every variety of suffering was experienced by Him. He tasted *poverty* in its severest rigor. Born in a stable, owning no property on earth, dependent upon the charity of others (Luke 8:3), oftentimes being worse situated than the inferior orders of creation: Matthew 8:20. He suffered *reproach* in all its bitterness. The most malignant accusations, the vilest aspersions, the most cutting sarcasm, were directed against His person and character. He was taunted with being a glutton, a winebibber, a deceiver, a blasphemer, a devil. Therefore do we hear Him crying, "Reproach hath broken my heart" (Psa. 69:20). He experienced *temptation* in all its malignity. The Prince of darkness assailed Him with all his ingenuity and power, causing his infernal legions to attack Him, coming against Him like "strong bulls of Bashan," gaping on Him with their mouths like ravening and roaring lions (Psa. 22:12, 13). Above all, He suffered the *wrath* of God, so that He was "exceeding sorrowful, even unto death" (Matt. 26:38), in "an agony" (Luke 22:44), and ultimately, "forsaken of God."

What then is the explanation of these unparalleled "sufferings"? Why was the most perfect obedience followed by the most terrible punishment? Why was unsullied holiness visited with unutterable anguish? David declared, "Yet have I not seen the righteous forsaken" (Psa. 37:25); why, then was the Righteous One abandoned by God? Only one answer is possible; only one answer fully meets all the facts of the case; only one answer clears the government of God. In taking the place of offending sinners, Christ became obligated to discharge all their liabilites, and this involved bearing their sins, being charged with their guilt, suffering their punishment. Accordingly, God dealt with Him as the Representative of His criminal people, inflicting upon Him all that their sins merited. As the sin-bearing Substitute of His people, Christ was justly exposed to all the dreadful consequences of God's manifested displeasure.

Of old the question was asked, "Who ever perished being innocent?" (Job 4:7), to which we may, without the slightest hesitation, answer, None. God never has and never will smite the innocent, Therefore before His punitive wrath could fall upon Christ, the sins of His people must first be transferred to Him, and this is precisely what Scripture affirms. Remarkably was this foreshadowed of old in the great type of Israel's annual Day of Atōnement, "And Aaron shall lay both his hands upon the head of the live goat, and confess over him all the iniquities of the children of Israel, and all their transgressions with all their sins, *putting them upon* the head of the goat" (Lev. 16:21). So too was it plainly prophesied, "The Lord hath laid *on Him* the iniquity of us all . . . He *bare* the sin of many" (Isa. 53:6, 12). So also is it expressly affirmed in the New Testament, "So Christ was once offered to *bear* the sins of many" (Heb. 9:28). Once again we would point out there is not a hint in these passages that Christ bore the sins of His people *only* while He was hanging upon the Cross. We are aware that many have so affirmed, but in doing so they have not only been guilty of adding to the Word of God, but also of flatly contradicting it.

We have already pointed out that the expression of Romans 8:3, "made in the likeness of sin's flesh," clearly pre-supposes the *transfer* of His people's sins *to* Christ, and that what happened immediately after His birth was in full keeping with this fact, and cannot be understood apart from it. That He was "circumcised" (Luke 2:21) not only proved that He had been "made in the likeness of men" (Phil. 2:7), but also evidenced that He *had* been made "in the likeness of *sin's flesh.*" So too the ceremonial "purification" of His mother (Luke 2:22) and her presentation of a "sin-offering" (Lev. 12:2, 6), was in perfect keeping with the fact that, though His humanity was immaculate, yet He had entered this world officially guilty.

As little children we sinned — "the wicked are estranged from the womb; they go astray as soon as they be born, speaking lies" (Psa. 58:3) — and therefore as a child Christ suffered, suffered not only as our Substitute, but because our sins had been transferred to Him. In our youth we sinned, and as a youth Christ suffered, and suffered at the hands of God, as His own words clearly testify: "I am afflicted and ready to die from youth up: I suffer Thy terrors, I am distracted" (Psa. 88:15). In the prime of our manhood, we sinned, and in the prime of His manhood Christ suffered. Let us refer once more to His being assailed by Satan. Hebrews 2:18 tells us that He "*suffered* being tempted," and that very suffering was *penal*. That Christ's "suffering" under Satan was designed and appointed as an infliction *from God,* is proved by the statement that "Jesus was led up *of the Spirit* into the wilderness *to be* tempted of the Devil" (Matt. 4:1).

Man having allowed himself to be overcome by Satan, God has, by a just sentence, delivered him up as a slave to his tyranny; therefore was it necessary that Christ, as His sinful people's Substitute, should be exposed to the harrassings of the Devil, that in *this* respect also He might satisfy Divine justice. Most assuredly Satan and his agents could never have assailed Christ had He not been so (legally) charged with the guilt of our crimes, that God righteously exposed Him to injuries from them (Acts 2:23). The elect themselves, as sinners, were subject to Satan's power (Col. 1:13), and that by the righteous sentence of the Judge of all the earth; therefore were they not only the "prey of the mighty," but also were "*lawful* captives" (Isa. 49:24). Therefore, as Christ came here as Surety in their room, He, by virtue of God's sentence, also became subject to the buffetings of Satan.

"Christ's passive, or suffering obedience, is not to be confined to what He experienced in the garden and on the cross. This suffering was the culmination of His piacular sorrow, but not the whole of it. Everything in His human and earthly career that was distressing belongs to His passive obedience. It is a true remark of Jonathan Edwards, that the blood of

Christ's circumcision was as really a part of His vicarious atonement, as the blood that flowed from His pierced side. And not only His suffering proper, but His humiliation, also, was expiatory" (W. Shedd). "The satisfaction or propitiation of Christ consists either in His suffering evil, or His being subject to abasement . . . Whatever Christ was subject to which was the judicial fruit of sin, had the nature of satisfaction for sin. But not only proper suffering, but all abasement and depression of the state and circumstances of mankind (human nature) below its primitive honor and dignity, such as His body remaining under death, and body and soul remaining separate, are the judicial fruits of sin" (Jno. Edwards, 1743).

When the Scriptures speak of the Satisfaction of Christ, they ascribe it to His sufferings in general, as Isaiah 53:4, "Surely He hath borne our griefs and carried our sorrows," that is, He suffered all the pains and sorrows due to us from sin. It is to be most carefully noted that the inspired declaration "the Lord hath laid on Him the inquity of us all" (Isa. 53:6) comes *before* "He was oppressed" and before "He is brought as a lamb to the slaughter"; as it was at the commencement of His public ministry, and *not* while He hung upon the Cross that God moved one of His servants to cry, "Behold the Lamb of God" which taketh away the sin of the world. Christ was brought "to the slaughter" before the three hours of darkness, yet even then "affliction" lay upon Him, and our iniquity was exacted of Him. So too this very chapter (Isa. 53) ascribes our "healing" to the *stripes* which He received from *men* as plainly as other passages attribute our being delivered from the curse of the law through *God's* visiting Him with its curse.

"For even hereunto were ye called: because Christ also suffered for us, leaving us an example" (I Pet. 2:21). "To *suffer* here denotes to be in affliction: for all those sufferings are here intended, in which Christ has left us an example of patience. These sufferings he affirms to be *for* us, that is, undergone as well in our stead, as for our good. For this is ordinarily the signification of the word *huper,* and that this is the true meaning of Peter, we conclude hence, that in 3:18 he says, 'Christ suffered *for sins*', namely, that He might be the propitiation for our sins" (H. Witsius).

When the sovereign rights of God are emphasized there is generally raised the objection that we are hereby "reducing man to a mere machine." Many are they who are prepared to hold a brief for human responsibility. But rare indeed is it that we ever hear anything about *transferred responsibility*. Yet it is at this point lies one of the chief wonders and glories of the Gospel. The responsibility of God's people was transferred to Christ: He assumed their liabilities, made Himself chargeable with their debts, answerable to every demand of the law against them. Had this not been the case, how could God have righteously laid the iniquities of His people upon the head of His Holy Son? Still less could He have called for the sword of Justice to smite Him. It was because Christ was "made *sin*" for us, that He was also "made a curse" for us: the latter could not be without the former. As this is a point of such vital importance we must amplify a little further.

Hebrews 7:22 declares that Christ is "Surety of a better covenant": He was the Sponsor of His people, as Judah undertook to be for Benjamin. "I will be *surety* for him; of my hand shalt thou require him; if I bring him not unto thee, and set him before thee, then let *me* bear the blame for ever" (Gen. 43:9). Or, as Paul was for Onesimus, "If he hath wronged thee, or oweth ought, put that on *mine account;* I Paul have written it with mine own hand, I will repay it" (Philem. 18, 19). Just so did Christ engage Himself unto His Father for us: reckon to Me whatever they owe Thee, and I will satisfy for it. "A surety, whose name is put into a bond, is not only bound to pay the debt, but he makes it his *own* debt also, even as well as it is the principal's, so that *he* may be sued and charged for the debt. So Christ, when He once made Himself a Surety, He so put Himself in the room of sinners, that what the law could lay to their charge, it might lay to His" (T. Goodwin, 1680).

Christ must take on Him the guilt of our transgressions before He could take our punishment upon Him, and so satisfy Divine justice on our behalf. That He *did so,* is demonstrated by His own words. It is indeed remarkable to find how that Christ actually *owned* our sins as being *His*. First, in the 40th

Psalm. That this Psalm is a Messianic one we know from its quotation in Hebrews 10. That it contains the very words of Christ, is plainly evident from vv. 7-11. He is still the Speaker in v. 12, where He declared "For innumerable evils have compassed me about: *Mine* iniquities have taken hold upon me, so that I am not able to look up; they are more than the hairs of mine head: therefore my heart faileth me." What a proof that the sins of His people *had been* transferred to Him! Second, in the 69th, another great Messianic Psalm. There too we find Him saying, "O God, Thou knowest *my* foolishness; and *my* sins are not hid from Thee" (v. 5). How unmistakably do those words show our sins had been reckoned to Him! Those sins were His not by perpetration, but by imputation.

"Who his own self bare our sins in his own body on [to] the tree" (I Pet. 2:24). "'Our sins' here are our liabilities to punishment on account of our violations of the Divine law, and the necessary consequences of those liabilities; in other words, guilt in the sense of binding over to punishment, and punishment itself" (J. Brown). Those sins Christ "bare," endured as a heavy load. The prime meaning of the Greek verb is "to carry up," the allusion being to the typical animal which was carried up to the altar, which was always erected on an elevated place. The margin gives the preferable rendering—"*to* the tree": the preposition is the same as in the next verse, "ye are returned *to* the Shepherd." The reason why the Cross is here termed "the tree" we will state a little later.

There was a needs-be for Christ taking on Him the guilt of our transgressions in order for Divine justice to punish Him, for "we are sure that the judgment of God is according to truth" (Rom. 2:2). Whomsoever God punishes for sin must be guilty *of* sin. Therefore we read, "For He hath made Him sin for us, who knew no sin" (II Cor. 5:21). Each word here calls for a separate paragraph. The opening "for" assigns the ground on which the message of reconciliation (vv. 19, 20) rests. V.19 states that God does not impute trespasses unto His people; v. 21 tells us why: because they were imputed to Christ. Here the Atonement is traced back to its source. "God was in Christ reconciling": *He* made Christ to be sin—when? In the everlasting covenant, by the mutual agreement of the

Father and the Son. Then we beheld the *fitness* of Christ to make atonement: He was personally sinless, it was *God* who so adjudged Him! "Who knew no sin" is the negative way of saying that His obedience was perfect. The law had no fault against Him, either of omission or commission. Nevertheless, "He [God] made him [legally constituted Christ] to be sin for us," not in mere semblance, but in awful reality, and this, from the moment of His incarnation.

In entering the law-place of His people, Christ became *answerable* to the righteousness of God on their behalf: whatever they owed, must be exacted from their Sponsor: He must pay their debts, suffer the full penalty of their iniquities, receive sin's wages in their room. Christ now became exposed to all that the holiness of God must inflict upon sin. Therefore we read, "Christ hath redeemed us from the curse of the law, being made a curse for us: for it is written, Cursed is every one that hangeth on a tree" (Gal. 3:13). "The cross was accursed, not only in the opinion of men, but by the decree of the Divine law. Therefore when Christ was lifted up upon it, He rendered Himself obnoxious to the curse" (Calvin).

The very *mode* of death which God appointed for His Son reveals to us the *penal* nature of it. The Cross was no mere "accident," as though it made no difference what form His death took. Fundamental reasons rendered it expedient and necessary that the Surety should die a death which was *accursed of God*; hence the frequent reference in the New Testament to the "cross" and the "tree"—cf. John 12:32, 33. At Calvary God's terrible curse on sin was publicly displayed, of which the cross was not the cause but the symbol: cf. John 3:14. Under the Mosaic law (to which the apostle refers in Gal. 3:13), hanging on a tree was a death reserved for great criminals. Hence the force of the word "tree" in I Peter 2:24. Christ hanging upon the tree was the *public* testimony to *God's* curse on Him. "The *cause* of the curse was not the hanging on the tree, but the sin with which He was charged; and that mode of punishment exhibited that He was the object of God's holy displeasure; not indeed because He was suspended on the tree, but because He was the sin-bearer, and the punishment of the offences for which that ignominious penalty was allotted was then inflicted. Divine wisdom appointed that He who bore the sin of the world should be exposed as a curse, for the Divine displeasure was there most awfully displayed" (G. Smeaton).

As to why *this* means and method of death was selected by God out of all others possible—poisoning, stoning, beheading, etc,—Genesis 3 supplies the answer: "As the fatal sin which diffused the curse over the human race was connected with the forbidden 'tree,' God wisely ordered that the last Adam should expiate sin by being suspended on a tree: and He appointed in the law (Deut. 21:22, 23) such a symbol of the curse as reminded all men of the *origin* of the Divine curse on the world. He would not have the curse removed in any other way" (G. Smeaton). Among the Romans, death by crucifixion was the deepest possible humiliation. It was the most degrading of punishments, inflicted only on slaves and the lowest of the people, and if freemen were at any time subjected to crucifixion for great crimes, such as robbery, high treason, or sedition, the sentence could not be executed till they were put into the catalogue of slaves, and that, by the utmost humiliation. Their liberty was taken from them by servile stripes and scourging, as was done to Christ. Thus the curse of God's law was executed upon the Head and Substitute of His people. To "preach Christ crucified" (I Cor. 1:23) is to proclaim and expound His being "made a curse for us."

Because Christ was "made sin" and "made a curse" for His people, the wrath of God's holiness flamed against Him and the sword of His justice pierced Him. "Awake, O sword, against my shepherd, against the man that is my fellow, saith the Lord of hosts: *smite* the shepherd" (Zech. 13:7), and cf. Matt. 26:31. God inflicted punishment on Christ as if He had been the personal offender. "It pleased the Lord to bruise him; *He* hath put him to grief: when *Thou* shalt make his soul an offering for sin" (Isa. 53:10). As all the sufferings of men, whether inflicted immediately by God or mediately by Satan or men (Jer. 2:15-17), arise from the demerits of sin; so *all* the sufferings of Christ, from man, Satan, God, arose from the demerits of His peoples' sins imputed to their Substitute.

The punishment which God meted out to Christ was the *very* punishment which was due His people. That He was accursed of God is seen from His hanging on the tree. That He received sin's wages was evidenced by God's forsaking Him. That He was numbered with transgressors was exhibited by His dying between two thieves. True, He did not suffer eternally, for the eternity of our punishment was only a circumstance arising from *our incapacity* to suffer the whole weight of God's wrath in a brief season, and therefore the brevity of duration of Christ's sufferings is no valid objection against the *identity* of penalty which He received. Moreover, the infinite dignity of *His* person more than compensated the law. "To the enlightened eye, there is found on the cross another inscription besides that which Pilate ordered to be written there: The Victim of guilt. The Wages of sin" (J. Brown).

CHAPTER EIGHT

THE ATONEMENT—ITS NATURE (CONCLUDED)

We have pointed out in the preceding chapters that the particular aspect of Christ's Satisfaction which is now before us constitutes the very heart of this mighty subject. As the physical heart is to the human body, so is the *nature* of the Atonement to the whole of this wondrous theme. When a man's heart becomes seriously affected, the whole of his constitution suffers. In like manner, when we err in our views of the precise *character* of Christ's obedience and sufferings, the whole of our system of truth suffers injury in exact proportion. The acid test of a theologian's views and a preacher's capability to expound the Gospel, is his orthodoxy at this particular point. Hence, because, *this* part of the Truth is of such vital importance we have prayerfully sought to examine it with sevenfold thoroughness, and set before our readers at some length the results of our investigation.

First, we have shown that the work of Christ was *federal* in its character: that is, Christ became legally one of His people. He came here not to strangers, but to His "brethren" (Heb. 2:12). He came here not to procure a people for Himself, but to secure a people already His (Eph. 1:4; Matt. 1:21). The place we occupied was "under the law." We were placed under it at creation, and perfect obedience was made the condition of our well-being. By our fall in Adam we became incapable of obeying the demands of the law and subject to its unrelaxable penalty. The law remained over us, therefore, as an inexorable taskmaster, demanding the impossible, and as the organ of immutable justice, insisting upon our death. Therefore to be our Saviour the Son of God was "made under the law" (Gal. 4:4): He was, by God's ordination, transferred to that position. Thus, the place He took was our law-place. In taking that place He necessarily assumed all our responsibilities: obedience as a condition of life, suffering as a penal consequence of disobedience.

Second, we have shown that the work of Christ was *vicarious* in its character. Substitution has been thus defined: "A 'substitute' is one who does or suffers the same thing which the person or persons for whom he is substituted would have done or suffered." The Scriptures teach us plainly that Christ's obedience was as truly vicarious as was His suffering, and that He reconciled us to the Father by the one as well as the other. It is for this reason we have chosen the term "Satisfaction" in preference to the more popular "Atonement." "The word Atonement signifies only the expiation of our guilt by Christ's vicarious sufferings, but expresses nothing concerning the relation which His obedience sustains to our salvation, as that meritorious condition upon which the Divine favour and the promised reward have by covenant been suspended. On the other hand, the word Satisfaction exactly expresses *all* that Christ has done as our Substitute, in our stead, and for our sakes, to the end of satisfying in our behalf the federal demands of the law, and of securing for us the rewards conditioned upon their fulfillment. His whole work was of the nature of a satisfaction" (A. A. Hodge).

Third, we have shown that the work of Christ was *penal* in its character. This follows of inevitable necessity. In becoming one with His criminal people, Christ entered their law-place before God. In acting as the Substitute of His people, Christ must receive that which was due them from God. Because the sins of His Church were transferred to Christ, He must be paid their wages. Because He took our law-place, the curse of the law must fall upon Him. Because He was "made sin" for us, the sword of Divine justice must smite Him. As I Corinthians 15:3 declares, the God-man not only died "for us," but "Christ died for *our sins,*" which was only made possible by our sins having been federally placed upon

Him. Because our sins were imputed to Him, the wrath of God fell upon Him, and He was visited with all that our sins merited. We are now ready to show—

4. IT WAS A SACRIFICIAL WORK

From the many passages which set forth this aspect of Christ's redemption, we may cite the following. "When thou shalt make his soul *an offering* for sin" (Isa. 53:10). "Christ our passover is *sacrificed* for us" (I Cor. 5:7). "Christ also hath loved us, and hath given himself for us an offering and *a sacrifice* to God for a sweetsmelling savour" (Eph. 5:2). "Who needeth not daily, as those high priests, to offer up sacrifice . . . for this he did once, when he *offered up himself*" (Heb. 7:27). "How much more shall the blood of Christ, who through the eternal Spirit *offered himself* without spot to God, purge your conscience from dead works to serve the living God" (Heb. 9:14).

Ere attempting to define the character of Christ's sacrifice, let us first remind ourselves that He presented Himself a sacrifice to God *by covenant agreement.* As we are told in Romans 3:25, "Whom God hath *foreordained* a propitiation through faith in his blood." God can be pleased only with that which He has appointed. The Everlasting Covenant furnishes the key to many a verse of Scripture. For instance, when Christ was about to go to the Cross, He said, "Now is the Son of Man *glorified*" (John 13:31). But how could that be? Was it not rather His degradation? No, for the eternal Three had assigned to the God-man the work of mediation, and *that* was a high honor. So the Son of man viewed it. It is our "glory" too to bow to God's will and keep His appointments.

Second, though Christ offered Himself a sacrifice according to Divine appointment, it was also by His own *free consent.* As in all our obedience there are two principal ingredients to the true and right constitution of it, namely, the matter of the obedience itself, and the principle or fountain of it in us; in other words, the deed, and the will behind it—which latter God accepts in us, oftentimes without (II Cor. 8:12) and always more than the outward deed—so in Christ's obedience, which is both the pattern and measure of ours, there are these two eminent parts which complete it — the obedience itself, His willingness thereto. First, Christ was willing from all eternity. This is clear from the Covenant, for *that* is a mutual agreement between two parties. It is also necessarily implied in His being made "a Surety" (Heb. 7:22), an undertaking on His part: a surety is a plighter of his troth, by "striking hands" as the phrase is in the original: Prov. 22:26. Again; His willingness from everlasting unto the time of His incarnation is evidenced from Proverbs 8:30, which shows in what or whom He delighted all that while.

Again: His willingness is seen in those words "He humbled Himself" (Phil. 2:8) actively, not "He was humbled," passively. Remarkably and blessedly is this also brought out in Hebrews 10:5-7. There we find His dedication of Himself unto His great work. "When He cometh into the world, He saith, Sacrifice and offering thou wouldest not, but a body hast thou prepared me . . . Lo, I come . . . to do thy will, O God." Here is the remarkable thing: the Holy Spirit has here been pleased to make known to us (as the great Secretary of the Covenant) the very words the Son used as He left the Father's presence to come to earth. To which we may add — amazing, heart-thrilling fact — the Holy Spirit has also been pleased to reveal to us the first words which were uttered by the Father when His Son returned to Him, "The Lord said unto my Lord, Sit thou at my right hand" (Psa. 110:1).

The point we are now dealing with is so precious that we would feign dwell upon it. There was no constraint laid upon Christ: all that He did was done freely and gladly. From the beginning of the days of His flesh He said, "Thou art my God from my mother's belly" (Psa. 22:9), and that, by His perfect choice. So too as He neared the end He could say, "I was not rebellious neither turned away back. I *gave* my back to the smiters, and my cheeks to them that plucked off the hair: I hid not my face from shame and spitting" (Isa. 50:5,6). Yes, Christ "*gave* Himself" (Gal. 2:20) for us.

Third, as it was of the Father's appointment, and the God-man's willing consent that He presented Himself a sacrifice, so also was it *by the Spirit's agency*. "How much more shall the blood of Christ, who through the eternal Spirit offered Himself without spot to God" (Heb. 9:14). The discharge of His entire Messianic office was by the enduement of the Holy Spirit. The very title, "Christ," means "the *anointed* One," and was given to Him because of the peculiar unction of the Spirit conferred upon Him, an unction which was unique in nature and degree. At the beginning of His public ministry He declared, "The Spirit of the Lord is upon me" (Isa. 61:1). He was "full of the Holy Spirit" (Luke 4:1), and the same Spirit which led Him into the wilderness (Matt. 4:1) also led Him as a willing Victim to the Cross. We shall now take note of the various characteristics of Christ's sacrifice:

A. *Christ's Sacrifice Was a Ransoming One*

"There are three several generic forms of conception under which the work wrought by Christ for the salvation of men is set forth. These are (a) that of an expiatory *offering* for sin: (b) that of the redemption of the life and liberty of a captive by the payment of a *ransom* in his stead, and (c) the satisfaction of the *law* by the vicarious fulfillment of its demands. These different conceptions are designed both to limit and to supplement each other in a manner strictly analogous to the combination of the different perceptions of the same object by the different bodily senses. The sense of sight, although when educated in connection with the concurrent and mutually limiting and supplementing perceptions of the organs of touch and hearing, is unmatched as to the extent and accuracy of its information, yet would, if left to itself never have risen beyond an infant's vague perception of a surface variously shaded, without any sense of relation in space.

"All our knowledge of the material world, considered as an object of sense, arises from the education of our minds in the use of our bodily senses *in combination,* and the habits of judgment and inference to which are thus produced. Men learn to interpret the impressions made upon them through their eyes by means of other impressions made upon them in connection with the same object, through the senses of touch and hearing, and vice versa. In like manner our knowledge of the true nature of the work of Christ and its bearing upon us results from all the various forms in which the Scriptures set it forth in *combination,* each at once limiting, modifying and supplementing all the others.

"It should be noticed, moreover, that the Scriptures do not present these several views as different sides of the same house to be taken in succession, but habitually present them in combination, as lights and shades blend together in the same picture in producing the same intelligible expression. Thus, in the same sentences it is said, 'We are *redeemed* with the precious blood of Christ, *as of a lamb* without blemish and without spot.' 'Christ hath *redeemed* us from the *curse of the law* being made a curse for us' (Gal. 3:13). That is, He redeems us not in the sense of making a pecuniary payment in cancellation of our debts, but by His vicarious suffering, like the bleeding sacrifices of the Mosaic ritual, of the penalty due our sins.

"The fact here noticed, that the same inspired sentences represent Christ at the same instance and in the same relations as a 'ransom' and as a 'sin-offering,' and as made to endure 'the curse of the law' for us, is worthy of careful study. The teaching of Scripture is not that Christ is a sacrifice, *and* a ransom, *and* a bearer of the curse of the law, but it is that He is that particular species of sacrifice which *is* a ransom; that His redemption is of that nature which is effected by His bearing the curse of the law in our stead, and that He redeems us by offering Himself a bleeding sacrifice to God. Thus, the teaching of the Holy Spirit is as precise as any ecclesiastical theory of Atonement. Christ saves us by being a sacrifice. He is specifically a sin-offering in the Jewish sense. More specifically yet, the offering of Himself a ransom for us, and to His bearing the curse of the law in our stead, and the design and effects of this ransom-paying, curse-bearing sacrifice of His, that He redeems us from the curse of the law. It is not any kind of a sacrifice, but a ransom-paying, curse-bearing sacrifice. It is not any kind of redemption, but a sacrificial redemption" (A. A. Hodge).

That the sacrifice of Christ was a *ransoming* one is clear, first, from Matthew 20:28, "Even as the Son of man came not to be ministered unto but to minister, and to give his life a ransom for many." This remarkable declaration calls for our closest attention. Christ came here not to be ministered unto as the Lord of all, but to give His life, not only in and by dying, but throughout the whole course of His earthly *service.* The word "give" emphasizes the fact that He acted voluntarily, without compulsion of any kind. The reason for His saying that He came to give His "life" or "soul" appears from the sacrificial language of Leviticus 17:11, "For the life of the flesh is in the blood: and I have given *it* to you upon the altar to make atonement for your souls." The life of the typical sacrifice represented the life of its offerer: the death-sentence executed on the former was what the latter had incurred. *That* was the fundamental idea of all the Old Testament sacrifices.

Christ came here to give His life "a ransom." This term necessarily connotes that the many for whom the ransom was paid were *captives,* in bondage, the slaves of sin (Titus 3:3), and as such, obnoxious to God's holy displeasure. There is an important distinction between "ransom" and "redemption": the former is the price paid to secure the latter. The first mention of a "ransom" in Scripture is in Exodus 21:30, where a valuable price was required for the deliverance of one who, through guilt, was worthy of death, cf. Ex. 30:12, etc. Christ's ransom was paid to satisfy God's justice: a life for a life; the ransom being a penal infliction. Christ gave His life a "ransom *for* many": the Greek preposition is "anti" which, except in the few instances where it means "against," is always used in a *substitutionary* sense. His life was not "given" in any vague, indefinite way for the good of others, but was a specific quid pro quo, dying in the very room of His people. The "many" is in contrast from the one life.

"The church of God, which he hath *purchased* with his own blood" (Acts 20:28). The prominent idea of "ransom" is that of payment, of vicarious substitution, of one thing standing in the place of another. No figure can so fully convey this idea as of one drawn from purchases with money. The very idea of *purchase* necessarily involves that of substitution. I go into a shop and ask the price of a book. It is one dollar. I put down the money, and I am at liberty at once to take up the book. It is mine. On what principle? Of substitution. I substitute the money *for* the book. In *this* way Christ bought His people. To the Corinthian saints Paul wrote, "Ye are not your own; for ye are *bought* with a price" (I Cor. 6:19,20).

"Ye were not redeemed with corruptible things, as silver and gold . . . but with the precious blood of Christ" (I Pet. 1:18,19). Sinners are the prisoners of Divine justice. True, they are the captives of the Devil; but *who* delivered them up to him? The Lord: Satan is but the executioner of His righteous sentence. And their salvation is not a simple discharge without compensation. Neither is the salvation of guilty sinners an act of power only, effected by the interposition of an arm full of might to secure their escape. Gratuitous favor and almighty power *are* both concerned in it, but there is more: there is a price paid, a ransom laid down, every way equivalent to the redemption for which it is offered; and that price was Christ's satisfaction.

B. *Christ's Sacrifice Was a Priestly One*

This has been denied by Socinians, and it is sad to see those who believe in the Deity of Christ adopting this vain reasoning upon the sacerdotal nature of our Saviour's oblation. Through a misunderstanding of Hebrews 8:4, they insist that Christ only entered upon His priestly office consequent upon His ascension. That Christ was High Priest and *acted* as such while He was here on earth is abundantly plain from Hebrews 2:17, for He made "propitiation" for the sins of His people on the Cross! It is true that others besides priests offered sacrifices to God in Old Testament times, but the New Testament represents Christ not only as Priest, but as the great "*high* Priest" of His people, and if the character, purpose and scope of that office be interpreted (as it must be) in the light of the inspired types, then there is no room left for doubt as to the meaning of the anti-type.

Israel's high priest represented the people before God. Taken from among men, he was ordained to act in the behalf of men in those matters which related *to God,* so that he might bring near to God both gifts and sacrifices (Heb. 5:1). As the general character of the prophet was that of one qualified and authorized to speak from God to men, so the general idea of the priest is that of one qualified and authorized to treat in matters of men with God. The high priest was he in whom the entire priesthood culminated, and he, especially, acted in all respects as the literal representative of the entire holy (separated) nation. First, he bore the names of each tribe graven on the stones on his shoulders, and on the breastplate over his heart (Ex. 28:9-29). Second, he made atonement in behalf of all the people, confessing over the head of the scape-goat all their sins (Lev. 16:15-21). Third, if he sinned, it was regarded as the sin of all the people (Lev. 4:3). His chief function was to offer bleeding sacrifices for propitiation and to make intercession for the people. The antitypical fulfillment of this is shown us in the epistle to the Hebrews, where Christ is called Priest six times, and high Priest twelve times. Let us, very briefly, point out the several details of this.

First, in Hebrews 2:17, 18 we are told that Christ became incarnate "*That he might be* a merciful and faithful high Priest," etc. Second, in 5:4-6 we learn that Christ was chosen by God *to this office.* Third, 5:7; 8:3; 9:11-15, 25-28; 10: 12-19, etc., show that Christ literally discharged the functions of a priest, offering to God a sacrifice for all His people, which, through God's acceptance thereof, brought to an end all the typical offerings. Conclusive proof of this was furnished by God in rending the veil of the temple, thereby setting aside the whole system of the Levitical priesthood. The priestly sacrifice of Christ had now superseded theirs.

That Christ *was* high Priest on earth is also clear from Hebrews 4:14: "Seeing then we have a great high Priest, that is passed into the heavens" etc. Aaron was high priest when he entered the holy of holies, yet he was also a high priest *before,* or he could not have entered at all. If Christ be a priest He must have a sacrifice, for the very nature of the sacerdotal office required it. The entire employment of the high priest, as priest, consisted in offering sacrifice, with the performance of those things which did necessarily precede and follow it. Now Christ was both Priest and Sacrifice. He offered Himself to God. What could be plainer than Ephesians 5:2, "Christ . . . hath given himself for us an offering and a sacrifice *to God* for a sweet-smelling savour"? He had to do with God as He stood in the relation and respect of a "sacrifice." In His dual person He was Priest: in His human nature, He was the sacrifice offered. In the term "flesh" — "condemned sin in the flesh" (Rom. 8:3) — the Holy Spirit refers to the whole manhood of Christ, and *it* was the "sacrifice" for sin *by which* sin was "condemned."

"For every high priest is ordained to offer gifts and sacrifices: wherefore it is of necessity that this man have somewhat also to offer" (Heb. 8:3). And *what* was it that He did "offer"? His "own blood" (Heb. 9:12), His "body" (Heb. 10:10), His "soul" or "life" (Isa. 53:10), "Himself" (Heb. 9:14). In Christ's sacrifice there was an "altar" too, namely, His Godhead: "The altar that sanctifieth the gift" (Matt. 23:19). The Deity of Christ not only sustained and strengthened His human nature in being a sacrifice therein, but it also gave merit and efficacy to His sacrifice. How did that *one* sacrifice avail for all the sins of all God's people, but from the fact that He who offered up Himself was God as well as man! Christ abides in His office of priesthood (Heb. 8:1), not to offer fresh sacrifice (10:12), but to intercede (7:25).

C. *Christ's Sacrifice Was a Propitiatory One*

By Adam's fall a sad breach was made between God and man. Sin greatly incensed the holy God against His rebellious creatures, nay, there was a mutual enmity constrained between them. On the one hand, we read of God, "Thou *hatest* all workers of iniquity" (Psa. 5:5), "But they rebelled, and vexed His Holy Spirit: therefore He was turned to be their *enemy*, He fought against them" (Isa. 63:10). Of man we read, "The carnal mind is *enmity against* God" (Rom. 8:7); "You that were sometimes alienated and *enemies in your mind* by wicked works, yet now hath He reconciled" (Col. 1:21). Now Christ came here to effect reconciliation between these alienated parties, to bring God and men together again in amity and love. By His bloodshedding, Christ appeased the righteous wrath of

God. By His sacrifice, He pacified the claims of Divine justice. Some have asked, How could the elect be "by nature the children of *wrath*" (Eph. 2:3), seeing that God always *loved* them (Jer. 31:3)? In the language of John Owen we reply, "He loved us, in respect of the free purpose of His will to send Christ to redeem us and satisfy for our sins; He was angry with us, in respect of His violated law, and provoked justice by sin."

The leading New Testament scriptures which present this particular aspect of Christ's sacrifice are the following: "Whom God hath foreordained *a propitiation* through faith in His blood to declare His righteousness" (Rom. 3:25). "For if, when we were enemies, we were *reconciled* to God [not by the Holy Spirit's work in us, nor by our laying down the weapons of our warfare but] *by the death of his Son*" (Rom. 5:10). We were "reconciled" through Christ's averting God's anger from us and procuring our acceptance in His legal favor. "All things are of God, who hath *reconciled* us to Himself by Jesus Christ" (II Cor. 5:18). "And having *made peace* through the blood of his cross" (Col. 1:20). "That he might be a merciful and faithful high Priest in things pertaining to God to *make propitiation* for the sins of the people" (Heb. 2:17). "If any one sin, we have an Advocate with the Father, Jesus Christ the righteous: And he is the *propitiation* for our sins" (I John 2:2).

Now the above passages are best understood in the light of the Old Testament types. There we read, "And Moses said unto Aaron, Take a censer, put fire therein from off the altar, and put on incense, and go quickly unto the congregation and *make an atonement* for them: For there is *wrath* gone out from the Lord; the plague is begun. And Aaron took as Moses commanded . . . and made an atonement for the people . . . and the plague was stayed" (Num. 16:46-48). Again, we read, "The Lord said to Eliphaz the Temanite, My *wrath* is kindled against thee, and against thy two friends . . . therefore take unto you now seven bullocks and seven rams, and go to my servant Job, and offer up for yourselves a burnt offering; and my servant Job shall pray for you: for him will I accept," etc. (Job 42:7-9). What could be plainer? The wrath of

God was appeased by bloodshedding! It remains to be pointed out that the Hebrew word for "atonement" and the Greek word for "propitiation" are one and the same.

D. *Christ's Sacrifice Was an Expiatory One*

The whole of Christ's humiliation and suffering from His birth to the Cross were invested with a priestly and sacrificial character, as constituting His once-offering up of Himself a sacrifice, as propitiatory of God and expiatory of His people's sins; yet the emphasis of Scripture shows that Christ's oblation of Himself as victim was principally manifested and concentrated in His pouring out of His soul unto death. Faith is directed to the Cross, as presenting not merely the historical terminus and climax, but the logical and indispensable completion of all that preceded, for sin not only entails suffering but *death*.

"Propitiation" defines the bearing which Christ's sacrifice had *Godwards*: it placated Him. "Expiation" has reference to the bearing which Christ's sacrifice had *manwards*: it removed the sins of His people.

"This is my blood of the new covenant, which is shed for many for the *remission* of sins" (Matt. 26:28). "Remission" is a judicial term, and signifies the annulling of guilt, the removal of all ground of punishment. "Once in the end of the age hath He appeared to *put away* sin by the sacrifice of himself" (Heb. 9:26). Christ has so "put away" all the sin of His people that they are perfectly and finally acquitted in the high court of God, so that *no* charge can evermore be laid against them (Rom. 8:33). Blessedly and gloriously has the Old Testament type been fulfilled, "On that day shall the priest make an atonement for you, to *cleanse* you, that ye may be clean from *all* your sins *before the Lord*" (Lev. 16:30). Thus are God's believing children able to say, "The blood of Jesus Christ His Son *cleanseth* us from *all sin*" (I John 1:17).

This was one of the chief ends of Christ's Satisfaction saintwards: to take upon Him the sins of His people, and so atone for them that an *end* was made of them. Those who are not sheltered beneath the precious blood of Christ have to say, "Thou hast set our iniquities before Thee, our secret sins in the light of thy countenance" (Psa. 90:8). But they who, by marvelous sovereign grace, have been brought to trust in the Lamb, may exclaim, "As far as the east is from the west, so far hath he *removed* our transgressions from us" (Psa. 103:12). Our guilt has all been annulled. We have been completely freed from a deserved punishment. No longer is there a single charge on God's docket against us. Proof of this is that, "This man, after he had offered one sacrifice for sins forever, *sat down* on the right hand of God" (Heb. 10:12). Therefore "unto them that look for Him shall he appear the second time *without sin* unto salvation" (Heb. 9:28). Hallelujah!

CHAPTER NINE

The Atonement — Its Design

What was the purpose of the Eternal Three in sending Christ Jesus into this world? What was the incarnation of the Son of God intended to accomplish? What were His sufferings and obedience ordained to effect? Concerning this all-important matter the most erroneous ideas have been entertained, ideas at direct variance with Holy Scripture, ideas most dishonoring to God. Even where these awful errors have not been fully espoused, sufficient of their evil leaven has been received to corrupt the pure truth which many good men have held. In other instances, where this great subject has been largely neglected, only the vaguest and haziest conceptions are entertained. Sad it is to see what small place this vital theme now has in most pulpits, and in the thoughts and studies of the majority of professing Christians.

"Known unto God are all his works from the beginning of the world" (Acts 15:18). Everything God does is according to design: all is the working out of "the eternal purpose which He purposed in Christ Jesus our Lord" (Eph. 3:11). God had a design in creation: Revelation 4:10. He has a design in providence: Romans 8:28. And He has a design or purpose in the Satisfaction which was wrought by Christ: I Peter 1:20. What, then, was that purpose? This is not a speculative question, but one of the utmost moment. Surely the right answer to it must be the one which upholds the glory of God. Therefore any answer which carries with it the inevitable corollaries of a dishonored Father, a disgraced Saviour and a defeated Holy Spirit, *cannot* be the right one. Redemption is the glory of all God's works, but it would be an everlasting disgrace of them if it should fail to effect whatsoever it was ordained to accomplish.

One conception, now widely held, is that Christ came here to remove certain barriers which stood in the way of God's grace flowing forth to fallen creatures. This theory is that Christ's death took away that hindrance which the Divine justice interposed to mercy being extended to trangressors of the law. Holders of this view suppose the great Atonement was merely the procuring unto God a right for His pardoning of sin. The words of Arminius are: "God had a mind and will to do good to humankind, but could not by reason of sin, His justice being in the way; whereupon He sent Christ to remove that obstacle, so that He might, upon the prescribing of what condition He pleased, and its being by them fulfilled, have mercy on them." Sad it is to find so many today echoing the errors of this misguided man.

The error in the above theory is easily exposed. If it were true that the design of Christ's satisfaction was to acquire a right unto His Father, that notwithstanding His justice He might save sinners, then did He rather die to redeem a liberty *unto God,* than a liberty *from evil* unto His people; that a door might be opened for God to come out in mercy to us, rather than that a way should be opened for us to go in unto Him. This is certainly a turning of things upside down. And where, we may ask, is there a word in Scripture to support such a grotesque idea? Does Scripture declare that God sent His Son out of love to Himself or out of love unto us? Does Scripture affirm that Christ died to procure something for God, or for His people? Does Scripture teach that the obstacles were thrown out by Divine justice or that our sins were what Christ came here to remove? There can be only one answer to these questions.

Again: this theory would reduce the whole work of Christ to a costly experiment which might or might not succeed, inasmuch as according to this conception, there is still some condition which the sinner himself must fulfill ere he can be benefited by that mercy which God would bestow upon him. But *that* is a flat denial of the fatal effects of the Fall, a repudiation of the total depravity of man. Those who are spiritually dead in sins are quite *incapable* of performing any spiritual conditions. As well offer to a man who is stone blind a thousand dollars on condition that he sees, as offer something spiritual to one who has *no* capacity to discern it: see John 3:3; I Corinthians 2:14. Such a view as this is as far removed from the truth as is light from darkness. Such a view, reduced to plain terms, comes to this; if the sinner believes, then Christ died for him; if the sinner does not believe, then Christ did not die for him; thus the sinner's act is made the cause of its own object, as though his believing would make that *to be* which otherwise was not. To such insane absurdities are the opposers of grace driven.

How different the plain teaching of the Word! Christ came here to fulfill His agreement in the Everlasting Covenant. In that covenant a certain work was prescribed. Upon His performance of it a certain reward was promised. That work was that Christ should make a perfect satisfaction unto God on behalf of each and all of His people. That reward was that all the blessings procured and purchased by Him should be infallibly bestowed on each and all of His people. "God out of His infinite love to His elect, sent His dear Son in the fulness of time, whom He had promised in the beginning of the world; to pay a ransom of infinite value and dignity, for the purchasing of eternal redemption, and bringing unto Himself all and every one of those whom He had before ordained to eternal life, for the praise of His own glory. So that freedom from all the evil from which we are delivered, and an enjoyment of all the good things that are bestowed on us, in our traduction from death to life, from hell and wrath to heaven and glory, are the proper issues and effects of the death of Christ, as the meritorious cause of them all" (John Owen). We are now ready to answer our opening question. The design of Christ's Satisfaction was

1. THAT GOD MIGHT BE MAGNIFIED

"The Lord hath made all things for himself" (Prov. 16:4). The great end which God has in all His works is the promotion of His own declarative glory: "For of him, and through him, and *to him,* are all things: to whom be glory for ever. Amen" (Rom. 11:36). It must be so. There is nothing outside Himself which can possibly supply any motive for Him to act. To assert the contrary would be to deny His self-sufficiency. The aim of God in creation, in providence, and in redemption, is the magnifying *of Himself*. Everything else is subordinate to this paramount consideration. We press this, because we are living in an age of infidelity and practical atheism.

God predestinated His people unto "the glory of His grace" (Eph. 1:6). Christ has "received us to the glory of God" (Rom. 15:7). All the Divine promises for us are in Christ "Amen, to the glory of God" (II Cor. 1:20). The inheritance which we have obtained in Christ is in order that "we should be to the praise of His glory" (Eph. 1:12). The Holy Spirit is given us as the earnest of our inheritance "unto the praise of his glory" (Eph. 1:14). The very rejoicing of the believer is "in hope of the glory of God" (Rom. 5:2). Our thanksgiving is that it may "redound to the glory of God" (II Cor. 4:15). This is the one design of all the benefits which we obtain from the Satisfaction of Christ, for "we are filled with the fruits of righteousness which are by Jesus Christ unto the glory and praise of God" (Phil. 1:11). While every tongue shall yet "confess that Jesus Christ is Lord to the glory of God the Father" (Phil. 2:11).

God had both a subservient and a supreme design in sending Christ into this world: the supreme design was to display His own glory, the subservient design was to save His elect unto His own glory. The former was accomplished by the manifestation of His blessed attributes, which is the chief design in all His works, pre-eminently so in His greatest and grandest work of all. The remainder of the chapter might well be devoted to the extension of this one thought. Through Christ's obedience and death God magnified His *law*: Isaiah 42:21. The law of God was more honored by the Son's subjection to it, than it was dishonored by the disobedience of all of Adam's race. God magnified His *love* by sending forth the Darling of His bosom to redeem worthless worms of the earth. He magnified His *justice*, for when sin (by imputation) was found upon His Son, He called for the sword to smite Him: Zechariah 13:7. He magnified His *holiness*: His hatred of sin was more clearly shown at the Cross than it will be in the lake of fire. He magnified His *power* by sustaining the Mediator under such a load as was laid upon Him. He magnified His *truth* by fulfilling His covenant engagements and bringing forth from the dead the great Shepherd of the sheep: Hebrews 13:20. He magnified His *grace* by imputing to the ungodly all the merits of Christ. This, then, was the prime purpose of God in the Atonement: to magnify Himself.

2. That the God-man Might Be Glorified

Christ is the Center of all the counsels of the Godhead. He is both the Alpha and Omega of their designs. All God's thoughts concerning everything in heaven and in earth begin and end in Christ. "God created all things by Jesus Christ" (Eph. 3:9), and all things were created "for Him" (Col. 1:16). As Mediator He is the only medium of union and communion between God and the creature. "That in the dispensation of the fulness of times he might gather together in one all things *in Christ,* both which are in heaven, and which are on earth; in him" (Eph. 1:10). Christ is the one universal Head in which God has summed up all things. Therefore was the stupendous work of redemption given to Him that He might reconcile all things in heaven and earth unto himself, and this, that a revenue of glory might come to Him.

The man Christ Jesus was taken up into union with the essential and eternal Word, God the Son, so that He might be Jehovah's "Fellow" (Zech. 13:7). The man Christ Jesus was predestinated unto the ineffable honor of union with the second person in the Trinity. As such He is the Head of the whole election of grace, called by the Father, "Mine elect, in whom my soul delighteth" (Isa. 42:1). As the God-man, the Father covenanted with Him, appointed Him as Surety, and assigned Him His work. As God-man, He had a covenant subsistence before He became incarnate. This is clear from John 6:62: "What and if ye shall see the Son of *man* ascend up where he was *before?*" It was as the God-man the Father "sent" forth Christ on His errand of mercy, and that for His personal glory.

As Judas went out to betray Him, Christ said, "Now is the Son of man glorified" (John 13:31). Within a few hours

His stupendous undertaking would be accomplished. The Mediator was honored, supremely honored, by God's having committed to His care the mightiest work of all, a work which none other was capable of performing. To Him was entrusted the task of glorifying God here on earth; of vanquishing His arch-enemy, the Devil; of redeeming His elect. To this He makes reference in John 17:4, "I have glorified thee on earth; I have finished the work which thou gavest me to do." He had completed God's vast design, executed His decrees, fulfilled all His will.

Having so gloriously glorified the Father, the Father has proportionately glorified the Mediator. He has been exalted high above "all principality and power, and might and dominion, and every name that is named, not only in this world, but also in that which is to come" (Eph. 1:21). He has been elevated to "the right hand of the Majesty on high" (Heb. 1:3). He has been given all authority in heaven and in earth (Matt. 28:18). He has been given "power over all flesh, that He should give eternal life to as many as the Father hast given him" (John 17:2). He has been given a name which is above every name, before which name every knee shall yet bow (Phil. 2:11). Speaking of Christ's finished work and the Father's rewarding thereof, the Psalmist said, "His glory is great in thy salvation: honour and majesty hast thou laid upon him. For thou hast made him most blessed forever: Thou hast made him exceeding glad with thy countenance" (Psa. 21:5, 6). This was the grand design of the Trinity: that the God-man should thus be glorified.

3. That God's Elect Might Be Saved

"For the Son of man is come to seek and to *save* that which was lost" (Luke 19:10). How different is this plain, positive and unqualified statement from the tale which nearly all preachers tell today! The story of the vast majority is that Christ came here to make salvation *possible* for sinners: He has done His part, now they must do theirs. To reduce the wondrous, finished, and glorious work of Christ to a merely making salvation possible is most dishonoring and insulting to Him.

Christ came here to carry into effect God's sovereign purpose of election, to save a people already "His" (Matt. 1:21) by covenant settlement. There are a people whom God hath "from the beginning chosen unto salvation" (II Thess. 2:13), and redemption was in order to the *accomplishing* of that decree. And if we believe what Scripture declares concerning the person of Christ, then we have indubitable proof that there can be no possible failure in connection with *His* mission. The Son of man, the Child born, was none other than "the mighty God" (Isa. 9:6). Therefore is He omniscient, and knows where to look for each of His lost ones; He is also omnipotent, and so cannot fail to deliver when they are found.

Observe that Luke 19:10 does not say that Christ came here to seek and to save *all* the lost. Of course it does not. Two thirds of human history had already run its course before Jesus was born. Half the human race was already in Hell when He entered Bethlehem's manger. It was "*the* lost" (see Greek) for which He became incarnate. That is the awful condition in which God's elect are by nature. Lost! They have lost all knowledge of the true God, all liking for Him, all desires after Him. They have lost His image in which they were originally created, and have contracted the image of Satan. They have lost all knowledge of their own actual condition, for their understanding is darkened (Eph. 4:18), they are spiritually dead in trespasses and sins (Eph. 2:1). Totally unconscious of their terrible state they neither seek Christ nor realize their need of Him.

Christ did not come here to see if there were any who would seek after Him. Of course not. Romans 3:11 emphatically declares "there is *none* that seeketh after God." *Christ* is the seeker. Beautifully is that brought out by Him in His parable of the lost sheep. A strayed dog or a lost horse will usually find its way back home. Not so a sheep: the longer it is free, the farther it strays from the fold. Hence, if that sheep is ever to be recovered, one must go after it. This is what Christ did, and which by His Spirit He is still doing. As Luke 15:4 declares, He goes "after that which is lost until He *find* it." But more: Christ came here not only to seek and find, but also to *save*. His words are, "For the Son of man is come to seek and to *save* that which was lost." Note it is not merely that He offers to, nor helps to, but that He actually *saves*. Such was the emphatic and unqualified declaration of the angel to Joseph, "Thou shalt call his name Jesus, for he *shall save* his people from their sins"—not try to, not half do so, but actually *save* them.

Christ came here with a definitely defined object in view, and being who He is there is no possible room for any failure in His mission. Hence, before He came here, God declared that He should "see of the travail of his soul and *be satisfied*" (Isa. 53:10). As the Mediator He solemnly covenanted with the Father *to* save His people from their sins. He actually *purchased* them with His blood (Acts 20:28). He has wrought out for them a perfect salvation, therefore is He "mighty to save" (Isa. 63:1). Blessedly is this illustrated in the immediate context of Luke 19:10. To Zacchaeus He said, "Make haste, and come down; for today I *must* abide at thy house . . . This day is salvation come to this house, forsomuch as he also is a son of Abraham" (vv. 5,9). Yes, "a son of Abraham," one of the elect seed. Therefore we boldly say to the reader, If you belong to the sheep of Christ, you *must* be saved, even though now you may be quite unconscious of your lost condition. Though, like Saul of Tarsus, you may yet "kick against the pricks," invincible grace *shall* conquer you, for it is written, "Thy people shall be willing in the day of thy power" (Psa. 110:3).

"I am come *that* they might have life, and that they might have it more abundantly. I am the good Shepherd: the good Shepherd giveth his life for the sheep" (John 10:10, 11). Here again we have clearly defined the *design* of Christ's mission and satisfaction. His sheep once possessed "life," possessed it in their natural head, Adam. But when he fell, they fell; when he died, they died. As it is written, "In Adam all die" (I Cor. 15:22). But by Christ, through His work, and in Him their spiritual Head, they obtain not only "life," but "more abundant" life; that is, a "life" which as far excells what they lost in their first father, as the last Adam excells in His Person, the first Adam. Therefore is it written, "The first Adam was made a living soul; the last Adam a quickening spirit" (I Cor. 15:45).

"As the Father hath life in himself, so hath he given to the Son to have life in himself" (John 6:26), which speaks of Christ as the God-man, the Mediator, as is clear from the words "given to." But that "life" had to be "laid down" (John 10:17) and received again in resurrection before it could be, efficaciously, bestowed on His people: John 12:24. It was as the Risen One that Christ was made "a quickening spirit." The first Adam was "made a living soul" that he might communicate natural life to his posterity; the last Adam was "made a quickening spirit" that He might impart spiritual life to all His seed. As the soul dwelling in Adam's body animated it and so made him to be a "living soul," so the man Christ Jesus being united to the second of the Trinity, has constituted Him a "quickening spirit," i.e., quickening His mystical body, both now and hereafter. The life of the Head is the life of His members.

The Christian first has a federal life *in* Christ before he has a vital life *from* Christ. Being legally one with Christ, this must be so. When Christ died His people died, when Christ was quickened His people were quickened "together with" Him (Eph. 2:5). It is to this union with the life of Christ that Romans 5:17 refers: "For if by one man's offence death reigned by one; much more they which receive abundance of grace and of the gift of righteousness shall reign in life by one, Jesus Christ." Yes, there is a "much more": the abundance of grace is greater than the demerits of sin, and the gift of righteousness exceeds that which was lost in Adam. The righteousness of God's elect far surpasses that which they possessed in innocence by the first Adam, for it is the righteousness of Christ, who is God. To this, neither the righteousness of Adam nor of angels can be compared. Those redeemed by Christ are not only recovered from the fall, but they are made to "*reign* in life" to which they had no title in their first parent. Since Christ is King, His people are made "kings" too (Rev. 1:6).

The same aspect of truth is brought before us again in II Corinthians 5:14, 15: "For the love of Christ constraineth us: because we thus judge *that* if one for all died, then all died. And for all He died, *that* they who live no longer to themselves should live, but to Him who for them died and was raised again" (Bagster's Interlinear). The American Version is misleading here. Many have supposed that the last clause of verse 14 refers to those who are "dead in sins," but *that* was true apart from the death of Christ! Nor does the spiritual death of Adam's fallen descendants render them capable of "living unto" Christ, but the very reverse. No, it is, "If one for all died" (i.e., for all His people), then they all died *in Him.* Then in verse 15 we have stated the consequence and fruit of this: as the result of His rising from the dead, they "live." His act was, representatively, their act. The atoning death of Christ, on the ground of federal union and substitution, was also our death; see Galatians 2:20. So too His resurrection was, representatively, our resurrection: see Colossians 3:1. Thus, in Christ, God's elect have a "more abundant" life than they ever had in unfallen Adam.

The same truth is set before us in I Peter 2:24, "Who his own self bare our sins in his own body on the tree, *that* we, being dead to sins, should live unto righteousness." The first part of this verse has been before us in a previous chapter. The second half of it expresses the Divine design in appointing Christ to be federally and vicariously the Bearer of His peoples' sins. Christ's death was their death: they are "dead to sins," not to "sinning"! Let the reader compare Romans 6:2 and the apostle's exposition in the next nine verses. Further, Christ's resurrection was their resurrection: they "live," legally and representatively, "unto righteousness" in Christ their risen Head, of whom it is written "He liveth unto God" (Rom. 6: 10). We quote below from John Brown's lucid exposition of I Peter 2:24.

"To be 'dead to sins' is to be delivered from the condemning power of sin; or, in other words, from the condemning sentence of the law, under which, if a man lies, he cannot be holy; and from which, if a man is delivered, his holiness is absolutely secured. To 'live unto righteousness' is plainly just the positive view of that, of which 'to be dead to sins' is the negative view. 'Righteousness,' when opposed to 'sin,' in the sense of guilt or liability to punishment, as it very often is in the writings of the apostle Paul, is descriptive of a state of justification. A state of guilt is a state of condemnation by God; a state of righteousness is a state of acceptance with God. To live unto righteousness, is in this case to live under the influence of a justified state, a state of acceptance with God; and the apostle's statement is: Christ Jesus, by His sufferings unto death, completely answered the demands of the law on us by bearing away our sins, that we, believing in Him, and thereby being united to Him, might be as completely freed from our liabilities to punishment, as if we, in our own person, not He Himself, in His own body, had undergone them; and that we might as really be brought into a state of righteousness, justification, acceptance with God, as if we, not He, in His obedience to death, had magnified the law and made it honorable."

"God sending His own Son in the likeness of sinful flesh, and for sin, condemned sin in the flesh: *that* the righteousness of the law might be fulfilled in us" (Rom. 8:3, 4). Here again the *design* of Christ's mission is clearly stated. God sent His Son here in order that (1) the punishment of His peoples' guilt should be inflicted upon their Head, (2) that the righteous requirements of the law — perfect obedience — might be met by Him for us. This righteousness is said to be "fulfilled *in* us" because representatively, we were "in Christ" our Surety: He obeyed the law not only "for" our good, but so that His obedience should become actually ours by imputation; and thus Christ purchased for us a *title* to Heaven.

A parallel passage to Rom. 8:3, 4 is found in II Cor. 5:21, "For he hath made him sin for us, who knew no sin; *that* we might be made the righteousness of God in him." The purpose of Christ's vicarious life and death was that a perfect righteousness should be wrought out for His people and imputed to them by God, so that they might exclaim, "*In the Lord* have I righteousness" (Isa. 45:24). This will come before us more fully when we take up the *results* of Christ's Satisfaction, yet a few words upon it are here in place. The righteousness of the believer is wholly *objective;* that is to say, it is something altogether outside of himself. This is clear from the antithesis of II Cor. 5:21. Christ was "made sin" not inherently, but imputatively, by the guilt of His people being legally transferred to Him. In like manner, they are "made the righteousness of God *in Him*", not "in themselves," by Christ's righteousness being legally reckoned to their account. In the repute of God, Christ and His people constitute one mystical person, hence it is that their sins were imputed to Him, and that His righteousness is imputed to them, and therefore we read: "Christ is the end of the law for righteousness to every one that believeth" (Rom. 10:4).

"For Christ also hath once suffered for sins, the Just for the unjust, *that* he might bring us to God" (I Pet. 3:18). This wondrous declaration gives us a remarkably clear view of the substitutionary punishment which Christ endured, with the design thereof, namely, to restore His people to priestly nearness and service to God. Four things in it are worthy of our most close attention. First, Christ "suffered." *Sin* was the cause of His suffering. Had there been no sin, Christ had never suffered. To "suffer" means "to bear punishment," as in ordinary speech we say, a child suffers for the sins of its parents. Christ suffered for "us," the whole election of grace: it was for their sin He was penalized. Second, He suffered "once." This must not be understood to signify that His suffering was confined to the three hours of darkness, but means "once for all" as in Hebrews 9:27, 28. The "suffering" which pervaded the whole of Christ's earthly life culminated at the Cross. That suffering was final. His all-sufficient Atonement possesses eternal validity.

Third, Christ Himself was personally sinless: it was the "Just" or "Righteous" One who suffered. To affirm that He was "righteous" means that He was approved of God as tested by the standard of the law. He was not only sinless, but One whose life was adjusted to the Divine requirements. As such, He suffered, the pure for the impure, the innocent for the guilty. His sufferings were not on His own account, nor were they from the inevitable course of events or laws of evil in a sinful world; but they were the direct and necessary consequence of His vicariously taking the place of His guilty people. Christ received the punishment they ought to have suffered. He was paid sin's wages which were due them.

Fourth, the end in view of Christ's substitutionary sufferings was to bring His people *to God*. This was only possible by the removal of their sins, which separated them from the thrice Holy One: Isa. 59:2. By His sufferings Christ has procured for us access to God. "But in Christ Jesus ye who sometimes were far off, are *made nigh* by the blood of Christ" (Eph. 2:13). "That he might bring us to God" is the most comprehensive expression used in Scripture for stating the design of Christ's Satisfaction. It includes the bringing of His people out of darkness into marvelous light: out of a state of alienation, misery and wrath, into one of grace, peace and eternal communion with God. By nature they were in a state of enmity, but Christ has reconciled them by His death: Rom. 5:10. By nature they were "children of wrath" (Eph. 2:3), obnoxious to God's judicial displeasure; but by grace they have been accepted into His favor: Romans 5:2. By nature they were spiritual lepers, but by one offering Christ hath "perfected forever them that are sanctified" (Heb. 10:14).

Here then, in brief, is the Divine *design* in the Satisfaction of Christ; that God Himself might be honored; that Christ might be glorified; that the elect might be saved by their sins being put away, an abundant life being given them, a perfect righteousness imputed to them, and their being brought into God's favor, presence and fellowship.

CHAPTER TEN

The Atonement—Its Efficacy

In our last chapter we considered the Divine design in Christ's Satisfaction; in this we propose to show from Scripture that that design *must be* accomplished. Two widely differing views have been taken concerning the effectuation of what the mediatorial work of the Lord Jesus was meant to achieve. Some have affirmed that the Atonement possesses only a *conditional* efficacy, others that it is vested with an *infallible* efficacy. These two views are known as the Arminian and the Calvinistic interpretations. They are completely antagonistic and utterly irreconcilable. The difference between them is that of Truth and error, Light and darkness, Jehovah and Baal, God and the Devil. Before attempting to set forth some of the sure grounds on which rests the certain accomplishment of God's purpose in the obedience and suffering of Christ, we will first glance briefly at the contrary view and expose its fallacy.

It is high time that some voice was raised in protest against the fearful perversions of Divine truth which are now being given out by many, who, though posing as the champions of orthodoxy, are nothing more than wolves in sheep's clothing, blind, leading those who follow their pernicious heresies into the ditch. The omnipotency of God is now frittered down to a persuasive power which He brings to bear upon sinners, but which is so feeble that it fails to move the great majority who are subject to it: more than this "persuasion" must not be affirmed, lest man be reduced to a "mere machine." The all-efficacious Atonement, which has actually redeemed everyone for whom it was made, is degraded to a "remedy" which sin-sick souls may use if they feel disposed to. The invincible work of the Holy

Spirit is supposed to be nothing more than an "offer" of the Gospel which sinners may accept or reject as they please. That such frightful errors should now be accepted in "churches" calling themselves "Fundamentalists," only shows how far the Apostasy has advanced.

The horrible and blasphemous idea of Arminians is that the wondrous and perfect Atonement of Christ has made sure and certain the salvation of none, that it has only made *possible* the salvation of all who hear the Gospel. When this "possibility" is carefully examined it is found to be an impossibility! The supposed "possibility" is that fallen man, while dead in trespasses and sins, must fulfill a certain condition, must of himself perform a certain act which God is said to require of him, before the sacrifice of Christ can be of any avail. That "condition" is faith; that "act" is that he must believe. Now to reduce the "great salvation" which Christ procured and secured to a bare possibility, as something which is available for everyone but sure for no one, is to say that Christ did no more for Peter and Paul than He did for Pilate and Judas. Everything is thus left to chance and uncertainty.

To make the efficacy of Christ's Atonement depend upon an act of man's will is highly dishonoring to our blessed Saviour. To say that the success of the greatest of all God's works is left contingent upon the creature's pleasure is most insulting to the Almighty, impeaching as it does His wisdom, goodness and justice. To teach that salvation lies within the sinner's own power to secure, is to flatly deny Christ when He said "with men this is *impossible*" (Matt. 19:26). Alas, nearly all preachers today speak of faith in Christ as a comparatively easy matter, as though it were well within the range of the sinner's own ability. But the Scriptures teach far otherwise. They teach that man by nature is spiritually bound with fetters, such as none but God can break (Gal. 5:1), that he is shut up in darkness (Eph. 4:18), and is in a prison-house (Isa. 61:1). *The salvation of no man is "possible" apart from the effectual operations of God's invincible grace.*

To affirm the "possibility" of an unregenerate sinner believing in Christ to the saving of his soul, is to deny that "men loved darkness rather than light" (John 3:19), that "they that are in the flesh *cannot* please God" (Rom. 8:8), that the "carnal mind is enmity against God." In short, it is to repudiate the fact that man is, by nature, a fallen creature, *dead* in trespasses and sins. Carnality cannot thirst after holiness. An evil tree cannot produce good fruit. A corpse cannot quicken itself. Man's will, like all his other faculties, has been disabled by the fall. His only hope is the intervention of sovereign and omnipotent grace: that God will perform upon and within him a miracle of mercy: that Divine power will lift him out of the grave of sin and make him a new creature in Christ Jesus. Until he is born again he can no more love God, savingly believe in Christ, or walk in the Spirit, than he can create a world.

We have not said that faith is unnecessary, nor that God does not call on man to believe the Gospel. What we do say is that faith is God's gift, that this gift was *purchased* by Christ for all for whom He died, and that in due time this gift is imparted to them. As this will come before us again we shall say no more upon it now; instead, we proceed to call attention to some of the many infallible proofs which demonstrate the certain efficacy of Christ's Satisfaction.

1. The Purpose of God

All the designs of a Being possessed of infinite wisdom and almighty power must be fulfilled. It is impossible that they should be frustrated. In Ephesians 3:11 we read of "the eternal purpose which He purposed in Christ Jesus our Lord." The context shows what that "eternal purpose" concerned. It was a "dispensation of the grace of God" (v. 2) toward poor sinners. It was that elect Jews and elect Gentiles should be "fellow heirs and of the same body, and partakers of His promise in Christ by the gospel" (v. 6). It was that these should be partakers of "the unsearchable riches of Christ" (v. 8). It was that by means of the Church the "manifold wisdom of God" should be exhibited (v. 10). This same "eternal purpose" of God is revealed in I Thessalonians 5:9, "For God hath not appointed us to wrath, but to obtain salvation by our Lord Jesus Christ."

Now the purpose of God is absolutely certain of fulfillment. He Himself emphatically declares, "My counsel shall stand, and I will do all my pleasure" (Isa. 46:10). He insists that, "There is no wisdom nor understanding nor counsel against the Lord" (Prov. 21:30). Neither the malice of man nor the enmity of Satan can prevent the infallible accomplishment of whatsoever God hath ordained. To affirm the contrary is blasphemy. In Proverbs 19:21 we are told that "there are many devices in a man's heart, nevertheless the counsel of the Lord, that shall stand." There were many "devices" in the heart of Pharaoh against Jehovah and His people, nevertheless the "counsel" of the Lord stood fast. There were many "devices" in the heart of Saul of Tarsus against Christ and His church, and though he kicked against the pricks, nevertheless, the "counsel" of the Lord was accomplished.

"The counsel of the Lord standeth forever, the thoughts of his heart to all generations" (Psa. 33:11). This is the firm and glorious confidence of His saints. No ingenuity of man and no plotting of the Devil can overthrow it, no, nor so much as hinder it. "Our God is in the heavens: He hath done *whatsoever* He hath pleased" (Psa. 115:3). Hath He "from the beginning chosen us unto salvation"? (II Thess. 2:13) Then saved we must be. Hath He "predestinated us unto the adoption of children by Jesus Christ to Himself, according to the good pleasure of His will"? (Eph. 1:5) Then that will must be fulfilled. God's purpose is immutable (Heb. 6:17), invincible (Psa. 2:6), triumphant (Isa. 14:26, 27). Before there can be the slightest failure in the accomplishment of the Divine design in the Atonement of Christ, God must cease to be! But this is impossible.

2. THE COVENANT OF GOD

Now it is obviously impossible to have any clear views of what the Lord Jesus died to achieve, if we have no real knowledge of the Eternal Agreement between the Father and the Son *in fulfillment of which* His death took place. Yet, today, deplorable to say, even the great majority of those considered evangelical — to mention no others — have scarcely any such knowledge. The very fact that that Covenant was proposed, accepted and drawn up before the foundation of the world, proves beyond all shadow of doubt that it was unconditional so far as man is concerned, for *he* then had no existence! Therefore he cannot be a party to it, even though his eternal well-being is the object of it.

It must be admitted that, in effecting salvation, God acts agreeably to a preconceived plan or designed arrangement. We say "must," for to deny this is to impute to the infinitely wise God conduct such as is found only among the most thoughtless and foolish among men, conduct such as is exemplified in no other department of His works, for in all of them we discover such order and regularity as clearly evince the existence of an original plan or design. Hence, to direct attention to the Everlasting Covenant is but to show that God is now working according to an eternal purpose. The Scriptures plainly represent the Divine persons as entering into a federal agreement for the salvation of men. In that covenant the Father is the representative of the Godhead, and the Son the representative of those who are to be redeemed. He is, on that account, called the "Surety" (Heb. 7:22) and "Mediator" (Heb. 8:6) of the covenant. Whatever He did as Surety or Mediator must, therefore, have been done in connection with the covenant.

The great Architect of the universe drew up His plans before ever a creature was brought into existence. Everything concerning Christ and His Church was firmly settled beyond possibility of alteration. All that concerns the being and well-being of His people is done according to God's covenant-enactment. As Ephesians 1:11 declares, God "worketh all things after the counsel of His own will." Yes, "He will ever be mindful of His covenant" (Psa. 111:5). There were no contingencies, no uncertainties, no peradventures. All the affairs of the elect were settled by the mutual consent of all the persons of Deity. The Father made choice of the elect (Eph. 1:4), the Son accepted that choice (John 17:10), the Spirit recorded it in the Lamb's book of life (Rev. 13:8). The Father decreed salvation, the Son consented to purchase it, the Spirit pledged Himself to the communication of it.

Now as stated in an earlier chapter, a covenant is an agreement between two parties who are under mutual engagements. Something is to be done by one of the parties, in consequence of which the other party binds himself to do something in return. When a master, for example, enters into an agreement or covenant with a servant, he prescribes certain duties to be performed by the servant and promises to recompense him with suitable wages. By consenting to the compact, the servant becomes bound to perfom the stipulated work, and the master is bound to bestow the reward when the term of labor is finished. Such an agreement, such a compact, was entered into between the Father and the Son before the foundation of the world. Clear proof of this is found in Isaiah 49:1-19; II Timothy 1:9. In Isaiah 53:10-12 we have recorded the promises which God made to the Mediator. In John 17:24 we hear Christ putting in His claim to the fulfillment of that promise.

The covenant is "ordered in all things and sure" (II Sam. 23:5). It is "sure" in its ordinations, operations, communications, preservations, and consummations. Yes, it is a salvation *worthy of God!* Well might the late Joseph Irons say, "O the vast importance of getting at and possessing an infallible Christianity! The Devil knew well of what worth and importance that word was, and, therefore, he carried it off to Rome, that the vilest of wretches might claim it as theirs and talk about infallible heads, and infallible decrees, and infallible councils and infallible vicars of Christ. I wonder the earth does not swallow them up as it did Korah, Dathan, and Abiram; It is such blasphemous presumption. They talk about infallibility, and then run away to Gaeta to take care of it; they talk about infallibility, and then are obliged to have an army of infidels from France to reestablish and to preserve it. I would not give a straw for such infallibility. I want the infallibility of the throne of God, the infallibility of the existence of Deity, the infallibility that is sworn to by the Persons of Godhead, that is ratified in the oaths of His Word, embraced and enjoyed in my own soul; all the members of Christ secure in His hands, so that none shall pluck them thence; all the purposes of grace infallibly settled; and all that the Father gave Him be infallibly brought home, to behold His glory and see Him as He is."

The Satisfaction of Christ was the one and only "condition" of the Covenant. It was stipulated as the condition of His having a seed to serve Him, that He should make His soul an offering for sin, that He should bear their iniquities, that He should pour out His soul unto death. In reference to this, we find Him saying to His apostles on the eve of His crucifixion, "This is my *blood of the new covenant,* which is shed for many for the remission of sins" (Matt. 26:28). The blood of Christ was not shed by accident, nor was it poured out at random or on a venture. No, He laid down His life by commandment: He had received orders from His Father so to do: John 10:18. The blood of Christ was the *sealing* of the Covenant, and by it He has actually *purchased* to Himself the Church of God: Acts 20:28.

At the close of His earthly career we find Christ saying to the Father, "I have glorified thee on the earth: I have finished the work which *thou gavest* me to do" (John 17:4). On the ground of this He prays, "And now, O Father, glorify thou me with thine own self" (v. 5). Furthermore He said, "Father *I will* that they may behold my glory" (v. 24). Having faithfully discharged His part of the Contract, the Father is now in honor bound to bring to Heaven every one for whom Christ died. So far as the elect are concerned, the design of the Mediator's work was not that God might, if He would, but that He *should,* by virtue of His engagement with the Surety, actually *bestow* on the Church all that He merited for it. Therefore we boldly affirm that, before there can be the slightest failure in the Divine design of the Atonement, the Father must betray the Son's confidence in Him and prove false to His own stipulation with Him. That is impossible.

3. THE VERACITY OF GOD

In the past eternity the Father made definite promises to the Mediator. From these we may cite the following: "I the Lord have called thee in righteousness, and will hold thine hand, and will keep thee, and give thee for a covenant of the people, for a light of the Gentiles; To open the blind eyes, to bring out the prisoners from the prison" (Isa. 42:6, 7). "In the Lord *shall* all the seed of Israel [namely "the Israel of God", Gal. 6:16] be justified, and shall glory" (Isa. 45:25). "Thus saith the Lord, the Redeemer of Israel, his Holy One, to him whom man despiseth, to him whom the nation abhorreth, to a servant of rulers, Kings shall see and arise, princes also *shall* worship, because of the Lord that is *faithful*" (Isa. 49:7). "He *shall* see of the travail of his soul, and be satisfied: by his knowledge *shall* my righteous servant justify many: for he shall bear their iniquities. Therefore will I divide him a portion with the great, and he *shall* divide the spoil with the strong" (Isa. 53:11, 12). "Ask of me, and I *shall give* the heathen for thine inheritance, and the uttermost parts of the earth for thy possession" (Psa. 2:8). In view of these promises, Christ had a joy "set before him," for which joy he endured the Cross and despised the shame (Heb. 12:2).

Now if one man enters into a solemn engagement with another which is duly ratified, signed, sealed and witnessed to, for him to attempt to break it would be to violate his honor, forfeit his good name, and make him an object of contempt to all righteous people. But the man who is honorable and upright, respects his pledges: his word is his bond. Infinitely more so does all this hold good of Him who is the God of Truth. "God is not a man, that He should lie; neither the Son of man, that he should repent: hath he said, and shall he not do it? or hath he spoken, and shall he not make it good?" (Num. 23:19). God not only entered into formal covenant with Christ, not only made Him definite promises, but solemnly placed Himself on oath to the certain fulfillment of them: "My covenant will I not break; nor alter the thing that is gone out of my lips. Once have I sworn by my holiness that I will not lie unto the beloved" (Psa. 89:34, 35).

Here then is another sure and unchanging ground of confidence. The very perfections of Deity stand pledged unto the triumphant issue of Christ's Satisfaction. The honor of God is involved in it. His faithfulness is at stake. His veracity is eternally pledged for the fulfillment of every iota of the grand Charter between Himself and the Mediator of His people. Therefore not a promise can fail, not one elect vessel of mercy be cast out. There can be no failure, for nothing is left contingent on the creature. As Psalm 111:5 declares "He will ever *be mindful of* His covenant." Here is security indeed. God will not change His mind, revoke His choice, or violate His pledge. Therefore we boldly affirm that, before there can be the slightest failure in the Divine design concerning the Atonement, the Father would have to falsify His promises, lie to His Son, and go back upon His most solemn oath. Such is utterly impossible.

4. THE POWER OF GOD

The work of Christ, of itself, never did, never will, and never can, save a single soul. God must carry that death into effect. If the efficacy of Christ's sacrifice should be left for men to receive or reject, men to help forward or impede the prosperity thereof, then His death would be utterly in vain. But the Lord Jesus did not leave the virtues of His Atonement to depend upon the creature. No, He committed His cause and interests unto the Father. Hear Him saying. "And now I am no more in the world, but these are in the world, and I come to thee. Holy Father, *keep* through thine own name those whom thou hast given me, that they may be one, as we" (John 17:11). Unto the keeping power of the Father did Christ entrust those for whom He died.

We have shown in previous chapters that Christ died not as a private person, but as the federal Head of the whole election of grace; therefore His final act on the Cross must be understood as signifying "Father, into *thy* hands I commend *my* [mystical] spirit" (Luke 23:46). And what was the Father's response? Psalm 110 tells us. The Father not only exalted Christ to His own right hand, but solemnly assured Him that, "The Lord shall send the rod of thy strength out of Zion . . . thy people shall be willing in the day of thy power" (v. 2, 3). Thereby He promised to make the preaching of the Gospel successful unto the saving of His "people." Invincible grace should open hearts to the reception of its message (Acts 16:14), and they should be "*kept* by the *power* of God through faith unto salvation" (I Pet. 1:5). Therefore we boldly say that, before there can be the slightest failure in the Divine design concerning the Atonement, God must be stripped of His omnipotence But that is impossible.

5. THE JUSTICE OF GOD

"There are many who plead for the atonement of Christ, who, in effect, deny it, as well as its open opposers. They suppose that it is a conditional atonement, of efficacy only to those who comply with certain terms. It is evident, however, that a conditional atonement is no atonement in the proper sense of the word; for an atonement *must* expiate the sins atoned for, just as a payment cancels a debt. Where, then, there has been an actual atonement made, the sins atoned for never can be punished again, any more than a debt once paid can be charged a second time. It would be unjust in God to charge the debt to the account of man that was fully paid by man's Surety. It may be alleged that one man may pay another man's debt upon certain conditions; and that if those conditions are not fulfilled, the debt will be still chargeable upon the debtor. But it is evident that, in such a case, the surety either does not actually pay the debt till the conditions are fulfilled, or if he has conditionally paid it, he is refunded before it is chargeable upon the debtor. In every such case, the debt is not really paid. But Jesus *has paid* the debt. He has already made atonement; and if they for whom He died are not absolved, the debt is charged a second time. Christ can never be *refunded.* His blood has been shed; and there is no possibility that what He suffered can be now either more or less. They, then, who suspend the efficacy of the atonement of Christ upon conditions to be complied with by man, in effect *deny* that atonement has been truly made" (Alex. Carson, 1847).

Shall not the Judge of all the earth do right? Assuredly. His very perfections move Him to give every one His due. This principle is exemplified time after time in Holy Writ. Then shall God make an exception of His Son? No, indeed. God ever acts sovereignly, but He never acts unrighteously. Just as He will not, cannot (Ex. 34:7), remit sin without satisfaction, so He will not, cannot (Job 4:7), punish sin where satisfaction *has been* received. To condemn one for whom an atonement has been accepted, would be as incompatible with perfect equity as to ignore sin without an atonement. If the punishment of sin has been borne, the remission of the offense follows, of course. God never punishes twice for the same crime. Thus, inasmuch as the oblation of Christ was a legal satisfaction for sin, all for whom it was offered *must* enjoy the remission of their transgressions.

It is a matter of bare justice that those blessings which Christ intended to procure for His people *should be* actually bestowed upon them. First, because this was promised Him as the reward of His obedience and sufferings; that reward has been fully earned. Second, because He actually *purchased* salvation for them. The enmity of the carnal mind may object that such a conception is a "commercializing" of Divine love, but Scripture does not hesitate to employ pecuniary terms: "Ye are bought with a price" (I Cor. 6:20). What has been paid for, the purchaser has a right to. To deny that to him would be unjust. Again, the Word speaks of our sins as "debts" (Matt. 6:12): if then Christ has discharged them, He has the right to demand the exemption of all for whom He acted as Sponsor. Therefore we boldly affirm that, before there can be the slightest failure in the Divine design of the Atonement, God must cease to hate iniquity, and love righteousness. But that is impossible.

6. THE GOVERNMENT OF GOD

The law of substitution, which is a principle appointed by the Divine government, requires the salvation of all those whom Christ represented. "Perfect suretyship, whether we regard the supreme instance and exemplification of it in the work of Christ in our behalf, or the most common and familiar instances of it as exemplified among men, is always and manifestly suretyship which, in its own nature, *secures* and *necessitates,* the reinstatement of every one in whose behalf it is undertaken" (John Armour). Now as Christ fully met every demand of the Law, both preceptive and penal, against His people, its claims having been satisfied, cannot be again enforced.

In the fifth chapter of this series we sought to define with care the meaning of the term "substitution." We pointed out that substitutionary suffering is that which is endured in the stead of others, in their actual place. Such suffering inevitably carries with it the *exemption* of the party or parties in whose room it is endured. What is done or suffered by a substitute, completely absolves those whom he represents from doing or suffering the same thing. Christ so satisfied the law of God in behalf of His people that the law can now make no claim whatsoever upon them. The death of Christ was as truly and actually a substitutionary one as was the death of those animals sacrificed in Old Testament times in lieu of the death of the transgressor offering them. Thus the substitutionary satisfaction of Christ *requires* Divine justice *to* remit the sins and to reinstate in Divine favor all for whose sake it was made.

Substitution necessarily involves two parties: an offender and one who takes his place, a debtor and one who discharges it for him. It is equally self-evident that substitution involves a two-fold effect; the position of *each* is changed in relation to the law. The one who before was innocent now becomes guilty, and the one who before was guilty now becomes innocent. This is a palpable fact and not a fine-spun theory. If then Christ bore the sins of His people, no sin can rest on them. If on their behalf He was made a curse, the law cannot now curse them. With the apostle we triumphantly exclaim, "Who shall lay anything to the charge of God's elect?—God that justifieth! Who is he that condemneth?—Christ that died" (Rom. 8:33, 34). Therefore we boldly affirm that, before there can be the least failure in the Divine design of Christ's Atonement, the Throne of God, which is founded upon "righteousness and judgment" (Psa. 97:2), must be overturned. But that is impossible.

7. THE GLORY OF GOD

No lengthy argument is needed to establish the fact that the glory of God *requires* the mediatorial work of Christ should be completely efficacious, i.e., that it should infallibly accomplish all it was designed to effect. If there were any failure in the *fruits* or *results* of the Atonement, then the purpose of God would be foiled, His covenant broken, His veracity forfeited, His power defeated, His justice sullied, and His glory dishonored. Few seem to realize the fearful implications which necessarily follow the principles they hold and advocate. To predicate an Atonement which fails to atone, a Redemption which does not redeem, a Sacrifice which secures not the actual remission of sins, is a horrible reflection upon all the attributes of God. To make the efficacy or success of the greatest of all God's works dependent upon the choice of fallen and depraved creatures, is to magnify man at the cost of dethroning his Maker.

The manifestative glory of God is bound up in the person and work of Christ. Our Lord Jesus revealed this plainly when, facing the crucial hour, He cried, "Father glorify *thy* name" (John 12:28). Again He declared, "Now is the Son of man glorified, and God is glorified *in him*" (John 13:31). Compare also John 14:13. If Christ be dishonored, God is dishonored. But if Christ be glorified by the Father's acceptance of His work and by the Spirit's infallible application thereof, so that every effect is produced which it was intended to bring forth, then is God supremely glorified. Therefore we boldly declare that, before there can be the slightest failure in the Divine design of the Atonement, God must cease to have any respect for His own honor. But that can never be.

CHAPTER ELEVEN

The Atonement — Its Application

"If the righteous scarcely [literally "with difficulty"] be saved where shall the ungodly and the sinner appear?" (I Pet. 4:18). It seems that comparatively few of the Lord's people have an adequate conception of the obstacles in the way of their salvation, of all that is involved in God's overcoming of them, and of the manner in which His salvation becomes theirs. Rightly did John Owen affirm, "So great and glorious is the work of saving believers unto the utmost, that it is necessary that the Lord Christ should lead a mediatory life in heaven, for the perfecting and accomplishment of it." Yet how few today recognize the needs-be for this. There has been such a one-sided emphasis laid upon the death of Christ, that the relation of His resurrection, ascension and intercession to the *salvation* of His people is now little understood even in orthdox circles.

If it were more clearly grasped that the redemptive work of Christ is a strictly *priestly* one, and if His *priestly* work were interpreted in the light of the Old Testament types we should experience less difficulty in perceiving the necessity, the meaning and the value of His present intercession on High. At the Cross Christ offered Himself to God, in all the merits of His life of perfect obedience, as a Satisfaction for His failing people. But what Christ did for His people, and their actual entering into the good of what He did for them, are two totally different things. That which He *purchased* for them has to be *applied* to them. It is at this point that so much confusion exists in the minds of many. God has left nothing uncertain, *nor is anything contingent on the creature*. Full provision was made by the wisdom of God for securing the results or fruitage of His Son's work: "He *shall* see of the travail of his soul and shall be *satisfied*" (Isa. 53:11) guarantees this. It is by the present ministry of Christ on High and by the operations of His Spirit on earth that this is attained. The first of these will now engage our attention.

The offices of Christ, the great Mediator between God and men, are the foundation of our hopes and the spring of our peace and joy, His priestly office particularly so. The exercise of His priestly office concerns two principal parts: His making full satisfaction to God by dying for His people, and His intercession at the right hand of God. "To offer and to intercede, to sacrifice and to pray, are both acts of the same sacerdotal office, and both required of him who is high priest, so that if he omit either of these, he cannot be a faithful *priest* for them; if either he doth not offer for them, or not intercede for the access of his oblation on their behalf, he is wanting in the discharge of this office by him undertaken" (John Owen). To which we may add that the *third* act of the high priest is his coming forth to "bless" those for whom he has offered an atonement: Lev. 9:22; I Chron. 23:13; Heb. 9:28.

But, as we have said above, through a one-sided conception of the death of Christ many fail to see the need for His present intercession as being requisite to their *salvation*. Their difficulty may be expressed thus: If our salvation was secured by the "one offering" of Christ, why must He now intercede for us? On the other hand, if our salvation "unto the uttermost" (Heb. 7:25) be obtained by Christ's intercession, what need was there for His atonement? We will answer in the words of H. Martin, "*Apparently* they mutually exclude each other, because they do *really* mutually and reciprocally *include* each other. The offering by which alone we are perfected is not passive endurance or suffering of the cross, but that *active* priestly offering of the cross which is prolonged without suffering into the function of intercession. And the Intercession, by which alone we are saved even unto the uttermost, is just the *perpetual presentation* of the 'continual burnt offering' of Calvary, which, as an active *offering*, subsists in perpetuity, and belongs to eternity, while the *suffering* of the cross belongs to the history of the past, and the Atonement, had it been mere suffering would have belonged to the past too."

The last quotation places the emphasis where it rightfully belongs. Had the Satisfaction of Christ consisted merely of His passively enduring the wrath of God, then everything required of Him as Mediator had been accomplished when He died. But in such case the "much more" of Romans 5:10 and the "yea rather" of Romans 8:34 had been rendered nugatory. Moreover, the sacrificial types of the Old Testament had been emptied of their meaning. Yea, the whole plan devised by God for the glorifying of Himself and the saving of His elect had been thrown into confusion. But allow that the Satisfaction of Christ is a *priestly* work, in which He is *active* throughout, and these difficulties are at once removed, for the types and the exposition of them in the epistle to the Hebrews show plainly enough that the work of atonement is not, in all respects, completed at the death of the victim. The intercession of Christ is just as requisite, just as vitally necessary, in order to save His people, as were His incarnation, obedience and death.

In support of what has just been said, we would call careful attention to one or two of the details found in Leviticus 16, where we have the fullest Old Testament type of Christ's high priestly office and work. As we hope to devote a separate chapter to the subject, in a later one of this book, we shall now confine ourselves to that which bears immediately upon the present aspect of our theme. First, in v. 11 we read of Aaron *killing* the bullock for a sin-offering, then, in v. 14, of taking its blood within the veil and *sprinkling* it upon the mercy seat. In like manner, in v. 15 we find the goat treated in the same way; something more than its blood being shed at the altar, namely brought within the veil. The antitype of this is found in Hebrews 9:12, where we read of Christ entering heaven "by his own blood," and in 9:24, where we are told that He has gone there "to appear in the presence of God for us."

Again, "The two altars of Sacrifice and of Incense were combined and correlative instruments of official action to the priest in the one complete office of his priesthood; and they constituted component and indispensable factors of one complete act of sacrificial worship. The same functionary or officebearer transacted at both: he transacted for the self-same person or persons; the blood of the self-same sacrifice that he had slain and offered on the altar, he sprinkled or put upon the horns of the other. To dislocate or derange this co-ordination would be to negate his official action in its intrinsic import, to annihilate the gracious results of his priestly intervention, and indeed to evert his office utterly. His action at the altar of Atonement was pre-requisite to his approach to the altar of Incense: and the successful achievement which signalized his action at the latter, revealed beyond the possibility of doubt the nature and efficacy of the services which he had accomplished at the former; while only in virtue of the two, in their combination and synthesis, was Aaron's priesthood a real priesthood at all" (H. Martin).

The intimate relation which existed between the brazen and the incense altars of Israel may be seen from their being linked together (Psa. 84:3): "Thine *altars*, O Lord of hosts." The close connection between them is revealed in a number of Scriptures. For instance, we gather from Leviticus 16:12, 13, and Numbers 16:46 that the fire on which the incense was laid upon the golden altar, was taken from the brazen altar, where the sin-offering was consumed. Thus, the activities of the one were based upon those of the other, the incense being kindled by that fire which had first fed upon the sacrifice; thus identifying the priest's service at both. This, in figure, tells us that our great High Priest pleads for no blessings which His blood has not purchased, and asks pardon from Divine justice for no sins for which He did not atone. The measure of the blessings for which Christ pleads is God's estimate of the life which He gave.

The wondrous scene portrayed in Isaiah 6 shows us again the inseparable connection between the two altars. There the prophet beheld the Lord of hosts, in His ineffable majesty and exalted glory, seated upon the throne in His heavenly temple, above which stood the seraphim, with veiled faces, crying, "Holy, holy, holy." What he saw and heard was so overwhelming that he said, "Woe is me for I am undone; because I am a man of unclean lips, and I dwell in the midst of a people of unclean lips: for mine eyes have seen the King, the Lord of hosts"

(v. 5). Blessed is it to mark the sequel: "Then flew one of the seraphims unto me, having a live coal in his hand, which he had taken with the tongs from off the altar: And he laid it upon my mouth, and said, Lo, this hath touched thy lips; and thine iniquity is taken away, and thy sin purged" (vv. 6, 7). As another remarked, "The emblem of Divine holiness had already consumed the sacrifice and was also consuming the sweet incense. Thus, symbolically, the prophet's lips were cleansed according to God's estimate of the value of the sacrifice and person of our Lord."

1. THE NATURE OF HIS INTERCESSION

"Christ maketh intercession, by His appearing in our nature, continually before the Father in heaven, in the merit of His obedience and sacrifice on earth, declaring His will to have it applied to all believers, answering all accusations against them, procuring for them quiet of conscience, notwithstanding daily failure, access with boldness to the throne of grace, and acceptance of their persons and sacrifices" (T. Ridgley). This definition seems to embody the essential features of the present intercession of our great High Priest. Having done everything on earth which God required from the Surety of our salvation, both in the removing of what would hinder it (sins and the curse) and procuring what would effect it (perfect obedience or righteousness), He has now gone into heaven, there "to appear in the presence of God for us" (Heb. 9:24).

First, He "appears" in our nature. The Mediator is "the Man Christ Jesus" (I Tim. 2:5) and to "intercede" *is* to *mediate.* He did not cast off the human nature when He left this earth, but carried it into heaven, retaining the same body, though glorified, as He had in the day of His humiliation. The same body in which He offered Himself as a sacrifice to God, He now *presents* in heaven — "a Lamb as it had been slain" (Rev. 5:6). The apostle does not say in Hebrews 9:24 that Christ entered heaven, to appear there in glory and majesty, as if His appearance there had been for Himself only; but "to appear in the presence of God for *us.*" As He was born, lived and died for us, so He ascended to heaven and appears in our nature at the right hand of God *for us* (cf. Hebrews 6:20).

Second, He appears as our "Advocate" to present His people and their cause unto God. When Aaron was to enter the most holy place to intercede for Israel, he was to bear the names of the twelve tribes upon his heart and shoulders (Ex. 28:12, 29): thus he went there not in his own name, but in the name and behalf of His people. As our Advocate (I John 2:1) Christ replies to the accusations of Satan (Rev. 12:10). A typical adumbration of this is found in Zechariah 3, where we see Joshua—type of the Church—charged by Satan. Christ, "the Lord," by His intercession with the Father, pleads that instead of Joshua, his accuser might be rebuked and confounded; acquitting and justifying the accused. No charge will have any better success which is formed against those for whom Christ appears as Advocate: see Romans 8:33, 34.

Third, He presents His meritorious sacrifice to God, pointing to His obedience and death in the stead of His people, to His blood which was shed for them. The typical high priest, when he was to mediate for Israel before God, brought in the blood of sacrifice and solemnly presented it (Heb. 9:7); so Christ, "by His own blood" has gone into heaven, thereby to "make intercession for the transgressors" (Isa. 53:12). Christ's blood "speaketh better things than Abel" (Heb. 12:24), crying for mercy, as Abel's did for vengeance. Its efficacy is so potent, and has as much the virtue of intercession, as if it had an articulate voice. The virtue of Christ's blood is still as fresh and powerful as if it were but just now shed—note "new and living" in Hebrews 10:20.

Fourth, He presents His will and desire that His people might have all which He purchased for them: the will of the Divine nature as He is God, the desires of His human nature as He is man. This is revealed to us most fully in that wondrous 17th of John, where we are permitted to hear the breathings of our great High Priest. There we find Him asking of the Father those things which are most requisite for His people in their time-state. There we behold Him putting in His claim on their behalf: "Father, *I will* that they also, whom thou hast given me, be with me where I am; that they may behold my glory, which thou hast given me" (John 17:24).

Fifth, by the intercession of Christ *access* to the throne of grace is obtained for His people. Though they have been delivered from the curse of the law, the flesh still remains within them, daily producing its evil fruit, defiling their service and interrupting their communion. As the conscience is made aware of this, the thought of drawing nigh unto the ineffably holy God would terrify, were it not that the Scriptures assure us we have One at His right hand pleading our cause. It is the realization of this blessed fact that gives us "boldness to enter into the Holiest by the blood of Jesus" (Heb. 10:19). Imperfect as are our approaches, unworthy as we are in ourselves, feeble though our petitions be, yet, there is One on High who has been given "*much* incense" and that "that He should add it to the prayers of all saints upon the golden altar which was before the throne" (Rev. 8:3). Thus may we "offer up spiritual sacrifices acceptable to God *by Jesus Christ*" (I Pet. 2:5).

2. THE NECESSITY OF HIS INTERCESSION

In an humble endeavor to ascertain the reasons why God has appointed the intercession of Christ, respect should be had unto the Divine honor, the Mediator's glory, and His people's peace and security. Underlying the whole plan of redemption God has determined that we should be saved in a way and manner which most contributed to His own honor and praise, in a way which would most glorify His Son, and in a way which should make our salvation most sure and steadfast. Let us seek, then, to reverently ponder the needs-be for our Saviour's present mediation in the light of these basic considerations.

The first reason, then, respects God Himself. "In general, God will be dealt with withal like Himself, in and throughout the whole way of our salvation, from first to last, and carry it all along as a superior wronged, and so keep a distance between Himself and sinners; who still are to come to Him by a Priest and a Mediator (Heb. 7:25), upon whose mediation and intercession their salvation doth depend; and therefore through Christ, in His dispensation of all *to us downward* doth carry it as a *king*, as one having all power to justify and condemn, yet *upward toward God*, He carries it as a *priest*, who still must intercede to do all that which He has power to do as king. Therefore, in the 2nd Psalm after that God has set Him as 'King upon his holy hill' (v. 6), namely, in heaven, and so has committed all power in heaven and earth to Him; then He must yet 'ask' all that He would have done—'*Ask* of me and I will give thee' (v. 8) God says to Him; for though He be a king, yet He is God's king—'I have set *my* King,' and by asking from Him God will be acknowledged to be above Him—i.e., above Him *as Mediator*.

"More particularly, God hath two attributes which He would have most eminently appear in their highest glory by Christ's effecting our salvation, namely, justice and free grace; and therefore hath so ordered the bringing about of our salvation, as that Christ might apply Himself in a more especial manner unto each of them, by way of satisfaction to the one, of entreaty to the other. Justice will be known to be justice, and dealt with upon its own terms; and grace will be acknowledged to be free grace, throughout the accomplishment of our salvation. You have both of them joined together in Romans 3:24, 26: 'Being justified *freely by his grace* through the *redemption* that is in Christ Jesus; that He might be *just*, and the justifier of him that believeth.' Here is highest justice and freest grace both met to save us, and both ordered by God to be 'declared' and 'set forth.'

"Our salvation depending and being carried on, even in the application of it, by a continuation of grace in a free way, notwithstanding satisfaction unto justice, therefore His free grace must be sought to, and treated with like itself, and applied upon in all, and the sovereignty and freeness of it acknowledged in all, even as well as God's justice had the honor to be satisfied by a price paid to it, that so the severity of it might appear and be held forth in our salvation. Thus God having two attributes eminently to be dealt with, His justice and His free grace, it was meet that there should be two eminent actions of Christ's priesthood, wherein He should apply Himself to each, according to their kind, and as the nature and glory of each doth require. And accordingly in His death He deals with justice, by laying down a sufficient price; and in His intercession He entreateth free grace, and thus both come to be alike acknowledged" (T. Goodwin).

What has been said above supplies the key which unlocks the blessed meaning of Hebrews 4:16, where Christians are encouraged to "come boldly to the throne of grace," and that, because they have "a great High Priest that is passed into the heavens," the "therefore" of v. 16 looking back to what is said there in v. 14. Observe well that it is called "the *throne of grace*" at which our High Priest now officiates: it is so designated because it is *chiefly* "grace" which His sacerdotal office now deals with and sues unto: therefore does He there treat with God by way of intercession. Of this throne of grace in heaven the mercy-seat in the holy of holies was the type, and as Aaron brought the blood and the mercy-seat together (Lev. 16:14), so has Christ. But more: Aaron not only entered the holiest with blood, but with incense too (Lev. 16:12) — the figure of prayer (Rev. 8:3) — to show that heaven is opened unto God's people not by mere justice (bloodshedding), but by grace also, yet grace which must be intreated.

Thus it is that there is the unfinished work of Christ in heaven, as well as His finished work on earth. In the one He dealt with justice here below, in the other He is treating with mercy in heaven. All the grace which Christ now bestows on His people He first *receives* from God, and that, in answer to His petitions. In Acts 2:33 it is said that, consequent upon His ascension, "He *received* of the Father the promise of the Holy Spirit, which He [Christ] hath shed forth," namely, on the day of Pentecost. Yet, if we go back to John 14:16 we learn that Christ received the Spirit (that as Mediator He might send Him forth) in answer to His intercession: "And I will *pray* the Father, and He shall give you another Comforter." So too in Ephesians 4:11 we read that the ascended Christ "gave" gifts unto His Church, but, if we go back to Psalm 68:18, we learn that He *"received* [from the Father those] gifts for men," and that, as the fruit of His intercession.

In the second place, God had respect unto the glory of His beloved Son. In ordering our salvation to be accomplished by His work of intercession, God had in view the honor and praise of Christ too, that "all might honour the Son even as they honour the Father" (John 5:23). Thus, for the maintaining of His honor and the manifestation of His glory, it was appointed that He should continue to intercede. None of His offices were to lie idle. All offices have work assigned them, and all work (properly done) has honor as its reward. When, then, Christ had finished His work here upon earth, as pertained to the *meriting* of our salvation, God appointed this perpetual work in heaven for the applying and bringing His people *into possession of* His salvation, and that, as a Priest, by praying in the virtue of the one oblation of Himself: see Hebrews 7:24.

For the same reason it became Him that the whole work of salvation from first to last, in every step and degree of its accomplishment, should be so ordered that *Christ* would still continue to have as great a hand in its application and consummation as He had in laying the first foundation thereof. This we have expressed in Hebrews 12:2, "Looking unto Jesus the Author *and Finisher* of our faith." In what immediately follows, two things are said of Him, as the two causes of two effects, concerning each of which faith needs to be "looking unto" Him. First, He is to be "looked" at as dying—"enduring the cross"; second, as "set down at the right hand of the Majesty on high," there interceding. We need to look to Him as dying as the "Author," or "beginning of our faith," and at His sitting at God's right hand as an Intercessor, for the "finishing of our faith," and so of our final salvation. Christ is both the Alpha and Omega.

In the third place, God had respect unto the comfort and security of His people. "God would have our salvation made sure, and us saved all manner of ways, over and over. First, by ransom and price (as captives are redeemed), which was done by His death, which of itself was enough. Second, by power and rescue; so in His resurrection, ascension, and sitting at God's right hand, which also was sufficient. Third, by intercession, a way of favour and entreaty, and this likewise would have been enough, but God would have all things concur in it, whereof notwithstanding not one could fail; a threefold cord, whereof each strand was strong enough, but all together must of necessity hold" (T. Goodwin).

The whole *application* of Christ's Satisfaction, both in justifying and saving us, first and last, has a special dependence upon His intercession. The leading difference between the influence of His death, and that of His intercession, unto our salvation, is this: the one was the means of procuring or obtaining it for us, the other the means of securing and applying it unto us. Christ purchased salvation by the one, but we are possessed of it by the other. It was not until Christ was "perfected through suffering" that He became "the Author [or "applying cause"] of eternal salvation" (Heb. 5:7). The two things were united at the cross: "He bore the sins of many *and* made intercession for the transgressors" (Isa. 53:12). That while the death of Christ procured our salvation, it did not (of itself) secure it, seems very evident from I Corinthians 15:17: "If Christ be not raised your faith is vain, ye are yet in your sins."

Those for whom Christ intercedes are they whose sin He bore (Isa. 53:12), namely, those given to Him by the Father (John 17:9). That for which He intercedes is what He purchased for them by His Satisfaction, namely, "eternal redemption" (Heb. 9:12), which includes the gift of the Holy Spirit to apply unto them all the virtues of His perfect work. That which the Holy Spirit communicates to them is life, light, love, faith, repentance and perseverance in obedience. As we shall devote the whole of the next chapter to an amplification of this deeply important yet greatly neglected aspect of our theme, only the briefest statement thereon can now be made. By His death Christ meritoriously procured for all of His people an actual participation in the blessings of redemption, and this is infallibly applied to them by His Spirit. By the operations of the Spirit the elect are brought to saving faith and repentance, so that every requirement of God's government is fully met.

3. THE EFFICACY OF HIS INTERCESSION

First, this is fully assured by the fact that Christ's petitions are grounded upon indisputable *merit,* and therefore must prevail in the high court of Justice. His obedience unto death was infinitely meritorious and did deserve for His people that which, as Intercessor on their behalf, He pleads for. He fully satisfied every demand of the law, perfectly performed the work which He came to do, paid to the last mite all His people owed, and therefore, because of the intrinsic value of what He did, He must, in very righteousness, be granted that which He purchased.

Second, the success of Christ's intercession is fully assured by the fact that He sues only for that which is agreeable to His Father, and therefore is the Father entirely ready to grant His requests. He pleads for nothing but what is according to the will of God: Hebrews 10:7-9. God's will was that Christ should be a sacrifice, and it is upon the ground of having perfectly performed His will, that His plea proceeds; such being the ground, it *must* prevail. Were it not effectual, the will of God were ineffectual. But, it is *God* that justifieth, so as none can condemn. How so? It is Christ that maketh the intercession: Romans 8:33, 34.

Third, the success of Christ's intercession is fully assured because it is a commemoration of His sacrifice. That which Christ pleads before God is His own blood, which is "precious" in His sight. The sacrifice of Christ is a "sweet-smelling savour" unto God (Eph. 5:2). He is infinitely pleased with it, and in view of it He cannot but grant Christ, upon His personal application, that which it was offered to procure. If the blood of bulls and of goats, and the ashes of an heifer sprinkling the unclean sanctified to the purifying of the flesh, "how much more shall the blood of Christ" prevail as He pleads its merits before God (Heb. 9:12, 13)!

Fourth, the success of Christ's intercession is fully assured by the fact that He is the Beloved of the Father. In Him the Father is so well pleased that He can deny Him naught that He asks. Christ Himself declared, "Thou hearest me always" (John 11:42). When Esther appeared before King Ahasuerus to intercede for her people condemned to destruction, he gave her this assurance, "What is thy request? it shall be even given thee to the half of the kingdom" (5:3). Christ was given still greater assurance before He entered upon His sacrificial work, "Ask of me," God said, "and *I will* give thee the Gentiles for thine inheritance and the uttermost parts of the earth for thy possessions" (Psa. 2:8). This is the greatest thing for which Christ does ask, the sum of all He intercedes for.

Finally, the success of Christ's intercession is fully assured by the fact that nothing, in, of, from, or by His people can possibly countervail it. "Wherefore He is able also to save them *to the uttermost* that come unto God by Him, seeing He ever liveth to make intercession for them" (Heb. 7:25). If Christ has once taken a person into His prayers, He will never, under any circumstances, cast him out. A man may be cast out of good men's hearts and prayers as Saul was out of Samuel's, and apostate Israel was out of Jeremiah's, but no man was ever cast out of Christ's prayers when He once took him in. The only possible danger could be through *sinning,* but Christ's prayers see to it and prevail and prevent them from apostatizing (John 17:15), which is the only sin for which there is no forgiveness. "If any one [of the family] sin, we *have* an Advocate with the Father, Jesus Christ the righteous" (I John 2:1).

How infallibly certain it is, then, that Christ shall "see of the travail of his soul and *be satisfied*" (Isa. 53:11). He sees to it Himself that nothing which He purchased by His obedience unto death shall be lost. The application of His Satisfaction is as sure as the impetration of it. He is Himself constantly engaged in maintaining the interests of those for whom He died. There is not only an "access" into the grace of God "through our Lord Jesus Christ," but there is also a *standing* in the same (Rom. 5:1,2), and that continued "standing" is expressly attributed to His "life" (Rom. 5:10), which, as it is interpreted for us in Hebrews 7:25, means His ever living to intercede. "We owe our standing in grace every moment to His sitting in Heaven and interceding every moment. There is no fresh act of justification goes forth, but there is a fresh act of intercession. And as though God created the world once for all, yet every moment He is said to create, every new act of Providence being a new creation; so likewise is Jesus continually, through His continuing out free grace to justify us at the first, and this Christ doeth by continuing His intercessions; He continues 'a Priest forever,' and so we continue to be justified for ever" (T. Goodwin).

CHAPTER TWELVE

THE ATONEMENT – ITS APPLICATION (CONCLUDED)

We cannot do better than begin this chapter by transcribing the opening words from chapter 1, book 3 of Calvin's *Institutes*. "We are now to examine how we *obtain* the enjoyment of those blessings which the Father has conferred on His only begotten Son, not for His own private use, but to enrich the poor and needy. And first it must be remarked, that as long as there is a separation between Christ and us, all that He suffered and performed for the salvation of mankind is useless and unavailing to us. To communicate what He received from the Father, He must, therefore, become ours, and dwell in us . . . The sum of all is this – that the Holy Spirit is the bond by which Christ efficaciously unites us to Himself."

The Satisfaction of Christ rendered absolutely certain the salvation of those for whom He transacted, whose federal Head He was. Yet something further was necessary to make His people the actual participants of it: in the language of Acts 26:18 the Holy Spirit must be sent to "open their eyes, to turn from darkness to light, and the power of Satan unto God, that they may receive forgiveness of sins, and inheritance among them which are sanctified by faith." The beneficiaries of Christ's mediatorial work enter this world in a state of guilt and depravity, and it is the peculiar office of the Holy Spirit to bring them into a state of life and liberty. The Persons of the Godhead have shared and distributed the whole work of the salvation of the elect amongst themselves unto three several parts: election is appropriated to the Father, redemption to the Son, the application of both election and redemption to the Spirit. Here again we reach a vitally important aspect of truth concerning which few today have any light.

We showed in chapter 10, conclusively we hope, that the efficacy of the Atonement has not been left an open question, that the full accomplishing of God's design therein is not in any wise dependent upon man. What we would now press upon the reader is that the same God who ordained the end, also ordained all the means whereby that end is infallibly reached. The end God had before Him was the salvation of His people, their ultimate glorification, their being fitted to spend eternity in His holy presence. The means whereby that end was to be reached are the mediatorial work of Christ and the operations of the Holy Spirit. As the three Persons of the ever-blessed Trinity are undivided in their essence, so they are perfectly unanimous in their will and workings. Therefore those who have an interest in the good will of the Father, and the redemption of the Son, are likewise the subjects of the Spirit's gracious influence.

It is a great mistake and a serious error to separate the present mission and ministry of the Holy Spirit from the Atonement of Christ, just as it is to contemplate the sacrifice of the Son apart from the purpose of the Father. All of the Three Divine persons concurred in the terms and arrangements of the Everlasting Covenant. It is the special work of the Spirit to make effectual unto the souls of God's elect the gracious purpose of the Father and the meritorious purchase of the Son. That which Christ did *for* His people, the Spirit stands pledged to make good *in* them. The Holy Spirit has been sent here to free those captives for whose liberty Christ paid the Father the ransom-price. This the Father promised His Son on condition of His performing the work assigned Him. It needs to be steadily borne in mind that "*all* the promises in Him [i.e. in Christ] are yea, and in him amen" (II Cor. 1:20), and therefore that the promises made to Christ's seed, recorded in Scripture, are but the *transcripts* of the promises which God first made to their Head—cf. Titus 1:2! Let such passages as Isaiah 44:3; Ezekiel 36:25-27; Joel 2:18 be read in *that light*.

"Salvation is of the Lord" (Jonah 2:9), entirely so, from beginning to end. It is God's "great salvation," in its origination, in its effectuation, in its application and in its consummation. Man contributes nothing to it whatsoever. All the Trinity are concerned and engaged in it. The Father is the Author of salvation from sin, Christ the Purchaser, the Spirit the Conveyor. It is the Father who begets the elect (James 1:17, 18); yet, they are declared to be the "seed" of Christ (Isa. 53:10), while they are "born" of the Spirit (John 3:6). Though it has many aspects, and may be considered from various angles, nevertheless, it is one and the same salvation. It is the third aspect of it we are here contemplating, namely, the Satisfaction of Christ made efficacious by the infallible *application thereof* to God's elect. To take this up in detail, let us note:

1. THE HOLY SPIRIT'S OFFICE

What we wish to look at now is the particular relation which the Holy Spirit sustains to the *economy* of Redemption. In this He is *subordinate to* Christ the Mediator. There are a number of passages which clearly teach this. John the Baptist declared concerning Christ, "He shall baptize you with the Holy Spirit" (Mark 1:8). The *communication of* the Spirit was to be the distinguishing mark of the Saviour's ministry, in respect of which He would prove to be greater and mightier than the herald who was sent to prepare His way. In John 20:22 we find the risen Redeemer imparting this Divine gift to His apostles: "He breathed on, and saith unto them, Receive ye the Holy Spirit." In Revelation 3:1 He is spoken of as "He that *hath* the seven Spirits of God." These, and other passages which might be quoted, show that, in the administration of the Everlasting Covenant, the Spirit is now subject to Christ. Hence is He called, "The Spirit of Christ" (Rom. 8:9).

That the Holy Spirit *should be* subject to Christ, that the Saviour should direct the Spirit's operations, was promised Him in the Everlasting Covenant. In Acts 1:4 He is referred to as "The *promise* of the Father." Observe now when John the Baptist's prediction was fulfilled and Christ baptized His people with the Holy Spirit, Peter explained the supernatural phenomena attending it, by saying, "Therefore being by the right hand of God exalted, and having received of the Father the *promise* of the Holy Spirit, He hath shed forth this, which ye now see and hear" (Acts 2:33)! So again in Galatians 3:14 we read, "That the blessing of Abraham might come on the Gentiles *through* Jesus Christ; *that* we might receive the *promise* of the Spirit through faith." So too we read that believers are "sealed with that Holy Spirit of *promise*" (Eph. 1:13).

In the next place, we would point out how that Christ has

actually *purchased* the gift of the Holy Spirit for His people, that His coming to the redeemed is one of the consequences or fruits of Christ's Atonement. First, this is clearly implied in John 7:39: "But this spake He of the Spirit which they that believe on Him should receive: for the Holy Spirit was not (given) *because* that Jesus was not yet glorified." Whether we understand the "glorified" as referring to Christ's death (John 13:31) or to His exaltation (I Tim. 3:16), the coming of the Spirit is clearly a result thereof; by this we are to understand that the obedience of Christ was the *meritorious* cause of God's sending His Spirit to indwell His people. Again; we may note that Christ's communication of the Spirit to His apostles in John 20:22 was not till after His blood had been shed. Again, observe the double "that" in Galatians 3:14 following Christ's being made a curse for us in verse 13; it is the relation of cause to effect.

"But when the fulness of the time was come God sent forth his Son, made of a woman, made under the law. To redeem them that were under the law, that we might receive the adoption of sons. And because ye are sons, God hath sent forth the Spirit *of his Son into* your hearts" (Gal. 4:4-6). Here we have three things: the Son's being sent forth to redeem God's elect; this, that they might receive the adoption of sons; in consequence thereof the Spirit's being sent into their hearts. The elect were adopted into God's family before the foundation of the world (Eph. 1:4-5), hence they *"are* sons" (Gal. 4:6), and this *before* they received the Spirit. The Spirit is not given to make them sons, for all the members of Christ were written in the book of life as sons and daughters before sin existed or time began. No, the Spirit was given to them because they are sons, and that, as the meritorious gift of Christ, purchased by His redemption.

To sum up this point. This choicest benefit we receive from God could not have come unless His justice had been fully satisfied, and His favor procured by a sufficient sacrifice. It was the death of Christ which appeased the anger of His holy Father, and opened those treasures of grace which by reason of our sins had otherwise been shut up from us. Wondrously is this brought out in the Old Testament types: the Rock

(Christ) must be *smitten* before the Water (the Spirit) could flow forth unto God's people (Ex. 17:6). The very design of the Spirit is to make manifest the fullness of God's love to His people, and how could that be until God had demonstrated it at the Cross: Romans 5:8! The Spirit is here to declare the means of salvation, and they are the obedience, death and resurrection of Christ.

We are now to consider the teaching of Christ in His paschal discourse on this most sacred and blessed subject. "But the Comforter, the Holy Spirit, whom the Father will send in my name" (John 14:26). Christ keeps the treasury of Grace in His own hands. He is so choice of it that He would not entrust its administration to angels. Angels were employed to strengthen Him, both at His temptation and in His agony in Gethsemane: and they are ministering spirits for the heirs of salvation, but they have not the custody of that which brings them into heirship. Christ employs none but the Spirit to be His Attorney and Deputy in this world. The Spirit is sent in *His* name: "But when the Comforter is come, whom *I* will send unto you from the Father" (John 15:26).

"Howbeit when he, the Spirit of truth, is come, he will guide you into all truth: for he shall not speak of himself; but whatsoever he shall hear, shall he speak: and he will show you things to come. He shall glorify me: for he shall receive of mine, and shall show unto you" (John 16:13, 14). There are three things in these verses which need to be particularly noted in this connection.

First, the Spirit would not speak of Himself, but only that which He should hear. He was to come as the Representative of Christ, and therefore He would reveal none other truth and communicate none other grace than what is in and by and from Christ Himself. Just as Christ declared, "I do nothing of myself; but as my Father hath taught me, I speak these things . . . I speak that which I have seen with my Father" (John 8:28, 38), so the Spirit would set His seal upon what Christ had taught. The Spirit was an equal participant in the councils of the Father and Son, being thoroughly cognizant of all that passed between them in the Everlasting Covenant. He has an infinite knowledge of their designs, for He "searcheth all things, yea, the deep things of God" (I Cor. 2:10);

therefore does He make intercession for the saints "according to God" (Rom. 8:27).

Second, "He shall glorify me," that is, the Lord Jesus. As Christ sought not His own glory, but ever had the glory of the Father before Him in all that He did, so the Spirit seeks not His own glory, but that of Him whom He now represents. This is the mission of the Holy Spirit, the design of His being sent here, the work He has come to do. "As the work of the Son was not His own work, but rather that of the Father who sent Him (John 5:17), and in whose name He performed it (Luke 2:49); so the work of the Spirit is not His own work, but rather the work of the Son who sent him, and in whose name He doth accomplish it" (John Owen).

"He shall receive of mine, and shall shew it unto you." The things of Christ may be reduced to two heads: "grace and truth" (John 1:17). From Christ the Spirit receives these; to His redeemed He effectually communicates grace and personally reveals the truth. Just as Christ declared "The Father loveth the Son, and hath given all things into his hand" (John 3:35), so hath Christ delivered all His interests into the Spirit's hand. Two great things accrue to us by Christ: *acquisition* of redemption, *application* of redemption. The one is wrought by His death, the other by His resurrection-life; the one was procured by Him immediately, the other is secured by the Spirit mediately.

2. The Spirit Regenerating

"That which is born of the Spirit is spirit" (John 3:6). And, what is it *to be* born of the Spirit? It is to be vitally united to Christ, so that "he that is *joined unto* the Lord is one spirit" (I Cor. 6:17). Therefore it is to be made the recipient of "eternal life" for "God hath given to us eternal life and this life is in His Son" (I John 5:11). And this is given to us on the ground of Christ's Satisfaction. This is brought out plainly in John 3, though nearly all writers on that chapter have quite missed the point. There we find our Lord pressing upon Nicodemus the imperative necessity of the new birth: "Marvel not that I said unto thee, Ye must be born again." The Pharisee was quite non-plussed, and asked, "How can these things be?" Christ's reply is found in verses 14-16,

Now to say Christ here taught that regeneration is effected by faith in Him as "lifted up," is to miss the main point in His words. The key to those verses lies in connecting the "must" of verse 14 with the "must" of verse 7. To be born again is to be made partaker of a new life: it is to have "eternal life." Now the very design of Christ's being "lifted up" and of God's love in "giving" Him was, "that whosoever believeth in him should not perish, but have *eternal life"* (v. 15). But no man could be born again, none could have eternal life, save as the result of a full satisfaction having been made to the claims of a holy and righteous God. Except the corn of wheat "fall into the ground and die, it abideth alone" (John 12:24). The Holy Spirit could not regenerate except on the ground of the atoning death of Christ. Let us present some further proofs of this.

"For the law of the Spirit of life in Christ Jesus hath made me free from the law of sin and death" (Rom. 8:2). In verse 1 we read that believers are exempt from all condemnation because of their *legal* union with Christ. In verse 2 we are shown the fruit of this: the Holy Spirit makes it good to the soul in a *vital* way. The "law" of the Spirit refers both to His authority and power. But what we would call special attention to is that, in the economy of redemption, the authority and power of the Spirit is "of life *in Christ Jesus."* In other words, the Spirit communicates to God's elect the very life which is in the Mediator. "The gift of God is eternal life through [or "in"] *Jesus Christ* our Lord" (Rom. 6:23). In Christ "dwelleth all the fulness of the Godhead" (Col. 2:9) therefore the Spirit both resides "in" and is dispensed "by" Him!

"And if Christ be in you, the body is dead because of sin; but the spirit is life because of righteousness" (Rom. 8:10). Because of our union with Christ, the whole body of sin (cf. 6:6; 7:24) is legally "dead." The "spirit" here refers to that which is born of the Spirit, and that is "life," and it is a life "*because of* righteousness," namely, the righteousness of Christ. The meritorious ground on which the Spirit imparts "life" to us is the Satisfaction of Christ. I live *because* Christ died and rose again for me.

"Not by works of righteousness which we have done, but

according to his mercy he saved us, by the washing of regeneration, and renewing of the Holy Spirit; which he shed on us abundantly *through Jesus Christ* our Saviour; That being justified by his grace we should be *made* heirs according to the hope of eternal life" (Titus 3:5-7). Nothing could be plainer. Here, the *ground on which* the Spirit regenerates is clearly referred to as the Redeemer's mediation. Many have wondered how it was possible for the *Holy* Spirit to take up His abode in a fallen and depraved creature. He could not do so but for one thing, namely, that the depraved creature has been legally cleansed by the precious blood of Christ. Beautifully was this foreshadowed in the Old Testament types. The "oil" (emblem of the Spirit: I John 2:20, 27) was always placed upon the "blood": see Leviticus 14:14-17.

Another beautiful type is found in Psalm 133:2, "Like the precious ointment upon the head, that ran down upon the beard, Aaron's beard: that went down to the skirts of his garments." Here Aaron foreshadowed our great High Priest receiving such a plenitude of that which spoke of the Holy Spirit, that all the members of His mystical body partake of the same. It is to this that Hebrews 1:9 refers, "Therefore God, Thy God, hath anointed thee with the oil of gladness above thy fellows." Here the Mediator is in view, as the words "Thy God" plainly show. Though He, by virtue of His humanity being taken up into union with the second person of the Godhead, has been anointed "above" His fellows, yet they *as* His "fellows" receive the same gracious and holy unction as He did.

"How much more shall the blood of Christ, who through the eternal Spirit offered Himself without spot to God, purge your conscience from dead works to serve the living God" (Heb. 9:14). This verse brings before us another aspect of the believer's regeneration, namely, the purging of his conscience, so that he may worship God. It is the Spirit who removes from the conscience the intolerable load of guilt, by giving him to see that Christ bore it away from Him. But what we would here emphasize is that this gracious operation of the Spirit is attributed to, is based upon, or is one of the fruits of, the "blood of Christ."

Now Christ, as Mediator, obtained for Himself a right to all the elect: "All mine are thine, and thine are *mine*" (John 17:

10). They are His "peculiar people" (Titus 2:14). Thus, at God's appointed hour Christ is entitled to claim each of them for Himself. This right He exercises. "When, according to the determinate counsel of God, the time of the gracious visitation of every one of the elect is come, He actually delivers them, as His property, by an outstretched arm. And why should He not, seeing He can easily effect it by the power of the Holy Spirit, turning and inclining their heart? Is it credible that He should suffer those who are His lawful right, to be, to remain, the slaves of Satan? Shall He suffer any of those to perish whom He purchased for His own possession by His precious blood? Christ Himself has taught us thus to reason: 'Other sheep I have, which are not of this fold: them also I must bring, and they *shall* hear my voice' (John 10:16). Because these sheep were of right His property, it therefore becomes Him actually to lay hold of them as His own, and bring them into His fold" (H. Witsius). This is done by the Spirit.

To sum up this point. The coming of the Spirit in regenerating power to God's elect is both a Covenant-promise and an Atonement-purchase. The *cause* of the Spirit's working is jointly from the Father and the Son. Only as this is maintained do we ascribe the glory which belongs to both by virtue of the Spirit's operations. The Spirit works from the Father's decree (II Thess. 2:13), and the Son's redemption; in other words, He is sent to effectuate what was determined upon in the Everlasting Covenant. To all the Father elected, and to all for whom Christ died, the Spirit is given. "The Holy Spirit is the bond of union between us and Christ. We are united to Him because we have the same Spirit Christ had; there is the same Spirit in Head and members, and therefore He will work like effects in Him and in you. If the Head rise, the members will follow after, for His mystical body was appointed to be conformed to their Head: Romans 8:29." (T. Manton, 1660).

3. Faith Imparted

That faith is, in some sense, essential unto salvation, it would, with an open Bible before us, be worse than idle to deny. But the important question is, Did Christ *purchase* the gracious operations of the Spirit and *all* His fruits for those for whom He died? Or, did He effect by His sacrifice nothing more than the removal of legal impediments out of the way of salvation, leaving them to provide their own faith and repentance? That Christ *must* have purchased these should be clear from the fact that, in their natural condition, the elect have no power to furnish any spiritual graces. It has been rightly pointed out that, "The Scriptures everywhere ascribe the *whole* ground and cause of our salvation to Christ. But if the differentiating grace which distinguishes the believer from the unbeliever is to be attributed to any cause external to Christ's mediation, then *that* cause, and not His redemption, is the real cause of salvation" (A. A. Hodge).

That faith is necessary in order to salvation is clear from such verses as Acts 16:31; Romans 1:16, etc. God never gives the one without the other, therefore both are inseparably connected in His eternal purpose thereunto: "God hath from the beginning chosen you to salvation *through* sanctification of the Spirit [the new birth] *and* belief of the truth" (II Thess. 2:13). Yet it is a mistake to say that faith is a "condition" of salvation in the sense of my paying for an article is the condition of obtaining the same. Every condition to the *right* of salvation has been fulfilled for us by Christ. Faith is rather the *connection* between the soul and God's salvation in Christ, and that connection is made by the Holy Spirit. The various steps in the outworking of God's eternal purpose are set forth in Romans 8:29, 30. The actual *application* of redemption commences with the effectual call of the Spirit, by which the elect are brought out of a state of nature into a state of grace.

There are two chief errors in connection with saving faith. The first is that fallen man is the author of it, that it is the product of the creature's will. This is a horrible delusion which must be firmly withstood. A dead man cannot believe. Believing in Christ in a spiritual and saving way is the result and fruit of "life" communicated to the heart. Christ declared that "No man *can* come to me, except the Father which hath sent me *draw* him" (John 6:44): this is accomplished in and by the Spirit's regeneration. It should be noted that John 1:12 is explained in 1:13, as that John 3:15, 16 are preceded by John 3:6, 7. Those who are born again believe. Those who believe *have been* born again: "Whosoever believeth that Jesus is the Christ *is* begotten of God" (I John 5:1 R. V.).

The second error is in separating the Spirit's communication of faith from the merits of Christ's sacrifice. "Why did we at first believe? Why do we still exercise that faith and walk by it? Only because it was covenanted for on our behalf when Christ undertook to die for us. It should help us to pray better, 'Lord, increase our faith' when we remember at what a cost that faith was procured for us. And certainly this alone will keep us from one of the subtlest of all Satan's snares, pride of faith . . . . How easy it is to live proudly on faith! Faith will do as well as works for Satan's purpose of leading us to give to man the glory that is Christ's" (From Papers of the Sovereign Grace Union Conference, 1923).

In order that Christ may have *all the glory* even for our believing in Him, it is most necessary to recognize that faith is not only God's gift, Ephesians 2:8, 9 (and therefore while we are saved "through" faith, we are *not* saved *for* faith), and that this faith is "of the operation of God" (Col. 2:12), i.e. of the Spirit's working, but also that the Spirit imparts it *on the ground of* Christ's redemption, i.e. that Christ *merited it* for us. It is because Christ appeased God's wrath and removed the obstacles from the outflow of His mercy toward us, that the Spirit is free to work in us. This is clearly stated in II Peter 1:1, "To them that have obtained a like precious faith with us *in the righteousness of* our God and Saviour Jesus Christ" (R. V.). God has treasured up all the store of grace and gifts in Christ, and it is out of His "fulness" the Spirit takes (John 16:14) and we "receive" (John 1:16). Only as this is held fast is the righteousness of Christ exalted and magnified.

In Ephesians 1:3 we are told that God "hath blessed us with *all* spiritual blessings in the heavenlies *in Christ*," and not the least of these is *faith!* In Romans 8:32 the question is asked, "He that spared not his own Son, but delivered him up for us all, how shall he not with him *also* freely give us *all* things?" Yes, "with" Christ, God freely bestows on us the Spirit, faith, repentance and all that is needed for time and eternity. In Philippians 1:29 we read, "For unto you it is given *in the behalf of Christ* not only *to believe* on him, but also to suffer for his sake." In I Peter 1:3 it is said, "Blessed be the God and Father *of our Lord Jesus Christ,* which according to his abundant mercy hath *begotten us*." It is *as* "the Father of our Lord Jesus Christ" that God begets us!

Salvation and all the blessings accompanying it were purposed, promised and purchased long before writer and reader first saw the light of day. Those for whom Christ died have an indefeasible *right* to what He bought for them, and that, long before they come into actual possession of the same. If it be asked, This being so, why do not the elect enter upon the enjoyment thereof as soon as they are born into this world? The answer is, because God has reserved to Himself the right and liberty to discharge the debtor *when* and *as* He pleases. As in the parable: some are called at the first hour, some at the third, sixth, ninth, and some at the eleventh (Matt. 20).

4. Repentance Given

"Him hath God exalted with His right hand a Prince and a Saviour *for to give* repentance to Israel, and forgiveness of sins" (Acts 5:31). Impenitence and unbelief are the thick clouds which dissolve under the blessed beams of the Sun of Righteousness.

Every spiritual gift and blessing we receive argues or presupposes the vicarious work of Christ. The grace of God is "given you by Jesus Christ" (I Cor. 1:4). It is by His having given Himself for our sins that we are delivered from "this present evil world" (Gal. 1:4). It is "*in him* also we have obtained an inheritance" (Eph. 1:11). Christ died to procure for us a subjective as well as an objective sanctification, which is accomplished by His Spirit's indwelling us: Titus 2:14; Ephesians 5:26, 27. It is because He has washed us from our sins in His own blood that "He hath made us kings and priests unto God and his Father" (Rev. 1:5, 6). God makes us "perfect in every good work to do His will, working in us that which is well-pleasing in his sight, *through Jesus Christ*" (Heb. 13:21).

Thus, all the graces of the Christian character and all the virtues of the Christian life which are wrought in us by the agency of the Holy Spirit, are imparted through Christ and received out of His meritorious fulness. Then, well may we join the saints in heaven in saying with a loud voice, "Worthy is the Lamb that was slain" (Rev. 5:12).

CHAPTER THIRTEEN

The Atonement—Its Results

Having sought to show from Scripture the *nature* of the Satisfaction which the Mediator offered unto God, and, by virtue of His acceptance of the same, its certain *efficacy* to procure and secure all that it was ordained to accomplish, we are now ready to contemplate in fuller detail some of the results which it has actually effected. By the "results" we mean the *consequences* which have flowed to the elect in their relation to God and His law. These are so many and so diversified that we shall not here presume an attempt to even enumerate them. Instead, following the emphasis of Scripture, we seek to direct attention unto the principle effects only. Once the Lord permits the regenerated soul to obtain a clear grasp of these, little difficulty should be experienced in apprehending the minor corollaries with which they are accompanied.

God Himself had a specific end in view when appointing the great Atonement, and in consequence of its having been made, certain things are effectually fulfilled and accomplished by it. As we sought to show in the 9th chapter of this book, the *supreme* aim of God in the Satisfaction of Christ is the advancement of His own declarative honor, and that by the manifestation of His glorious attributes therein. God's *subordinate* aim in Christ's Satisfaction, which aim is subservient to and is effectual unto His ultimate intendment, is the deliverance of His people from the curse and the restoring of them to His image and fellowship. To effect this, God has to be propitiated, sin expiated, and the elect sinner reinstated in the Divine favor.

Perhaps the most comprehensive single statement in Scripture upon the design and result of the Satisfaction of Christ is found in I Peter 3:18. There we read that "Christ hath also once suffered for sins, the just for the unjust, that he might *bring us to God.*" Bringing us to God is a general expression for the accomplishment of the *whole* work of our salvation, both in the removal of all hindrances and in the bestowal of all requisites. More specifically, in order for the elect — viewed as fallen in Adam — to be brought unto God, it was necessary that all enmity between them should be removed; in other words, that *reconciliation* should be effected. So too it was necessary that the guilt of all their transgressions should be cancelled; in other words, that they should receive *remission* of sin. Further, it was necessary that they should be delivered from all bondage; in other words, that they should be *redeemed.* Finally, it was necessary that they should be made, both legally and experimentally, *righteous.*

In the four words emphasized in the closing sentences of the last paragraph we have summed up the essential *results* which have accrued from the Satisfaction of Christ. As those results bear upon sin, it has been expiated; as they bear upon the elect, they have been emancipated; as they bear upon God, He has been propitiated. Lest this statement should create a false impression, let us at once add that the Atonement produced no actual change in God, any more than do His acts of creation or providence. The efficient purpose existed in the Divine mind from all eternity. He acted upon it from the fall of Adam, as though the atonement was actually accomplished. The infinite justice and the infinite love which were exercised in the sacrifice of Christ, were in the Divine mind from the beginning. The effect of Christ's Satisfaction was to render possible the *concurrent* exercise of Justice and Love in their treatment of the same persons. As these four "results" named are of such incalculable value and importance we shall devote a separate chapter to the consideration of each one.

1. RECONCILIATION

In II Corinthians 5, the Gospel of grace which God has called His servants to proclaim is spoken of thus: "And hath given to us the ministry of reconciliation" (v 18), and "hath committed to us, the word of reconciliation" (v. 19). This at once shows the great importance of having clear and Scriptural views upon this mighty subject, for otherwise it is impossible to honor

God in our preaching (which should ever be our first and chief concern), or to edify His people with wholesome doctrine. A mistake at this point seriously injures the whole of our evangelical ministrations and causes us to set forth a perverted presentation of God's saving truth. The realization of this ought to bow every minister of the Gospel before God in deep humility, earnestly entreating Him for Divine light and wisdom, that he may be so taught of the Lord that the Gospel trumpet may give forth no uncertain sound when it is placed to his lips. Far better not to preach at all, than to preach that which is contrary to Scripture, dishonoring to God, and injurious to souls. Let us now consider—

A. *Its Nature*

The word "reconcile" means to bring together again those who are alienated, to re-unite those who are at variance, to restore to amity and concord by removing that which hinders agreement and fellowship. It is most important to observe at the outset that the term "reconciliation" is itself *objective* in its signification. That is to say, reconciliation terminates upon the object, and not upon the subject. This is clear from Matthew 5:23, 24, where our Lord said, "If thou bring thy gift to the altar, and there rememberest that thy brother hath ought *against thee;* leave there thy gift before the altar, and go thy way; first be reconciled to thy brother." This is the *first* mention of the word in the New Testament. Here the offender is not bidden to reconcile himself, but the person whom he has offended. The person who has done the injury is to make up the difference. He is to propitiate or reconcile his brother to himself, by a compensation of some kind. Christ did not say, Conciliate thy own displeasure towards thy brother, but remove his displeasure against thee.

The teaching of Matthew 5:23, 24 is of basic importance in connection with our present inquiry. Its plain meaning is that the one who has offended should go and seek to appease the anger of the one who has been offended, obtaining his forgiveness, regaining his favor and friendship, by humbling himself before him, asking his pardon, and satisfying him for any injury which may have been done him. In like manner when Scripture speaks of God's having reconciled us to Himself by the blood of Christ's Cross (Col. 1:20) it does not refer to a subjective change which has been wrought in our hearts, producing our laying down of all enmity against God and our turning to Him in loving obedience; but it expresses one of the cardinal effects or results of His having graciously provided and accepted an atonement for us, so that instead of inflicting upon us the punishment we so richly deserve, we are, instead, received into His full favor *on Christ's account*. Thus we read in Romans 11:15, "For if the casting away of them be the reconciling of the world": here the reconciling of the world is contrasted from the rejection of the Jews, which must evidently be understood as signifying the extension of God's favor unto the Gentiles.

In the application of the term to God, "reconciliation" has to do with that which is *forensic*. That is to say, it contemplates God in His character as the Judge of all the earth, as the moral Governor of the universe, administering law and maintaining order. It concerns our relationship to Him not as our Creator, nor as our Father, but as our King. Thus, to affirm that through Christ God is now reconciled to His people, does not mean that there has been any change in either His nature, will, or disposition — to so affirm would be blasphemy. No, "reconciliation" means that transgressors of the Divine law have been restored to the *judicial* favor of God, through Christ's having closed the breach which sin had made between them. Reconciliation effects no change in God Himself, but it does in the administration of His government. His law now regards with approbation those against whom it was formerly hostile. There has been a change of relation between those for whom Christ died and the Judge of all. As this point is so little understood today, even by those claiming to be orthodox, we must amplify it a little further.

There is great need for exercising caution here, as in everything which pertains to our conceptions of the great God. Unless we are on our guard, our thought of Him will be but carnal. When one human being is reconciled to another there *is* an inward change: ill feelings are removed and good will is restored. But it is not so with the Lord God. It is greatly dishonoring to Him if we think of Him as possessing anything which corresponds to human passions. Reconciliation with God does not mean a change of heart in Him from an angry disposition to a friendly affection. Rather does it refer to an *effect* which has followed from that proper and full satisfaction which Christ offered to the violated law and offended justice of God. We repeat, it is God in His character of Judge, who insisting upon an atonement, has now no further demand to make, and therefore is most properly said to be appeased or reconciled to His sinful people. In order to understand this the better, let us next consider—

B. *Its Implications*

Conciliation is a state of peace, the mutual enjoyment of friendship. Reconciliation presupposes alienation and dis-fellowship. There is no occasion for reconciliation between parties who are in perfect accord with each other; but where that exists not, where instead there is discord and enmity, then the need for them to be reconciled is real. Thus, we say that the first implication in the term "reconciliation" is, that there has previously been a state of alienation. The second equally clear implication is that there was harmony before the discord; that, originally, peace and amity existed before strife and enmity broke it, for reconciliation is the *renewal* of lost friendship, the re-uniting of those who have been at variance. Thus, this one word "reconciliation" comprehends by implication the threefold relation which has existed between the elect and God, considered as their Governor or Judge. First, they were in happy fellowship together. Second, that fellowship was disrupted by the fall, and sin produced mutual alienation. Third, as the result of Christ's Satisfaction enmity is removed, peace is restored, and God and His people are re-united.

"God and man were once dear friends. Adam was the Lord's favourite. Till man was made, it was said of every rank and species of earthly creatures, 'God saw that it was good.' But when man was made, 'God saw every thing He had made, and behold, it was very good' (Gen. 1:31). God expressed more of His favour to him than to any other creature, except the angels: man was made after His own image (Gen. 1:26). He was fitted to live in delightful communion with his Maker. Man was His viceroy (Gen. 1:27). God entrusted him with the care, charge, and dominion over all the creatures; yea, he was capable of loving, knowing, or enjoying God. Other creatures were capable of glorifying God — of setting forth His power, wisdom, and goodness — objectively and passively; but man, of glorifying God actively" (T. Manton, Vol. 13, p. 255). Let it be carefully borne in mind that in Eden Adam stood not merely as a private person but as the representative of the race, and that the elect were all in him.

The condition of Adam was happy, yet mutable. Though created sinless, yea, "upright" (Eccl. 7:29), yet was he capable of falling. Alas how quickly he fell. God had forbidden him to eat of the tree of the knowledge of good and evil, and warned him that in the day he did so, he would surely die. But he heeded not. He apostatized. He disobeyed his Maker, and dragged down all his posterity with him (Rom. 5:12). By his fall, all his spiritual privileges were forfeited: he lost the image, favor and fellowship of God. God drove him out of Eden and stationed the cherubim at its entrance with flaming sword to bar his return. Thus sin separated between man and God (Isa. 59: 2). He, and all God's elect in him, were "alienated from the life of God" (Eph. 4:18).

As the consequence of the fall and man's becoming by practice a sinful creature, there was a mutual antagonism between God and man. Of man it is written, "the carnal mind is enmity against God" (Rom. 8:7). Of Christians in their unregenerate state it is said, "and you, that were sometimes alienated and enemies in your mind by wicked works" (Col. 1:21). The hatred of the sinner's heart for God was fully manifested when He became incarnate. Though He was full of grace and truth, went about doing good, preaching the Gospel, healing the sick, yet men despised and rejected Him, and were not satisfied until they hounded Him to death. Nor has the human heart changed one iota since then.

Sin has placed God and man apart from one another, so that all the harmony there was between them has been completely destroyed. By his sin man incurred the righteous hatred and wrath of God, which is "revealed from heaven against all ungodliness and unrighteousness of men" (Rom. 1:18). That God is alienated from the sinner and antagonistic to him is as clearly taught in the Scripture as is man's enmity against God. "Thou hatest all workers of iniquity" (Psa. 5:5). "God is angry with the wicked every day" (Psa. 7:11). "Though the Lord be high, yet hath he respect to the lowly, but the proud he knoweth *afar off*" (Psa. 138:6). "But they rebelled, and vexed his holy Spirit: therefore he was turned to be their *enemy,* and he fought against them" (Isa. 63:10). Herein then lay the need for reconciliation: that the breach which sin had made should be healed, the anger of God appeased, and peace and amity be restored. We are now ready to consider—

C. *Its Effectuation*

Many will not have it that the reconciliation is *mutual;* but God has been reconciled to His people, as truly as they to Him. Both there must be, for the alienation was mutual. God was angry with us, and we hated Him. As we have shown above, the Scriptures not only speak of enmity on man's part, but also of wrath on God's part, and that, not only against sin, but sinners themselves; and not only against the non-elect, but the elect too, for we "were by nature the children of wrath, even as others" (Eph. 2:3). Sin placed God and His people at judicial variance. We are the parties offending, God the party offended. Thus the alienation was on both sides, yet with this difference, that we were alienated in respect of affection, which is the ground and cause of Divine wrath; God in respect of the effects and issue of enmity and anger.

Now for Christ to make perfect conciliation it was required that He turn away the judicial wrath of God from His people. For this it was necessary for Christ to offer Himself a propitiatory sacrifice to God, Himself bearing that wrath which was due the sins of His people. This great fact was plainly typed out in the Old Testament again and again. For example, when Israel sinned so grievously in the making of the golden calf, we find Jehovah saying to Moses, "Now therefore let me alone, that my wrath may wax hot against them, and that I may consume them" (Ex. 32:10). But the immediate sequel shows us most blessedly how that the typical mediator interposed between the righteous anger of the Lord and His sinning people, turning away His wrath from them (vv. 11-14). Again, we read in Numbers 16 that upon the rebellion of Korah and his company, the

Lord said unto Moses, "Get thee up from among the congregation that I may consume them" (v. 5). Whereupon Moses said unto Aaron, "Take a censer, and put fire therein from off the altar. and put on incense, and go quickly unto the congregation, and *make an atonement* for them; *for* there is *wrath* gone out from the Lord, the plague is begun." Aaron did so, and we are told, "he stood between the dead and the living, and the plague was stayed" (v. 48)!

Nothing could be plainer than the above cases, to which many others might be added. All through the patriarchal and Mosaic economies we find that sacrifices were offered for the specific purpose of pacifying God's righteous vengeance on sin, appeasing His judicial displeasure, and turning away His wrath; the effect of which was expressly termed a "reconciliation": see Leviticus 16:20; II Chronicles 29:24; etc. Surely none is so mad as to suppose that Israelites offered sacrifices to turn away their own anger from God. Then, inasmuch as those Old Testament sacrifices were foreshadowings of Christ's Sacrifice, how can it be said that the great end of His work was to divert man's enmity from God, rather than to divert His wrath from us? But rather than rely upon mere reasoning, let us appeal to the clear teaching of the New Testament upon this vital point.

In Romans 3:25 we read, "Whom God hath set forth *a propitiation* through faith in his blood to declare his righteousness." Now a "propitiation" is that which placates or appeases by satisfying offended justice. Nor is the force of this verse in any wise weakened by the fact that the Greek word for "propitiation" is rendered "mercy-seat" in Hebrews 9:5, for the mercy-seat was a *blood-sprinkled one!* It was the place where the high priest applied the atoning sacrifice for the satisfying of God's justice against the sins of His people. The Hebrew word for "mercy-seat" signifies a "covering," and it was so designated for a double reason. First, because it hid from view the condemning law — the table of stone beneath it. Second, because the blood sprinkled upon it, covered the offences of Israel, from the eye of offended justice by an adequate compensation. That which it was fitly designed to typify was the averting of deserved vengeance by means of a *substitutionary* interposition.

Again in Romans 5:10 we are told, "For if, when we were

enemies, we were reconciled to God by the death of His Son, much more, being reconciled, we shall be saved by his life." We were "enemies," *God's* enemies, obnoxious to His righteous judgments. This word denotes the relation in which we stood to God as the objects of His displeasure, subject to the hostility of His law. We were "reconciled," that is, brought back again into His favor. And that, not by the Spirit's work in us, but "by the death," the propitiatory sacrifice, "of His Son." That this statement refers to the averting of *God's* anger from us, and the restoring of us to His favor, may be seen by the following considerations:

First, in that the immediate context is commending the amazing love of God *to us* (v. 8), whereof "reconciliation" is one of the highest proofs or manifestations. But if verse 10 were referring to the laying down of *our* enmity to God, it would rather be an instance of our love for Him, than of His for us.

Second, in that the terms of verse 10 are unmistakably parallel with those of verses 8, 9, and there we read, "while we were yet *sinners* Christ died for us," which can only mean, Christ died for us *as* "ungodly," to deliver us from the death which God's holiness required (vv. 6, 7), and died thus to bring us into favor of God.

Third, in that "reconciled to God by the death of His Son" is only another description of "being justified by His blood" in verse 9. Now to be "justified" is God's reconciliation to us, His acceptance of us into His favor, and not our conversion to Him; and that was in order that we should be "saved *from wrath*" (v. 9).

Fourth, in that in the following verse we are said to have "*received* the reconciliation" (v. 11), which cannot be meant of the laying down of our arms of rebellion: we cannot be said to "receive" our *conversion;* but we can that which Christ's sacrifice has procured for us.

"All things are of God, who hath reconciled us to Himself by Jesus Christ" (II Cor. 5:18). As this passage will come before us again in a later chapter, only a few words upon it can now be offered. "Who *hath* reconciled us." When did God do so? At the Cross, as verse 21 clearly enough shows. By whom were we reconciled? Not by the work of the Spirit within, subduing our enmity, but "by Jesus Christ." How were we reconciled? By Christ's being "made sin for us" (v. 21), and thus receiving in Himself the penalty of the law, and thereby appeasing God's justice. It was by His sacrifice that the Lord Jesus reconciled us to God, for the design of a sacrifice was to propitiate God, and not to reform the offerer.

"And that He might reconcile both unto God in one body by the cross, having slain the enmity thereby" (Eph. 2:15, 16). This important verse really calls for an exposition of its whole context, but we must content ourselves with a few brief words only. A careful analysis of verses 11-15 reveals the fact that both a double alienation and a double reconciliation is under discussion. There is first an antagonism between Jews and Gentiles, verses 11, 12. Second, there is a separation between God and His people, verses 12, 13. Conversely, through the Satisfaction which Christ has made unto God, elect Jews and elect Gentiles have been united in "one new man" (v. 15), and both have been reconciled unto God (v. 16). Thus, the "Christ is our peace" of verse 14 is amplified as: between ourselves mutually (v. 15), between us and God (v. 16); and in consequence therefrom "Through him we both have access by one Spirit unto the Father" (v. 18). "That he," that is, the incarnate Son of God, "Might reconcile," that is, restore to God's judicial favor. "Both," that is, elect Jews and elect Gentiles. "Unto God," that is, considered as the moral Governor of the universe. "In one body" that is, Christ's humanity — cf. Colossians 1:22. "In the body of his flesh." Our Lord's humanity is here designated "one body," because the Spirit is emphasizing the One for the many, as in Romans 5:17-19. It is the *representative* character of Christ's satisfaction which is here in view — Christ sustaining the responsibilities of all His people. It was in His humanity that He rendered obedience unto God; as it was His deity which gave value to all that He did. "Having slain the enmity thereby," that is, God's holy wrath, the hostility of His law. It should be carefully noted that the "enmity" of verse 16 cannot refer to that which existed between Jews and Gentiles, for *that* has been disposed of in verses 14, 15. "Enmity" is here personified ("slain"), as "sin" is in Romans 8:3. Thus, the verse means that all the sins of God's people met upon

Christ, and Divine justice took satisfaction from Him: in consequence, God's "enmity" has ceased, and they are restored to His favor. While the gracious provision originated in the love of God, the Atonement was the righteous means of removing His holy hatred against us.

Though the precise expression of "God being reconciled to us" is not found in so many words in Scripture, phrases of precisely equivalent import most certainly are. Thus, "O Lord, I will praise thee: though thou wast angry with me, thine anger *is turned away*" (Isa. 12:1). "Return, thou backsliding Israel, saith the Lord; I will not cause mine anger to fall upon thee, for I am merciful, saith the Lord; I will not *keep* anger forever" (Jer. 3:12). "And I will establish my covenant with thee; and thou shalt know that I am the Lord: That thou mayest remember, and be confounded, and never open thy mouth any more because of thy shame, when I am *pacified* toward thee for all that thou hast done, saith the Lord God" (Ezek. 16:63). To merely present a God who is *willing to be* reconciled to sinners is a wretched and wicked perversion of the Gospel.

Should it be humbly inquired, Why does Scripture throw the main emphasis on *our* being reconciled to God, we answer in the words of the Puritan, Thomas Manton, "First, because *we* are involved. It is the usual way of speaking amongst men: he that offendeth is said to be reconciled, because he was the *cause* of the breach; he needeth to reconcile himself and to appease him whom he hath offended, which the innocent party needeth not—*he* needeth only to forgive, and to lay aside his just anger. We offended God, not He us; therefore the Scripture usually saith, We are reconciled to God. Second, we have the *benefit*. It is no profit to God that the creature enters into His peace; He is happy within Himself without our love or service; but we are undone if we are not upon good terms with Him."

For Christ to make perfect reconciliation it was required that He should turn away the wrath of God from His people by removing their sin from before His face by means of a propitiatory sacrifice, as also that we should be brought to turn away from all our opposition to God and brought into voluntary and joyful obedience to Him. Until both of these are effected, reconciliation is not perfected. The one is secured by Christ's satisfaction, the other is accomplished by His sending His Spirit to renew us (Titus 3:5). A disposition must be produced in the rebel to return unto God and desire restoration to holiness and happiness in God, for "Can two walk together, except they be agreed?" (Amos 3:3). Hence the servants of God are bidden to go forth and beseech sinners to be reconciled to Him (II Cor. 5:20), obedience to which consists of faith's entrance into the peace which Christ has made (Col. 1:20); yet this will not be, till we cease from all fighting against God. When they do so, they are said to "have now *received* the reconciliation" (Rom. 5:11).

D. *Its Author*

This is the Father Himself. We do not entertain the idea for a moment that Christ died in order to render God compassionate toward His people. Not so; it was the love of God which gave His Son *to die* for them. The satisfaction of Christ was in order to the removal of those legal obstacles which our sins had interposed against God's love flowing out to us in a way *consistent with* the honor of His justice. Reconciliation was not the procurement of God's grace, but an effect thereof. God's reconciling us to Himself does not imply any change either in His will or disposition toward us. His infinite displeasure with sin, His disapprobation of our persons considered as offenders, and the engagement of Divine justice against us as transgressors, are perfectly consistent with His everlasting love to us and with His eternal and immutable approbation of our persons as viewed in Christ. If we distinguish sharply between personal resentment and judicial condemnation, all difficulty at this point vanishes. "God loved us, in respect of the free purpose of His will to send Christ to redeem us and to satisfy for our sins; He was angry with us, in respect of His violated law and provoked justice by sin" (John Owen, Vol. 9, p. 172).

That the Father *is* the Author of reconciliation is plain from II Corinthians 5:19, "God was in Christ reconciling the world unto Himself." After many hours of concentrated study upon it, we give it as our matured conviction that this expression covers the whole of our reconciliation, from its conception in the mind of God before the foundation of the world, till our final glorification in heaven. This expression "God was in Christ [a name of office, not of nature] reconciling" expresses the *agency* of the Father in the entire work of reconciliation. First, in choosing and appointing Christ for this work: Isaiah 42:1; Romans 3:25. Second, in the covenant and agreement with Him: Isaiah 49:3-6; Psalm 89:3, 4. Third, in calling and sending Christ into this world: John 10:36; Hebrews 5:4, 5. Fourth, in fitting Christ for this stupendous undertaking: Hebrews 10: 5; Isaiah 11:1-3; John 3:34: Fifth, in His dealings with Christ at the Cross: Isaiah 53:4, 5. Sixth, in accepting His expiatory sacrifice: Romans 4:24; 6:4. Seventh, in glorifying Christ: Matthew 28:18; Psalm 2:8.

E. *Its Scope*

"God was in Christ, reconciling a world unto Himself" (II Cor. 5:19). In II Peter 2:5 we read of "the world of the ungodly." Here in II Corinthians 5:19 it is the world of the godly or elect (as in John 6:33) – there is no "the" in the Greek. The expression is indefinite, though not universal. First, the "world" to show that men, and not angels (II Pet. 2:4), are intended – the sinning angels had neither Mediator nor Reconciler. Second, to show the amplitude of God's grace: confined not to the Jews – cf. Romans 11:15. Third, to denote the ground of the Gospel tender. All who are concerned, should be awakened to seek after this privilege. The Gospel offer is made indefinitely to all sorts and conditions of men. The added words in II Corinthians 5:19, "*not* imputing their trespasses unto them," is proof positive that all mankind are *not included* in the "world," for God *does* impute trespasses unto the wicked: Ephesians 5:5, 6, etc.

"And having made peace through the blood of His cross, by Him to reconcile all things unto Himself; by Him whether things in earth, or things in heaven" (Col. 1:20). The key to this verse lies in noting the particular epistle in which it is found. Here the apostle was refuting a false gnosticism with angelolatry and spirit emanations, which had been introduced by human philosophy to depose Christ as the *only* Mediator between God and men – see 2:18, etc. The Holy Spirit here shows the true relation of angels to Christ: they were *created* by Him (1:15,

16). Further, they too were the *gainers* by His Satisfaction (1:19-21). There had once been a union between angels and man, as fellow-citizens in one vast empire of God. But sin had dissolved that union. Sin is rebellion against God, and loyal angels could have no fellowship with sinners. But the great Atonement has restored the happy relationship between holy angels and God's elect: Ephesians 1:10. They too have gained by it. Christ has restored the disrupted harmony of the universe. A clear proof and blessed illustration of this is found in Revelation 22:9, where an angel, speaking of himself to John, says, "I am thy *fellow*-servant!"

It may help some if we give a summary of the whole subject. 1. Its *Origin* was the love of God: Romans 5:8; II Corinthians 5:18. 2. Its *Basis* was the everlasting covenant, the "counsel of peace:" Zechariah 6:13. 3. Its *Procuring-cause* was the satisfaction of Christ (Rom. 5:10), which has "made peace:" Colossians 1:20. 4. Its *Occasion* was the legal alienation between God and His people through sin: Ephesians 2:16. 5. Its *Need* lay in a satisfaction being required by Divine justice: Romans 5:9, 10. 6. Its *Nature* is a restoring to God's judicial favor: Colossians 1:21, 22. 7. Its *Communicator* is the Holy Spirit: Romans 14:17. 8. Its *Requirement* is that sinners be reconciled to God (II Cor. 5:20), which means the embracing of His offer of reconciliation through Christ, and this, by ceasing all opposition to Him: Psalm 2:12. 9. Its *Reception* is by faith: Romans 5:1, 11. 10. Its *Consequence* is sins remitted (II Cor. 5:19) and access to God: Ephesians 2:18. 11. Its *Publication* is by "the Gospel of peace": Ephesians 6:15. 12. Its *Extent* is the re-uniting of all holy beings in the universe: Ephesians 1:10.

CHAPTER FOURTEEN

The Atonement—Its Results (continued)

At the beginning of our last chapter we pointed out that the principle results secured by the Satisfaction which Christ offered unto God, may be summed up in these four words: reconciliation, remission, redemption and righteousness. It is indeed remarkable, and calls for our profoundest admiration, that God caused each of them to be shadowed forth on this earth-plane at the very time of our Lord's passion. Just as the *nature* of that unparalleled transaction which was taking place in the unseen between the Judge of all the earth and the Mediator was outwardly adumbrated in all the details of Christ's "trial" before Caiaphas, Herod and Pilate, so also were the leading *effects* secured by that transaction illustrated in concrete and visible form. A wonderful field of study, which has been entered by scarcely any, is here opened for our reverent exploration. Perhaps the few hints now dropped will be sufficient to bestir some to prayerfully investigate it.

Reconciliation is the bringing together again of two parties who have been alienated. Christ has, by His Satisfaction, reunited the Governor of the universe unto His sinning people. Strikingly was this adumbrated by what we read in Luke 23: 10, 11, "And Herod with his men of war set him at nought, and mocked and arrayed him in a gorgeous robe, and sent him again to Pilate. And the same day Pilate and Herod were *made friends* together: for before they were *at enmity* between themselves." Why has the Holy Spirit recorded this detail? Is it nothing more than a mere historical allusion? Of what interest to us is the relation which existed between Pilate and Herod? Why introduce this statement in verse 12 right after what is said in verse 11? For what reason does the Spirit emphasize "the *same* day"? The spiritually-minded should have no difficulty in supplying answers to these questions. It was God causing the glorious *consequence* of Christ's death to be tangibly imaged before the eyes of men.

Remission is the cancellation of guilt. Christ has, by His Satisfaction, propitiated the offended justice of God. He has made complete amends to the law for every injury which the sins of His people had wrought. He has, by His sacrifice, perfectly healed the breach which our transgressions had made. Christ has repaid all the wrongs which the iniquities of His people had done to the manifestative holiness of God: "I *restored* that which I took not away" (Psa. 69:4). In the light of this fact read what is recorded in Luke 22:50, 51, "And one of them smote the servant of the high priest, and cut off his right ear. And Jesus answered and said, Suffer ye thus far. He touched his ear and *healed* him." What a picture of Christ, on the very eve of His death, neutralizing the damage which His erring people had done!

Redemption is the liberating of sin's captives. Christ has, by His Satisfaction, emancipated those who were slaves of sin, the helpless serfs of Satan. He has delivered from prison those who were bound. He has brought from death unto life those who were cast in the sepulchre by Adam's transgression. "By one man sin entered into the world, and death by sin; and so death passed *upon* all men" (Rom. 5:12). From that dreadful state Christ has freed His people. God caused this too to be adumbrated in connection with Calvary, for in Matthew 27: 50-52 we read, "Jesus, when He had cried again with a loud voice, yielded up the spirit. And, behold, the veil of the temple was rent in twain from the top to the bottom; and the earth did quake, and the rocks rent; and *the graves were opened;* and many bodies of the saints which slept *arose.*"

Righteousness is that which qualifies the saint to stand in the presence of the thrice holy God. It is that which fits him for the Court of Heaven. As we read in Isaiah. 61:10, "I will greatly rejoice in the Lord, my soul shall be joyful in my God; for he hath clothed me with the garments of salvation, he hath covered me with the robe of righteousness." Such a righteousness cannot be wrought out by man, therefore was it secured for His people by the perfect obedience of Christ. This is the "best robe" of Luke 15:22, namely, the righteousness of Christ imputed. This also was shadowed forth on earth at the time our Saviour died. The soldiers took His garments. Among them was His coat, "without seam, woven from the top throughout"—emblem of the flawless unity of His life, lived out by power from above. That perfect robe became the property of one whose wicked acts were instrumental in crucifying the Lord of glory (John 19:23, 24). O my readers, what a truly *marvelous* book is the Bible! Having previously considered the first of the four consequences of Christ's Satisfaction, Reconciliation, let us now turn to—

2. Remission

That reconciliation and remission of sins are closely connected is clear from II Corinthians 5:19, "God was in Christ, reconciling the world unto himself, not imputing their trespasses unto them." That which was the ground of reconciliation is equally the ground of pardon. Necessarily so. Reconciliation implies in its very nature a release from the punishment of sin: on God's part it is the laying aside of His anger, and that was possible only because our sins were put away; on our part, of laying aside enmity and disobedience, which is possible only by an utter renunciation of sin. Again; the fruit of reconciliation is fellowship, and *that* is only promoted by the remission of sins, for two cannot walk together except they be agreed. In taking up this most blessed subject of remission, let us consider—

A. *Its Nature*

Remission is the sovereign prerogative of God as Judge, whereby He acquits the believing sinner from all liability to suffer punishment as a satisfaction to His law, and that on account of the Satisfaction of Christ, applied by the Spirit and appropriated through repentance and faith. Remission is God's declining to deal with His people according as justice required for their sins, and that because He has received full compensation for them from Christ in their stead. Because the Divine Creditor has received full payment from their Surety, the debtors are discharged. Thus, remission of sins is a cancellation of their guilt, a legal discharge, a removal of obligation to suffer the wrath of God. It is the verdict of the Lawgiver; a sentence of "not guilty."

The Greek word for remission, "aphesis," signifies "a sending away." It is translated "deliverance" and "liberty" in Luke 4:18, and "forgiveness" in Acts 13:38; Ephesians 1:7, etc. Thus remission of sins means that God refuses to charge them to the account of him who truly believes in Christ. It is a deliverance from the curse of the law, which holds us fast under its death-sentence until Divine grace revokes it. It is the privative or negative side of justification, whereby the sinner who flees to Christ for refuge is delivered from every claim which Divine justice had upon him. This is clear from Romans 4, where the apostle is expounding the truth of justification before God, and, after citing the case of Abraham, he appeals to the language of David in further proof: "Blessed are they whose iniquities are forgiven, and whose sins are covered. Blessed is the man to whom the Lord *will not impute* sin" (vv. 7, 8).

There are other expressions used in the New Testament of equivalent import. Thus, "When he had by himself *purged* our sins" (Heb. 1:3). The word "purged" is here used in a sacrificial way, and refers to the removal of them from before the face of the Judge: cf. Psalm 51:7 and its context. Again, in Hebrews 10:10 we read, "By the which will we are *sanctified* through the offering of the body of Jesus Christ once for all," and cf. 13:12. Here, too, "sanctified" is used in a *sacrificial* sense. "The blood of Jesus Christ his Son *cleanseth* us from all sin" (I John 1:7). By contracting guilt, the sinner is defiled, and becomes unclean in the sight of an holy God; but when his guilt is removed, he is said to be "cleansed."

It is important to note that I John 1:7 has no reference whatever to the purifying of the unholy nature which still remains within the believer: this is quite clear from the next verse. No, it predicates the taking off of the guilt of sin and our obligation unto wrath. Sin is the whole cause of God's displeasure against us, and that which makes us odious in His sight. Therefore when we are freed from sin by faith's appropriation of the death of Christ, we are said to be "cleansed." The same term was used in connection with Israel's annual day of atonement: "On that day shall the priest make an atonement for you, to *cleanse* you, that ye may be *clean* from all your sins before the Lord" (Lev. 16:30). Most certainly that does not and cannot mean that any internal purification was effected in their souls through Aaron's offering.

Three things are to be considered, and sharply distinguished, in connection with sin. First, its *fault.* This consists of a criminal *action,* a failing to render unto God that which is due Him, a transgression of His law. Now this is *not* taken away by the blood of Christ, nor, in the nature of the case, could it be. That which is done, cannot be undone. The sins we have committed, cannot be uncommitted. But though our sins as faulty and criminal actions are not annihiliated, they are — blessed be God! — "passed over" (Rom. 3:25, margin) and "passed by" (Micah 7:18) *as* the ground of guilt. That is to say, God no longer *imputes* them to the believer.

Second, its *guilt.* This is the *condemnation* of the law. Sin is "sin" simply because the law of God forbids it; when committed, it entails "guilt" because the law must punish it. Guilt is the law binding its transgressor to suffer its righteous penalty. Now remission does not mean that the offender is made intrinsically innocent, for having committed offenses he is still an offender. God never reputes a sinner to be in himself one who never omitted a duty or committed a transgression. Thus, guilt is not a quality, but a relation and obligation to punishment which the law has made the sinner's due, but which relation and obligation ceases when his sins are remitted.

Third, its *punishment.* When the believing sinner is pardoned neither his criminal *actions* themselves are destroyed, nor his personal *desert* of punishment removed, but because of Christ's sacrifice he is discharged from all *obligation to* punishment. Sin is no longer imputed unto condemnation. Nay more, the offender is dealt with (not "regarded") before the tribunal of the Divine Judge as if he were pure from all sin. He still *deserves* (in himself) *to be* accursed, but the penitent and broken-hearted culprit is accepted unto pardon and exempted from eternal punishment. "He that heareth my word, and believeth on him that sent me, hath everlasting life, and *shall not come into condemnation;* but is passed from death unto life" (John 5:24).

Neither the root nor the being of sin is removed from the believer when God pronounces sentence of forgiveness upon him. It is simply the guilt or obligation to punishment which is remitted; it is the revoking of the law's sentence against the sinner. He is legally discharged. And this because God is "not imputing their trespasses unto them" (II Cor. 5:19). This expression "not imputing" means that God is not laying them to the charge of His people, not reckoning them to their account. It is a metaphor taken from commercial transactions. Sin is a *debt*: Matthew 6:12. God is yet going to call sinners to account (Rom. 14:12), and charge their debt upon them: Matthew 25:19. Yes, people may now be gay and careless, but a day of reckoning lies ahead of them. But in that day of accounts, God will not impute the trespasses of them who are reconciled to Him by Christ — "Blessed is the man unto whom the Lord imputeth not iniquity" (Psa. 32:2).

"There is therefore now no condemnation to them which are in Christ Jesus" (Rom. 8:1). "Condemnation" here means the damnatory sentence of the law. It is not a question of our hearts not condemning us (I John 3:21), nor of *us* finding nothing within which is worthy of condemnation; instead it is the far more blessed fact that God Himself condemns not the one who has trusted in Christ to the saving of his soul. Because, by faith, they are in Christ, having fled to Him for refuge (Heb. 6:18), they shall never be adjudged guilty, nor shall a sentence of eternal death be passed upon them, for sins being remitted (guilt removed), no ground remains for it. "As far as the east is from the west, so far hath He removed our trangressions from us" (Psa. 103:12).

B. *Its Ground*

As the moral Governor of His universe, it becomes God's justice to deal with sin according to its deserts. Thus He spared not the angels that sinned, but "cast them down to hell and delivered them into chains of darkness" (II Pet. 2:4). Now all of God's elect are sinners: they were so in Adam, they have been and are so in themselves. How then shall Divine justice deal with them? Shall it ignore their sins and acquit them from punishment? Where then would be that inflexible righteousness which banished our first parents from Eden? What would become of God's own declaration that He "will by no means clear the guilty" (Ex. 34:7)? On the other hand, if they receive their due reward and are punished, how shall grace be shown them? On what ground are their sins remitted? Not on the basis of a belated reformation, for that would be no atonement for their past crimes. Not because of their repentance, for if sins could be pardoned at so cheap a rate then was there no need for Christ to die. "He that believeth not is condemned already" (John 3:18). Condemnation is a word of tremendous import, and the better we understand it, the more shall we appreciate the wondrous grace which has delivered us from its power. In the halls of a human court the sentence "condemned to death" falls with a dreadful knell upon the ear of a convicted murderer, and fills the spectators with sadness and horror. But in the Court of Divine Justice it is vested with a meaning and content infinitely more solemn and awe-inspiring. And to that Court every member of Adam's fallen race is cited. "Conceived in sin and shapen in iniquity" each one enters this world under condemnation—an indicted criminal, a rebel manacled. How then is it possible for anyone to escape the execution of the dread sentence? There was only one way, and that was by the *removal* from us of that which called forth the sentence.

That which entailed and demanded the sentence of the curse was the guilt which was inseparable from our sins. Let the guilt be removed and there could be no condemnation. But how could guilt be "removed"? Only by its being legally *transferred* to another. Divine holiness could not ignore it, but Divine grace could and did transfer it. As we are told, "The Lord hath laid on him [the Surety and Substitute of His people] the iniquity of us all" (Isa. 53:6). The punishment due His Church was visited upon its Sponsor. Christ, by virtue of His federal union with His people, which of His own accord He entered into, was dealt with by Divine wrath as though He had personally been the transgressor. God charged upon Christ and imputed unto Him all the sins of His elect, and proceeded against Him accordingly.

"There is therefore now no condemnation to them which are in Christ Jesus" (Rom. 8:1). The "therefore" here is an inspired and infallible inference drawn from the whole of the apostle's preceding discussion. Because Christ has been "set forth a propitiation through faith in his blood" (3:25), because He was "delivered [to justice] for our offenses, and was raised again for our justification" (4:25), because by "the obedience of One, many [saints of all ages] are made righteous," legally constituted so (5:19), because they have "judicially," "died to sin" (6:2), and "died" to the condemning power of the law (7:4), there is *therefore* no condemnation resting upon them. This is further opened in 8:3: "God sending his own Son in the likeness of sinful flesh, and for sin, condemned sin in the flesh." That which was the cause of condemnation is now condemned. The "no condemnation" of verse 1 is explained by the "condemned" of verse 3. Both must not be condemned: if sin itself be judged, punished, the believing sinner shall not be.

How marvelous are the ways of God! As death was destroyed by death, the death of Christ, so sin by sin. By the greatest sin that was ever committed — the murder of the Son of God — sin itself was put away. By God's imputing the trespasses of His people unto their Surety, Christ was condemned so that they might be acquitted. Christ first took our guilt upon Him, and then He bore its punishment, for guilt is obligation unto punishment. This is the very nature of suretyship: he takes the debt of another upon himself, and upon the debtor's insufficiency, becomes liable to payment thereof. By Christ's offering up of Himself in the stead of believers, all their sins were expiated. In consequence thereof we are able to triumphantly exclaim, "Who shall lay anything to the charge of God's elect?" (Rom. 8:33).

Just as Romans 8:1 is explained in 8:3, so II Corinthians 5:19 is amplified in 5:21. "God was in Christ reconciling the world unto himself, not imputing their trespasses unto them." And why? Because "He hath made him to be sin for us, who knew no sin; that we might be made the righteousness of God in Him." The non-imputation of sin to the believer is not only a consequent result of Christ's sacrifice, but was the cause of His death. Trespasses are not imputed to the members of His body, because they were imputed to the Head. "He," that is God the Mediator, "made him sin," legally constituted Him so, in accordance with the mutual agreement between them in the everlasting covenant. "Made him sin" means, appointed Him as the great Sinbearer, officially liable to wrath. Christ was "made sin for us" by the reckoning of our guilt to His account, not in mere semblance, but in dread reality. Because of this, Divine Justice took satisfaction from Him; because of this He died "the Just for the unjust."

Throughout His life and His death, the Lord Jesus was repaying all that injury which the sins of His people had done unto the manifestative justice of God. Therefore God now remits the sins of His believing people because He *has* received a vicarious but full satisfaction for them from the person of their Surety. Through Christ we are delivered from the wrath to come. Necessarily so, for an *accepted* Sacrifice obtained (not merely "made possible"), purchased, the remission of sins. Vividly and blessedly was this typified in Leviticus 5:5, 6, 10, "When he shall be guilty in one of these things, that he shall confess that he hath sinned in that thing: and he shall bring his trespass offering unto the Lord for his sin which he hath sinned . . . and the priest shall make an atonement for him, concerning his sin . . . and *it shall be forgiven him.*" So Christ's blood was shed "*for* the remission of sins" (Matt. 26:28). To this great and grand truth all the prophets bore witness (Acts 10:43). In Christ every claim of the law against the believer has been perfectly met. Thus grace reigns *not* at the expense of righteousness, but "*through* righteousness unto eternal life by Jesus Christ our Lord" (Rom. 5:21). Hallelujah!

C. *Its Scope*

"Who his own self bear our sins in his own body on the tree" (I Pet. 2:24). Whose sins? Believers'. Which sins? Not a few of them, not the majority of them, but *every one* which was on the docket against them. "Having forgiven you *all* trespasses" (Col. 2:13). Christ came here to "finish the transgression, and to *make an end of* sins, and to make reconciliation for iniquity" (Dan. 9:24). Rightly did James Wells say, "There is no mischief that sin hath done which He hath not repaired; there is no debt that sin has incurred that He has not paid; there is no foe under which sin has brought us that He hath not conquered; there is no fiery wrath which sin hath lighted up which He hath not quenched; there is no curse which sin hath entailed that He hath not borne; there is no mountain that sin hath rolled in upon us which He has not overturned; there is no distance between us and God which He has not filled up."

"There is *no* condemnation to them which are in Christ Jesus" (Rom. 8:1). "Thou hast in love to my soul delivered it from the pit of corruption: for Thou hast cast all my sins behind thy back" (Isa. 38:17) — as we turn our backs upon anything which we do not wish to behold. All our sins have been removed from the judicial eyes of God. God Himself declares that He "will not remember thy sins" (Isa. 43:25). Here our sins are likened unto a debt which has been cancelled; an act of oblivion has been passed upon them. "I have blotted out, as a thick cloud, thy transgressions, and, as a cloud, thy sins" (Isa. 44:22). Just as a dark cloud empties itself upon the earth and then melts away under the rays of the sun, so our sins have been dried up by Divine mercy, following the storm of judgment which was poured out at the Cross.

"Who is a God like unto thee, that pardoneth iniquity, and passeth by the transgression of the remnant of His heritage . . . and Thou wilt cast all their sins into the depths of the sea" (Micah 7:18, 19) — as the Egyptians were drowned in the Red Sea. God lays not aside our sins gently, but flings them away with violence, as things which He cannot endure the sight of, and which He is resolved never to take note of any more. Observe, "into the *depths* of the sea." Things cast into the depths of the ocean never appear again! Rivers may be turned and dried, but who could lave out the ocean? So Christ hath appeared "to put *away* sin by the sacrifice of himself" (Heb. 9:26). "As far as the east is from the west, so far hath he removed our transgressions from us" (Psa. 103:12). Hallelujah!

D. *Its Application*

This brings us to the most difficult aspect of our subject. *When* were the Christian's sins put away? This question is capable of more than one answer, according as it is viewed from different standpoints. Vicariously his sins were remitted when his Surety was raised from the dead. At His birth Christ assumed the full burden of His people's liabilities and responsibilities and He was not released from the same until God delivered Him from the grave. But *personally* we are not forgiven till we believe. We need to distinguish sharply between the results secured by Christ's death for God's elect, and their being, individually, made *partakers* of those effects. Christ purchased and procured a *right* unto our receiving forgiveness, but we do not enter into the *enjoyment* of this blessing until our faith is placed in Him. This may be illustrated by a young man who has been left an estate, but who cannot enter into possession of the same until he is thirty. Prior to that age he has a legal title to it, but he is not permitted to receive his inheritance: cf. Galatians 4:1-7.

"The blood of Jesus Christ his Son cleanseth us from all sin" (I John 1:7). The blood of Christ needs to be considered three ways: as shed, as pleaded, as sprinkled. As *shed*. This was necessary by way of satisfaction and merit, to *obtain* for us God's pardon of our sins, for "without shedding of blood is no remission of sins" (Heb. 9:22). It is *pleaded* by Christ in heaven. This is the very basis of His intercession. "By his own blood he entered in once into the holy place" (Heb. 9:12), and its merits He continually presents to the Father. It is also to be pleaded *by us* when we beg any blessing, especially the pardon of our sins: "Having therefore, brethren, boldness to enter into the Holiest *by the blood* of Jesus" (Heb. 10:19). But it is not enough that His blood be shed and pleaded, it must be actually sprinkled or applied to our conscience: "The blood of *sprinkling* which speaketh better things than that of Abel" (Heb. 12:24).

We must also distinguish between the general pardon received the moment we believed, and the specific forgiveness which we stand in need of repeatedly. To say that there is no need for Christians to pray for forgiveness because all their sins were atoned for at the Cross, betrays great confusion of thought and flatly contradicts Scripture. As well might an Israelite have argued against the offering of the *daily* lamb, because all his iniquities were remitted on the annual day of atonement (Lev. 16:21). So far as the Satisfaction of Christ has been offered once for all and is eternally valid before God, it allows of no repetition or addition. But considering forgiveness as the act of God as the moral Governor of the world, it is *continuous* unto the same persons. In the nature of the case sin cannot be formally pardoned before it is committed. As we daily commit trespasses, we are to daily ask for their forgiveness: Matthew 6:11, 12—note the "And" at the beginning of verse 12!

"Sins to come cannot be properly said to be pardoned, for till they are committed we are not guilty of them. This would not be so much a pardon as an indulgence and license to sin . . . Thus a man once converted could no otherwise than frivolously pray 'Forgive us our sin.' It would take away care of avoiding sin to come, and repentance for what is past. Daily sins displease God, and deserve death" (T. Manton, vol. 22, p. 52). At conversion we receive the Divine forgiveness of all our *past* sins (II Pet. 1:9) but forgiveness of present sins must be sued for daily. Keep short accounts with God, Christian reader! Constantly plead the promise of I John 1:9, "If we confess our sins, he is faithful and just to forgive us our sins, and to cleanse us from all unrighteousness."

E. *Its Requirements*

First, turning from sin unto God: "Let the wicked forsake his way, and the unrighteous man his thoughts: and let him return unto the Lord, and he will have mercy upon him; and to our God, for he will abundantly pardon" (Isa. 55:7). God will not remit the guilt while a man's heart remains in love with sin and he continues in the practice of it; if He did, He would compromise His holiness and encourage us in evil doing. "Christ died not to reconcile God to our sins, or to pardon our sins while we remain in them, but to bring us back again to the service and enjoyment of God" (T. Manton). The prodigal must leave the far country ere he can turn his face toward the Father's house.

Second, repentance: "Repent therefore of this thy wickedness, and pray God, if perhaps the thought of thine heart may be forgiven thee" (Acts 8:22). Repentance toward God signifies a willingness to return to the duty, love and obedience which we owe Him as our Creator, and from whence we have fallen by our folly and sin. "Him hath God exalted with His right hand to be a Prince and a Saviour, for to give repentance to Israel and forgiveness of sins" (Acts 5:31): as we must distinguish between God's viewing His elect in the purpose of His grace and in the sentence of His law, so we must between Christ's having purchased pardon and His now dispensing it according to the laws of His mediatorial kingdom.

Third, faith. The price of our forgiveness was paid when Christ died, but our actual admission into and possession of the privilege is not ours until we are planted into Him by a living faith. "Whosoever believeth in him shall receive remission of sins" (Acts 10:43): cf. 13:38, 39; 26:18. "By faith alone we obtain and receive the forgiveness of sin; for notwithstanding any antecedent act of God concerning us in and for Christ, we do not actually receive a soul-freeing discharge until we believe" (John Owen). Faith is as necessary in an *instrumental* way as Christ's satisfaction was in a *meritorious* way. Faith is the link of connection between the blessings purchased by Christ and the soul's enjoyment of them. Faith is that which appropriates the benefits of Christ unto itself.

What are the *marks*, or true evidences, of a pardoned man? First, genuine affection for God and Christ: "her sins, which are many, are forgiven; for she loved much" (Luke 7:47): the latter was the effect of the former. Second, a reverential awe for God: "There is forgiveness with thee, that thou mayest be feared" (Psa. 130:4): a pardoned soul will no longer rush heedlessly into sin. Third, a spirit without guile (Psa. 32:2), that is, a heart that is sincere in seeking the glory of God and desires to please Him in all things—cf. Ephesians 6:24. Where God pardons, He places His law in the heart (Heb. 8:10-12). Fourth, mourning for sin: where the heart is unbroken and unmelted, the condemnation of God rests upon it: cf. Luke 7:38. Fifth, the power of indwelling sin is broken: "He will *subdue* our iniquity, and thou wilt cast all their sins into the depths of the sea" (Micah 7:19): God never does the one without the other—justification and sanctification are inseparable. Sixth, praise and thanksgiving unto God: "Bless the Lord, O my soul . . . who forgiveth all thine iniquities" (Psa. 103:2, 3). Seventh, a genuine spirit of forgiveness toward those who wrong us: "Forgive us our sins, for we also forgive every one that is indebted to us" (Luke 11:4).

CHAPTER FIFTEEN

The Atonement — Its Results (continued)

In previous chapters we have pointed out the importance of distinguishing between the work which Christ performed and the results which that work produced. The need for so doing is great if we are to obtain anything more than a confused view of it. Unfortunately many have sadly failed at this point, so that neither they nor their readers have been able to apprehend separately the various parts of the vast whole. Noticeably has this been the case with that aspect of our theme which is now to be before us. Though the work of the Lord Jesus was one and indivisible, yet, as we saw when pondering its nature, it needs to be viewed from various angles. For this reason, among others, the typical altar of sacrifice was not round, but foursquare (Ex. 27:1). In like manner, though the result secured by Christ's work was also one and indivisible, namely, securing the eternal *salvation* of all for whom He transacted, yet that composite "result," that glorious "salvation," can best be understood when we contemplate its several sides. We now take up —

3. Redemption

Not a few have regarded "atonement" and "redemption" as being synonymous terms, but they are not so. Though closely, yea inseparably connected, they are, nevertheless, capable of being considered separately; the one being the cause, of which the other is the effect. Because Christ offered unto God a full and accepted satisfaction, the redemption of His people is the certain fruit, consequence and reward of the same. The "result" of Christ's mediation and the character of the salvation which He secured for God's elect can be most easily grasped when set out under these four words: reconciliation, remission, redemption, righteousness. By saying above that the "result" of Christ's satisfaction is as indivisible as the work itself, we mean that when one of these blessings is imparted, the other three always accompany it.

Near the beginning of our last chapter we pointed out how close is the connection between reconciliation and remission of sins (II Cor. 5:19), and to link up this one with the preceding, we would note how intimate is the relation existing between remission and redemption. In Ephesians 1:7 we read, "In whom we have redemption through his blood, the forgiveness of sins." Sins are "forgiven" or "remitted" by the redeeming blood. The preposition should be duly noted here: it is not *"through* whom we have redemption" (which presents another phase altogether), but *"in* whom." Redemption was the Christian's right, not only when the Spirit applied it to him at his regeneration, but also when Christ died. Just as we had condemnation in Adam before we were born into this world, so the elect have redemption in Christ since the time that He was raised from the dead: note that "believing" is not mentioned in Ephesians 1 till verse 12! "Redemption through his blood" is our forgiveness. Not that we are *actually* pardoned in the blood of His Cross before we believe, but that the pardon was procured by the redeeming blood, the grant of it was then sealed, and security given that it should in due time be made unto us.

The greatness of redemption may best be perceived by contemplating the person of the Redeemer. To none other than the Son of God was entrusted that work which was to secure redemption for His people. The greater the person who is employed in a work, the greater is that work; it is thus in the reckoning and ways of men, how much more shall it be so in the wisdom and ways of God! Kings do not send their sons out on petty errands or trivial services, but only upon that which is high and weighty; and can it be imagined that the King of kings would send forth His Son to redeem, unless that had involved a work of transcendent magnitude? The creating of the universe was a vast enterprise, but God dispatched it with a single fiat: He spake and it was done (Psa.

33:9). But to effect redemption, God sent His own Son from heaven to earth, to live and die. O how great a work was this; the greatest that Himself ever undertook. In approaching this blessed subject of redemption, let us consider,

A. *Its Signification*

"The term redemption is borrowed from certain pecuniary transactions among men, as the release of an imprisoned debtor by liquidating his debt, or the deliverance of a captive by paying a ransom. These are transactions with which mankind in general, and especially the Jews and primitive Christians, have been perfectly familiar. Accordingly, both in the Hebrew and Greek Scriptures, the deliverance of man from sin is frequently represented by language borrowed from such negotiations. The term before us is of this nature. It involves all the ideas included in atonement. It supposes sin, which is the cause of imprisonment or captivity. It supposes deliverance by a substitute, the captive or debtor being unable to effect his own escape. And, of course, it supposes also a clear emancipation or restoration as the result of the ransom being paid" (W. Symington).

The terms "ransom" and "redemption" when used in connection with the work of Christ are correlative in their import, the former denoting the price paid for the liberation of a prisoner, the latter marking the deliverance which is thus effected. The use of them in connection with our salvation, shows that this is brought about by the interposition of a Substitute, who procures the emancipation of the captive by the tendering of his ransom. By their sins men are brought under obligation to the law and justice of God, which He will not gratuitously fail to demand, and which they are quite incapable of discharging. To the law of God they are debtors; to the justice of God the prisoners. Their deliverance or salvation is not a manumission without price, that is, a simple discharge without compensation. Their salvation is not by an act of power only, effected by the intervention of an arm full of might to secure their escape. Both gratuitous favor (grace) and power *are* concerned, yet there was more. A price had to be paid, a ransom laid down, every way equivalent to the redemption for which it was offered.

Thus, "redemption" is *deliverance by ransom.* It is possible to conceive (in human affairs) of a price being paid and then, through some miscarriage of justice the prisoner not being freed; but in that case it would not be a "redemption," even though a ransom had been accepted. So also we may suppose a case where a captor, moved by compassion, freed his prisoner; yet though emancipated, he could not be said to have been "redeemed." Two things are absolutely necessary to a "redemption," a ransom paid, and the setting free of the subject or person purchased. The two things, though intimately related, are clearly distinguished in Jeremiah 31:11, "For the Lord hath redeemed Jacob, *and* ransomed him from the hand of him that was stronger than he." And again, "I will *ransom* them from the power of the grave; I will *redeem* them from death" (Hos. 13:14). Thus, we say again, Redemption is the payment of a ransom and the *release* of the ransomed. Hence *it is strictly limited to the people of God.* In no sense are the reprobate "redeemed." Election and redemption are of the same extent: they relate to the same individuals, to all such, and to none else. To affirm that any whom Christ redeemed are now in Hell is a flat contradiction in terms, for Hell is a *prison* (Matt. 5: 25; I Pet. 3:19).

The deliverance or redemption which the ransom-price paid by Christ to Divine justice has effected, consists of three parts.

First, there is a complete delivering of His people from the guilt or penalty of sin. This is their Justification. This is set forth in such Scriptures as the following: "Being justified freely by his grace through the redemption that is in Christ Jesus" (Rom. 3:24), "Christ hath redeemed us from the curse of the law, being made a curse for us" (Gal. 3:13).

Second, there is, in this life, a blessed deliverance from the dominion and bondage of sin. This is their Sanctification. This is set forth in such passages as these: "Who gave himself for our sins, that he might deliver us from this present evil world" (Gal. 1:4), "Forasmuch as ye know that ye were not redeemed with corruptible things, as silver and gold, from your vain conversation . . . but with the precious blood of Christ" (I Pet. 1:18, 19).

Third, there is, at the second coming of Christ, final deliverance from the very presence of sin. This is their Glorification. This is contemplated in Luke 21:28, "Lift up your heads, for your redemption draweth nigh," and "waiting for the adoption, the redemption of our body" (Rom. 8:23).

Redemption is the *setting free* of those who have been ransomed. The Greek word for "redemption" is actually rendered "delivered" in Hebrews 11:35: "Not accepting deliverance," which means, they refused to accept release from their afflictions on the terms offered by their persecutors, namely, upon the condition of renouncing their faith. Christ is therefore denominated not only "the Redeemer," but "the Deliverer" (Rom. 11:26). That from which He has emancipated His people is set forth in the following passages: "Christ hath redeemed us from the curse of the law" (Gal. 3:13). "Who hath delivered us from the power of darkness" (Col. 1:13). "Which delivered us from the wrath to come" (I Thess. 1:10). "That through death He might destroy him that had the power of death, that is, the devil; and deliver them who through fear of death were all their lifetime subject to bondage" (Heb. 2:14, 15). Let us next consider—

B. *Its Implication*

Redemption necessarily supposes *previous possession.* It denotes the restoring of something that has been lost, and that by the paying of a price. Thus we find Christ saying by the Spirit of prophecy, "I *restored* that which I took not away" (Psa. 69: 4)! This was strikingly illustrated in the history of Israel, who, on the farther shores of the Red Sea, sang, "Thou in thy mercy hast led forth thy people which thou hast *redeemed*" (Ex. 15:13). First, in the book of Genesis, we see the descendants of Abraham sojourning in the land of Canaan; cf. Hebrews 11:9. Later, we see the chosen race in cruel servitude, in bondage to the Egyptians, groaning amid the brick-kilns under the whip of their taskmasters. Then a ransom was provided in the blood of the pascal lamb, following which, the Lord by His mighty hand brought them out of serfdom and brought them into the promised inheritance.

In the above type we see three things: a people who were the Lord's; a people in bondage, lost to Him; a people recovered and restored to Him. Says someone, "But how can all these things hold good in the antitype? I can see that Christians were once the Devil's captives, now freed by Christ; but how were they His *before* He freed them?" Scripture supplies a satisfactory explanation. The type is just as true and accurate in the first point, as it is in the second and third. The redeemed belonged to Christ long before He shed His precious blood to ransom them. They were His by the eternal election of God, His by the Father's love gift: "Thine they were and thou gavest them me" (John 17:6). Yes, they were "chosen in him before the foundation of the world" (Eph. 1:4). But, "in Adam *all* died" (I Cor. 15:22), therefore did He come "to seek and to save that which was *lost*" (Luke 19:10). But through His blood He recovered them: "The church of God, which he hath *purchased* with his own blood" (Acts 20:28).

Thus, the implication of "redemption" is a double one. First, all the members of Christ's Church belonged to Him in eternity past. Second, through the Fall, they were brought into bondage. All men in their unrenewed state are slaves to sin and Satan, and under the wrath of God. "Whosoever committeth sin is the servant of sin" (John 8:34). Ere Christians were regenerated, "*serving* divers lusts and pleasures" (Titus 3:3) described their awful state. In the bondage of our ignorance, we supposed that we were free, imagining that liberty consisted of the power to do as we liked, instead of as we ought. Little did we dream that we were in the "snare of the Devil, who are taken captive by him at his will" (II Tim. 2:26). Nor could we free ourselves. Sin's chains were far too strong for human might to snap. Satan saw to it that we should not break out of his prisonhouse.

Man as a fallen creature is no more a "free agent" than he is a sinless being. "If the Son therefore shall *make you free* ye shall be free indeed" (John 8:36) would be quite meaningless, if the natural man already possessed liberty. But people will no more bow to this flesh-humbling truth today than they would when Christ Himself uttered it — "we be Abraham's seed and were never in bondage to any man" (John 8:33) was the haughty but lying boast of the Jews. Hence it is that so few seek the redemption which is in Christ Jesus: knowing not that *they* are bound, they suppose they are already free. This is one of the outstanding marks of these Laodicean days: men boasting that they are rich and increased with goods, and in need of nothing, knowing not that they are "wretched and miserable and poor and blind and naked" (Rev. 3:17). Yes, redemption presupposes bondage; happy the one who has had his or her eyes opened to see the need for a mightier hand than their own striking off the shackles of self-will, self-love and self-righteousness, which, by nature, bound and held them fast. We now turn to consider—

C. *Its Effectuation*

Sin is a debt, whereof God is the Creditor: Matthew 6:12. Debts render men liable to imprisonment for non-payment, so sin has caused God to "shut them all up in unbelief" (Rom. 11:32), nor can any escape till the uttermost farthing has been paid (Matt. 5:26). Man, by his disobedience to God, has been brought into a state of abject wretchedness, such wretchedness as Scripture often expresses by *captivity* (Isa. 61:1; Psa. 126:4; II Tim. 3:6). The Lord, because of our rebellion, both in Adam and personally, did, as the supreme Judge and Governor, deliver us unto Satan, and left us under the power of sin and death. Satan, as the jailor, led us captive at his will, making use of sin and the world as fetters to increase and continue our misery: "Wherein in time past ye walked according to the course of this world, according to the prince of the power of the air, the spirit that now worketh in the children of disobedience: among whom also we all had our conversation in time past in the lusts of our flesh" (Eph. 2:2, 3). From this dreadful state none but Christ could deliver us.

In every place in Scripture where our redemption in and by Christ is mentioned, there is an allusion to the law of redemption among the Jews. This law is set forth, most fully, in Leviticus 25, where we find regulations laid down for a two-fold redemption, of persons and possessions. None had a right to redeem but either the person himself, who had made the alienation, or some other that was near of kin to him. But inasmuch as none of Adam's race ever was, or ever will be, able to redeem himself, Another must interpose on his behalf if ever he is to be delivered. This is expressly affirmed by God: "None of them can by any means redeem his brother, nor give to God a ransom for him" (Psa. 49:7). Thus, poor sinners were entirely shut up to the merciful intervention of Christ. It was by Him and Him alone, this blessed promise was to be fulfilled: "Thus saith the Lord, Even the captives of the mighty shall be taken away, and the prey of the terrible shall be delivered: for I will contend with him that contendeth with thee, and I will save thy children" (Isa. 49:25).

The Redeemer must be *Kinsman*: "The man is near of kin to us, one that hath the *right* to redeem" (Ruth 2:20 margin). Thus the *covenant-oneness* of Christ and His people underlies the truth of redemption: "For both he that sanctifieth and they who are sanctified are all of one: for which cause he is not ashamed to call them brethren" (Heb. 2:11) — one from all eternity, one by Him having been appointed their Head. But not only must the Redeemer be federally united to those He redeems, but He must also take upon Him their nature and enter their circumstances, therefore are we told, "Forasmuch then as the children are partakers of flesh and blood, He also Himself likewise took part of the same; that through death He might destroy him that had the power of death, that is, the Devil; and *deliver* them" (Heb. 2:14, 15). So we read again, "God sent forth His Son made of a woman, made under the law, to redeem them that were under the law" (Gal. 4:4, 5).

The incarnation of the Son of God most strikingly fulfilled another Old Testament type of redemption. The Mosaic law provided that, in case any person was found murdered, then the nearest to him in blood was to prosecute the murderer and bring him to justice, and this nearest relation, thus avenging the murder, is called by the name of (Ga'al) *redeemer*, rendered "revenger" in Numbers 25:19. "Satan was the murderer from the beginning (John 8:44) who had given both body and soul a mortal wound of sin, which was certain death and eternal misery, and the Redeemer came to avenge the murder. He took our cause in hand, as being our nearest kinsman, and it cost Him His own life to avenge ours" (Wm.

Romaine, 1750). To which we may add, through His death, Christ "destroyed [rendered null] him that *had* the power of death" (Heb. 2:14).

Having accepted the office of Redeemer, having become one with His people in taking upon Him their nature, it was required that He should pay the ransom-price which Divine justice required. Now a "ransom" is something given in the stead of what is ransomed, and this was the vicarious life and death of the Lord Jesus: "The Son of man came, to give his life a ransom for many" (Matt. 20:28). Redemption views Christ as our "Surety" (Heb. 7:22), taking upon Him the liabilities of God's elect, and paying to God the price of their remission. Christ is the great Paymaster of His people's debts: "That by means of death, for the redemption of *the trangressions* under the first testament, they which are called might receive the promise of eternal inheritance" (Heb. 9:15). "Being justified freely by His grace through the redemption that is in Christ Jesus" (Rom. 3:24): in the first clause the inestimable blessing of justification is ascribed to the free grace of God, being altogether apart from our works, either before or after faith; in the second clause it is attributed to Christ's "redemption": though we are justified gratuitously, yet it is through the purchase of the Son of God.

Believers are said to have been "bought with a price" (I Cor. 6:20). *To whom* was the ransom-price paid? It seems strange that any Christian should experience difficulty in answering such a question, yet even some able Bible students have erred seriously on this point. Arguing that sinners were never in bondage to God, and that they are the captives of the Devil, a theory has been invented that the price of our ransom was paid to Satan himself, which theory can only be rightly denominated "diabolical redemption." Once this theory is held up in its naked hideousness, every renewed soul ought to shrink from it in horror. Surely there is a vast difference between sinners being the captives of the Devil, and his having any legitimate property-rights over them. That man is a slave of Satan is only a secondary result of his bondage. *Who* delivered him over to Satan, on account of his sins? Only one answer is possible: God Himself.

It is by Divine justice that the sinner is bound over to punishment. The Devil is only the *executioner* of God's righteous sentence. It is to God Himself the debt of obedience and suffering is due. It is God alone who has the right to detain him in prison. The detaining power is the equity of the Divine law and government, but for which, Satan could not hold him in thraldom a single moment. Therefore it was *to God,* to His inflexible justice, that Christ paid the ransom-price. Man had not sinned against Satan, but against the Divine Lawgiver, to whom alone it belongs to condemn or absolve. And God being satisfied, the Devil has no power over the redeemed, but is put out of office, as the executioner has nothing to do when the judge and the law is satisfied. To say that Christ offered Himself a ransom unto Satan is the most horrible blasphemy. Satan was to be conquered, not satisfied. Our enslaving foe was but the subordinate instrument of God's righteous judgment; why, he cannot so much as tempt men without the immediate permission of God, how much less could he demand from God the precious, precious blood of Christ.

The ransom which was paid for our redemption was the blood of Christ (I Pet. 1:19): this is sometimes set forth as a "price," sometimes as a "sacrifice." These are but one and the same thing under several notions. Now as the "sacrifice" was offered *unto God* (Eph. 5:2), so was the "price" paid to God, paid to His justice, paid to Him in His character of Judge and Governor. "Who hath delivered us from the power of darkness, and hath translated us into the kingdom of his dear Son: in whom we have redemption through his blood" (Col. 1:13, 14). The latter verse explains the particular nature of the "deliverance" in the previous one. It is not a mere release, as of a slave liberated by the compassion of his master, nor that of a debtor set free at his constant entreaties by his creditor; nor by the exercise of force only, as Abraham delivered Lot and David his followers from the Amalekites at Ziklag. But this "deliverance" from Satan's dominion is a *redemption,* a discharge by a ransom-price paid down; there was a rendering all that was due the law by a Substitute and Surety. The shedding of His blood was the last and greatest act of His mediatorial work on earth.

Thus Christ purchased His people out of the hands of vindictive Justice. Thereby He fulfilled that remarkable Messianic prophecy in Isaiah 45:13, "I have raised Him up in righteousness, and I will direct all His ways: He shall build my city, and he shall let go my captives, not for price nor reward, saith the Lord of hosts": the last clause signifies, it was not for personal gain that Christ did this: it was not "for price," though He effected it *by* price. Because Christ "bought" us (I Cor. 6:20), we are out of debt, free. There is not a single charge on the heavenly docket against any of His people. No debtor's prison now awaits them. "Thou shalt by no means come out thence, till thou hast paid the uttermost farthing" (Matt. 5:26): these terrible and hope-destroying words shall never be spoken to any of the *redeemed*.

Because the Representative of God's people was seized by the law, those whom Christ represented *must* go free. Beautifully was this adumbrated in John 18:8: "if therefore ye seek me, let *these go* their way." Christ's death was the believer's discharge: "Who is he that condemneth? It is Christ that died" (Rom. 8:33). "On that day shall the priest make an atonement for you, to cleanse you, that ye may be clean from *all* your sins before the Lord" (Lev. 16:30): if the typical blood so effectively cleansed the people ceremonially, how much more must the antitypical Sacrifice perfectly and eternally deliver from sin! The outcome of the ransom-price paid by Christ is the certain and actual redemption of His people.

There is *no unavailing* redemption in any of the Old Testament types. If land was "redeemed," *restoration* to its original owner was the *certain* outcome; if persons were "redeemed," then liberty was actually enjoyed by them. "*Deliver* him from going down to the pit, I have found a *ransom*" (Job 33:24), is God's authoritative fiat. Payment God cannot twice demand, first at my bleeding Surety's hand, and then again at mine. Because Christ paid to the full the whole debt which His people owed, Justice *demands* that the debtors should be liberated. Therefore the unqualifying word goes forth, "And the ransomed of the Lord *shall* return, and come to Zion with songs and everlasting joy upon their heads" (Isa. 35:10).

D. *Its Application*

"Blessed be the Lord God of Israel, for he hath visited and redeemed *his people*" (Luke 1:70). "The *Church of God* which he hath purchased with his own blood" (Acts 20:28). It is never said in Scripture that Christ died to purchase "salvation": it is always His flock, His people, His Church. "The Lord's portion is His people, Jacob is the lot of His inheritance" (Deut. 32:9), and the elect are not only God's inheritance, but His "*purchased* possession" (Eph. 1:14). By His death Christ paid the ransom-price, and made His people, whom sin had taken prisoners, His own. Therefore does the Father say to Him, "As for thee, by the blood of thy covenant I have sent forth *thy* prisoners out of the pit wherein is no water" (Zech. 9:11). Christ has a legal right to their persons, and therefore does God, by His strong arm (in His own appointed time), bring them forth. "He *sent* redemption unto His people" (Psa. 111:9).

Redemption is *unto an inheritance*: Galatians 4:5-7; Ephesians 1:14. Now just as an earthly parent reserves to himself the right to say (in his will) at what age his heir shall enter upon his estate, so God has appointed the time when each of His redeemed ones shall be freed from the dominion of sin, and when the whole election of grace shall enter their inheritance. As we have seen, the deliverance which Christ has procured for His people is threefold, so also is its application. *First,* they are freed from the guilt of sin when the Spirit first works faith in them and they are enabled to believe in Christ (Gal. 5:1). *Second,* they are gradually delivered from the power of indwelling sin, as through the Spirit they are led to "*mortify* the deeds of the body" (Rom. 8:13). *Third,* they are completely emancipated from the presence of sin when "there shall come out of Zion the Deliverer, and shall turn away ungodliness from Jacob" (Rom. 11:26, etc.). Each of these is redemption by *power,* in contrast from by price: cf. Exodus 6:6; Nehemiah 1:10; Psalm 77:15; for the same reason the resurrection of the body, by an act of Divine power, is called a "redemption" (Rom. 8:23).

E. *Its Manifestation*

Redemption is unto a *life of godliness.* "Being now made free from sin, and become servants to God, ye have your fruit unto holiness, and the end everlasting life" (Rom. 6:22). Those whom Christ has ransomed are given grace to live a holy life, freed from the bondage of their former corruptions: "redeemed . . . *from* your vain conversation . . . with the precious blood of Christ" (I Pet. 1:18). Those who are not delivered from their previous vain manner of life are not redeemed from hell and damnation, unless God gives them repentance. Let every reader test himself or herself by this sure and certain rule: you have not savingly believed that Christ laid down *His* life for you, unless *you* are now yielding up your life to Him: note the words, "in time past" in Ephesians 2:2. Christ has redeemed none that they might continue in a course of self-pleasing.

"That we being delivered out of the hand of our enemies might serve Him without fear, in holiness and righteousness before Him, *all* the days of our life" (Luke 1:74, 75). "Whenever God pardons sin, He subdues it (Micah 7:19). Then is the condemning power of sin taken away, when the commanding power of it is taken away. If a malefactor be in prison, how shall he know that his prince hath pardoned him? If a jailor come and knock off his chains and fetters, and let him out of prison, then he may know that he *is* pardoned: so if we walk at liberty (Psa. 119:45) in the ways of God, this is a blessed sign He has pardoned us" (Thos. Watson, 1690).

Let none make any mistake on this point. Scripture says "who gave himself for our sins, that he might *deliver us from* this *present* evil world" (Gal. 1:4). If, then, you are still in love with the world, a slave to its fashions, a follower of its ways, a companion of its people, you are yet in your sins. "Christ gave himself for us that he might redeem us from all iniquity, and purify unto himself a peculiar people, *zealous of good works*" (Titus 2:14). Christ offers Himself to none as a Saviour who are unwilling to submit to Him as their Lord. True, He has redeemed us from the "curse of the law," but most certainly not from the *righteous requirements* of the law. The people of God have been redeemed from their misery, but not from their duty. We have been redeemed "*to God*" (Rev. 5:9). Renunciation of the world, denial of self, and a daily walk to the glory of God, are the sure marks of *all* the "redeemed."

CHAPTER SIXTEEN

The Atonement—Its Results (continued)

Numerous and fearful have been the errors into which many have fallen when treating of the results of the perfect Satisfaction which Christ offered unto God on behalf of His people. Reconciliation has, on the one hand, been restricted to sinners throwing down the arms of their rebellion, whereas Scripture also plainly speaks of Christ's having "slain the enmity" of the Divine justice (Eph. 2:16); while on the other hand, some affirm that all (including the Devil himself) have been reconciled to God, when the Word declares there are many who shall be "punished with everlasting destruction *from* the presence of the Lord" (II Thess. 1:9). The remission of sins which Christ actually obtained for all He represented, has been whittled down to a mere possibility of forgiveness, which may or may not be procured by men according as their wills shall determine. While so terribly has the glorious truth of redemption been perverted that thousands believe there are multitudes in Hell for whom Christ shed His precious blood as a ransom-price. May it please the Lord to use the preceding chapters to dissipate the fogs of heresy from the minds of many of our readers.

4. Righteousness

This is, perhaps, the most wonderful of all the "results" obtained by the arduous Work of our blessed Saviour. Yet is it today, in most professing Christian circles, the least understood. If it be true that the blessed truths of reconciliation, remission and redemption have been grievously and grossly misrepresented by many who have posed as teachers sent from God, that which is now to be before us has been flatly denied, held up to ridicule, and branded as a serious error, by not a few of those who wished to be regarded as the champions of orthodoxy. It is indeed painful to find the writings of men who staunchly upheld the Divine inspiration of the Scriptures, the deity of Christ, His virgin birth and substitutionary death, defiled by a vicious repudiation of the principal consequence of His atoning sacrifice. But Satan is subtle, and the higher the reputation of a man for soundness in the faith, the happier is the enemy to employ him in his awful work of opposing God.

But today that inestimably blessed truth which we now desire to set before the reader (as the Lord is pleased to enable), is not so much denied, as it is *ignored*. That which is the crowning glory of the Gospel (Rom. 1:17), that by which God has supremely displayed His infinite wisdom (I Cor. 2:7), that which should most of all render the Redeemer precious to His people (Psa. 71:14-16), and that which ought to be the chief object of the believer's joy (Isa. 61:10), is now left out of almost all so-called evangelical ministry. Even where Christ is presented as the sinner's only hope, and His blood as the only cleanser of sin, that which secures a title for Heaven, that which alone can render a sinner acceptable before the Judge of all the earth, that which is the ground upon which He pronounces the ungodly *justified*, is missing from the best preaching and writings of this degenerate age. At best, only a half Gospel is being proclaimed, only the negative side of what Christ earned for His people is being set before them. Whether or not this criticism be too sweeping we leave the reader to decide after he has read the remainder of this chapter.

A. *Its Nature*

Following our usual custom, let us first show the connection between our present theme and that which was before us in our last chapter. "Being justified freely by his grace through the redemption that is in Christ Jesus" (Rom. 3:24): here we are shown the intimate relation which exists between the believer's righteousness and his redemption. To "justify" is the opposite of to "condemn": see Deuteronomy 25:1; Romans 8:33, 34; etc. Now to "condemn" a man is not to infuse evil into him, but is to pronounce him a transgressor. As the condemning of a man does not *make* him guilty, but simply announces that he *is* so, to "justify" a man is not to *make* him good, nor to infuse goodness into him, but is to declare that he *is* "just." Justification is that formal sentence of the Divine Judge whereby He pronounces the one before Him righteous. The *ground* upon which God pronounces this sentence is the "redemption which is in Christ Jesus."

As we showed in the last chapter, redemption is the consequence of a ransom-price having been paid. The ransom-price which the Lord Jesus offered unto the justice of God was that perfect Satisfaction which He gave to the Divine law, which consisted of the entire course of His virtuous and meritorious life, culminating in the laying down of His life at the Cross in obedience to His Father's command: John 10:18; 14: 31. Christ, then, "magnified the law and made it honourable" (Isa. 42:21), by keeping it in heart and life, in thought and word and deed; and therefore God, in His character of Law-administrator, the Judge of all the earth, has imputed the Saviour's obedience to all who believe on Him; and because they have that reckoned to their account, they are "justified," declared righteous in the High Court of heaven. The Christian is justified freely by God's "grace," because it was sovereign benignity which provided the Mediator and His ransom; yet that justification is not at the price of setting aside the claims of the law, but "*through* the redemption that is in Christ Jesus." Thus, grace reigns not at the expense of righteousness, but "*through* righteousness unto eternal life by Jesus Christ our Lord" (Rom. 5:21).

Old Testament prophecy not only announced that the Messiah and Mediator should "make reconciliation for iniquity," but also that He would "bring in everlasting righteousness" (Dan. 9:24). The two were equally needed by us: the one to deliver from Hell, the other to entitle unto Heaven. The taking away of our sins was not sufficient. In this world offenders are sometimes pardoned, so as to be no longer liable to punishment, yet without being at the same time received into favor, admitted to fellowship, and placed in a position of honor and privilege. But not so is it when a believing sinner is justified "through the redemption which is in Christ Jesus": he obtains not only pardon from God, but favor and acceptance; not only exemption from the penalty of sin, but a title to the reward of righteousness. Accordingly it is written, "Therefore being justified by faith, we have peace with God through our Lord Jesus Christ: by whom *also* we have access by faith into this *grace* [favor] wherein *we stand*" (Rom. 5:1, 2). And again, "That being justified by his grace, we should be *made heirs* according to the hope of eternal life" (Titus 3:7).

Two things were required in order for our acceptance by God: the removal of our sins, the making us righteous in the sight of His law. Man was impotent to effect the one as much as the other. We were no more able to get rid of our guilt, than the Ethiopian can change his skin or the leopard his spots. Equally powerless were we to render unto God that perfect obedience which His justice demands, and that because of the *weakness* ("without strength" Rom. 5:6) of the flesh (Rom. 8:3). "Therefore by the deeds of the law (that is, *our own* performances) shall no flesh be justified in his sight" (Rom. 3:20). Hence, if ever we were to be saved, One must come here and meet *both* these needs on our behalf: not only suffer the penalty which our transgressions entailed, but also render to the law active and passive obedience so as to merit righteousness for us. It is of the utmost importance to understand the distinction between obeying the law and enduring punishment. The mere suffering its penalty can never bring in righteousness, as the damned in Hell shall discover to their eternal anguish.

Christ, in the room and stead of His people, lived here a life of complete obedience to every demand of that law which they were responsible to keep, and then, in His death, He paid the full and entire penalty of that law which they had broken; and in this way He wrought out a complete righteousness for His church. Thus the *authority* of the law was fully vindicated, and its *breach* was fully avenged. There is a *double* exchange of place: Christ took ours, and we are given His. "For ye know the grace of our Lord Jesus Christ, that, though He was rich, yet for your sakes he became poor, that ye through his poverty might be rich" (II Cor. 8:9). There was therefore a two-fold identification: Christ was made one with us (Heb. 2:11, 14), we are made one with Him (Eph. 5:30). We had no righteousness of our own; now, as believers, we have received a perfect righteousness, by imputation, from Christ. "*Their* righteousness is *of me,* saith the Lord" (Isa. 54:17).

To affirm that the suffering of Christ was all that Divine justice required in order to redeem His people is blankly to deny the force and teaching of many Scriptures. For example, "As by one man's disobedience many were made sinners, so by the *obedience* of One shall many be made righteous" (Rom. 5:19). Just as light and heat are always united in the sun, so the righteousness of Christ's life and the efficacy of His death are conjoined in our justification. The blood of Christ ought never to be thought of as independent of or detached from His life of obedience: it was their *united* value which purchased our redemption. In their agency they were inseparable, though in our meditation, distinguishable. Christ yielded perfect obedience to the preceptive part of the law, and full satisfaction to its penal, on purpose that the merit of *all* might be made over to them who believe. This is the distinguishing glory of the Gospel: the blessed truth of free justification through the righteousness of Christ. Just as God transferred the guilt of His people to Christ, so does He transfer His obedience to them. Christ has not only made us accepted, but acceptable to God (Heb. 10:19)—accepted, because acceptable.

B. *Its Necessity*

"The claims of God's holy government in relation to man were made known at Sinai. There He promulgated His law, a law whose claims cannot be remitted or lowered, because they are founded on His own essential and unchanging holiness. The great *mandatory* commandment of that law is, Thou shalt love God perfectly, and manifest that love in thought and action. Perfectly and always. The great *prohibitory* commandment is, Thou shalt not covet (Rom. 7:7)—that is, thou shalt not desire anything of evil, anything that is forbidden by God.

"The law pronounced blessing and eternal life on any who should keep it; but it pronounced curse and judgment on all who should violate it even once, if only in thought. 'Cursed is every one that continueth not in all things which are written in the book of the law to do them' (Gal. 3:10). From Mount

Gerizim was pronounced the blessing; from Ebal, the curse. The law cannot remit or lower its claims; for its claims are founded on the essential and unchanging holiness of God. And the law having been promulgated, must be fulfilled: 'Verily I say unto you, Till heaven and earth pass, one jot or tittle shall in no wise pass from the law till all be *fulfilled*' (Matt. 5:18).

"The law demanded: 1. The absence of all wilful transgression. 2. The absence of sins of ignorance. 3. Perfectness in the inner man. 4. Perfectness of developed character in unreserved and unremitting devotedness to God. But we naturally have none of these things. Instead of being without wilful transgressions, and without sins of ignorance, in both we abound. Instead of perfectness in the inner man, unfathomable depths of corruption are therein. Instead of perfectness of character, the things that ought to be absent are present, and the things that ought to be present are absent. Instead of being unreservedly devoted to God, we are unreservedly devoted to ourselves. Such is our condition. And all this moral leprosy has come upon us as the result of the Fall. It is the result of Adam's first sin, for with him we had, by God's appointment, *a legal oneness*. He sinned, and his transgression brought upon him and upon us 'judgment unto condemnation': —one of the first and chief results of that judgment being the presence and dominance in us of indwelling sin, whereby all power of doing good is supplanted by the abiding presence of energetic evil. Who can tell the thrill of anguish and horror that must come on the soul, when, in eternity, it too late discovers the truth of these things?

"We are thus shut up into utter hopelessness. We find ourselves heirs of wrath, strong for evil, powerless for good. 'The law worketh wrath.' 'If there had been a law which could have given life . . . . But Scripture hath concluded all *under sin*' (Gal. 3:21, 22). The law can stir up the working of sin within us: it can work 'all manner of concupiscence' (Rom. 7); but it cannot deliver from those workings. 'The law entered that the offense might abound.' 'By the law is the knowledge of sin.' It is the prerogative of God alone to determine, and by His law to make known unto us, what is, and what is not, sin. Man is full of sin, yet he knows it not. 'I had not known sin but by the law, for I had not known lust (concupiscence, or desire) except the law had said, thou shalt not covet' (Rom. 7:7). In our flesh there is nothing but evil desire: 'the flesh lusteth against the Spirit,' and that evil desire is *sin*. Men refuse to acknowledge this. Wilful disobedience is the only form of sin they recognize.

"There never could have been any hope for such as we if God, in the infinitude of His grace, had not been pleased to declare that His holy courts admitted the principle of *substitutionary service*. For He announces that He has appointed for all 'who are of faith' a *Surety or Sponsor,* who, undertaking all their responsibilities is their *alter ego,* their other self, and accepted in their stead all that is needed to supply a valid and sure title of life and glory" (from *Atonement Saveth,* by B. W. Newton). Here then was the desperate need. The law could not abate its demand: flawless and continuous obedience. We have no ability to meet its demand: "There is none righteous, no not one" (Rom. 3:10), sounds the doom of the most punctillious moralist, equally as it does the most abandoned profligate. Therefore, if ever rebellious and guilty criminals were to be saved, it could only be by Another assuming their responsibilities and satisfying the law in their stead. This brings us to consider —

C. *Its Procurement*

"Atonement Saveth. The truth expressed by these words is the great keystone of our hopes for time and eternity. Atonement brings to all those who are under it (not salvability, but) *salvation*. All who are of the family of faith are under it. What then do we mean by Atonement? Atonement, or appeasement, is a priestly work of the Lord Jesus *directed toward God,* whereby, by one obligation, finished on the Cross, He has settled forever the claims of the Divine Government and procured for all His believing people, not only pardon, but acceptableness and rewardableness according to the value of His own meritorious obedience, which has been presented to God, and accepted by God for them . . .

"The eternal Son voluntarily undertook to be the Sponsor of His people. Humbling Himself to be born of a woman and made under the law (that so He might fulfill the Law), He formally assumed the responsibilities of all the family of faith, engaging to do everything and to suffer everything that was necessary *Godward,* in order to deliver them from wrath and secure to them an inalienable title to life and glory. His appointment to this Suretyship was founded upon the Justice of God, which required that all sin must be punished; and it was founded also on the Love of God, which determined not only to deliver from wrath, but to bring also to His own bosom and into His glory, those who personally deserved wrath. It was necessary, therefore, that the Substitute should, in the stead of His people (even all who should believe), meet every requirement of God's law, which demanded perfectness of obedient service; and likewise that He should bear all the penalties appointed to Him as the Substitute, because of our disobedience; for we owe unto God a *double* debt—a debt of obedience, and because of failure in that, a debt of penal suffering. Both must be paid. The penalty must be borne; and the perfect obedience rendered, otherwise, there could be no Atonement, and, in consequence, no salvation" (B. W. Newton, from *Atonement Saveth*).

The above quotation contains a succinct statement upon this important aspect of our theme. In seeking to amplify it a little, let us emphasize the fact that when the Beloved of the Father became Surety for us insolvent wretches, He made Himself subject to the *whole* law of God. Though its threatenings were set in terrible array, and though its commands peremptorily insisted on the very perfection of obedience, He asked for no mitigation of its severity, nor any abatement of its demands; but instead, with full but joyous submission to the Judge of all, He cried, "Lo, I come . . . I delight to do thy will, O my God: yea, thy law is within my heart" (Psa. 40:7, 8)—yes, "come" to pay the uttermost farthing of their debt, and to perform every jot and tittle of their duty. That perfect righteousness imputed to them, which is the ground upon which God justifies believing sinners, was *inaugurated* when God sent forth His son to be born under the law (Gal. 4:4); it was *perpetuated* throughout the whole course of the Saviour's life, when He did always those things which pleased the Father (John 8:29); it was *consummated* when Immanuel bowed His blessed head and cried with triumphant voice, "It is finished" (John 19:30). Let us examine this in fuller detail.

"What the law could not do, in that it was weak through the flesh, God sending His own Son in the likeness of sinful flesh, and for sin, condemned sin in the flesh: that the righteousness of the law might be fulfilled in us" (Rom. 8:3, 4). The last clause quoted states the ultimate end God had in view (so far as His elect were concerned) in sending His Son here, namely, that "the righteousness of the law," its holy and just demands, should be fulfilled for us in the person of our Representative, so that in the accounting of God *they* had themselves fulfilled it. "Righteousness" is a *judicial* term, and refers *not* to a state of mind or disposition of heart, but instead, to a *legal status* before the tribunal of God. The "righteousness of the law" signifies the full answering of all the requirements of the law, coming up to a perfect conformity to it, and that, by doing all it enjoins. It is this alone which gives title to enjoy its reward, namely, life everlasting. This "righteousness of the law" was and is "fulfilled in us" as we were and are *viewed in Christ,* just as verse 1 affirms, "there is therefore now no condemnation *to them which are in Christ Jesus"!*

Now in order for this "righteousness" to be wrought out for us by Christ it was necessary that He should, first, be "made under the law" (Gal. 4:4). "Christ was holy and righteous not as a private person, not for Himself alone, but for us sinners and our justification" (R. Haldane). Yet at this point great caution needs to be exercised lest we sully the honor and glory of the Mediator. There have been those who most erroneously affirmed that when the Son of God became incarnate it was obligatory upon Him *to* fulfil the law, that as Man, this was His personal duty. Not so. Had that been the case, His obedience had been of such a character that its merit could not have been imputed to others, for He would merely have been paying His own creature-debt to the law. Such is horrible blasphemy, proceeding from an altogether inadequate and faulty view of our Lord's manhood. As this error is now so fearfully prevalent, even in circles where few would expect to find it, something further needs to be said in order to its refutation.

The manhood of Christ never had an existence separate from the Godhead of the Son. When the "Word became flesh" (John 1:14), the second person of the adorable Trinity took into union with Himself an immaculate human nature, consisting of spirit and soul and body. We say "an immaculate human *nature*," for it was *not* a human *person;* instead, it was a Divine person who assumed that human nature. Carefully has the Holy Spirit guarded this very point in Luke 1:35, where it was said unto Mary, ". . . that holy *thing* which shall be born of thee shall be called the Son of God" – so denominated because that just as when a woman is united to a man in marriage she takes his name, so the humanity of the Saviour being taken into union with the second person of the Trinity, is called "the Son of God." Thus, because the holy manhood of the Redeemer became a part of the *person* of the Lord of glory, He was not only exempted from the common condemnation of all other men (inherent sin as the result of the Fall), but He was *not obligated* to be in subjection to the law as all other men are.

Let it be said with all possible emphasis that it was not as a private person, but as the public and *official* Representative of His people that the God-man was "made under the law." It was purely a voluntary act on His part, and in no sense compulsory. Therefore was His obedience infinitely meritorious, and capable of being imputed to His people. True, His being subject to the law and meeting its every requirement had been proposed to Him by the Father in the everlasting covenant, yet it must be expressly insisted upon that it was by His own free consent that those terms were accepted by Him. It was for the sake of His people, and not for Himself, that He became under the law. Even after He had become incarnate, the Saviour explicitly declared, "The Son of man is *Lord* also of the sabbath" (Mark 2:28), and if Lord of the Sabbath, therefore "Lord" of the whole law. The law had *no* claims upon *Him.* That obedience which He rendered to it was entirely voluntary, free, and on the behalf of and in the stead of His insolvent people.

"And being found in fashion as a man, *he* humbled himself, and *became* obedient" (Phil. 2:8). Weigh well these momentous words, and stand in awe at the amazing phenomenon which they present. *Who* "humbled" Himself? None other than the Maker of heaven and earth. When did He "humble' Himself? First, when He left the glory of heaven and entered into the virgin's womb. Unparalleled stoop was this; unprecedented condescension was that. But more; having assumed human nature unto Himself, He "humbled" Himself still further, and "became obedient." Notice the active, rather than the passive voice: it is not "he was humbled," but "he humbled himself." It was an act of His own, a voluntary act, *not* a duty, compulsorily laid upon Him! He "became obedient." Why? To render to God and His law that perfect service which was required in order to our being (legally) "made righteous." But not until we rightly estimate the surpassing dignity and excellency of the Surety's *person* shall we be able to value aright the *worth* of His obedience.

Think of *whose* obedience it is! "The obedience of CHRIST —obedience of Him who walketh in the circuit of the skies (Job 22:14), and all the kingdoms of the world are reputed as nothing before Him! The obedience of *Him* who doeth according to His will in the army of heaven and among the inhabitants of the earth (Dan. 4:35). The obedience of Him who is Alpha and Omega, the Beginning and the ending, which is, and which was, and which is to come, the Almighty (Rev. 1:8). Doubtless, *such* obedience must be deserving, of all that Grace and Glory which are, and will be communicated to His people, in every period of time and throughout all ages of eternity. *Worthy* is the Lamb that was slain. No wonder that *such* obedience shall 'justify the ungodly' (Rom. 4:5); should make us poor fallen creatures righteous — perfectly righteous in the sight of *God* — without the concurrence of any good works or any holy duties of our own.

"The infinitely most noble obedience of *Jesus Christ.* To this obedience I would have our thoughts continually directed. This surpasses the services of both angels and men, in all their various and wonderful orders. 'Tis true, compared with our duties, *Abraham's* obedience is like Saul's stature, who, from his shoulders upward, was higher than any of the people. But when the righteousness of *Christ* comes into view, it is somewhat like that magnificent Personage described in Revelation

10. Should such a sublime and majestic Being appear amidst an assembly of the most renowned monarchs of the world, how would their splendour be eclipsed, and all their grandeur dwindle into meanness! Before such an illustrious Potentate of heaven, who would take notice of Caesar, or bestow a look upon Alexander? So the righteousness of *Christ,* being the righteousness of Him who lay in the bosom of the Father from eternity, the righteousness of Him who now sits on the right hand of the throne of the Majesty in the heavens; this righteousness, being in itself most consummately perfect, and unspeakably ennobled by the dignity of the Performer, all other kinds, degrees, or forms of righteousness, shrink before it into the littleness of pygmies, of worms, of mites. Could they speak, the language of each would be, 'Look not upon me for I am dim, yea, I am black. But look upon your *Lord,* for His works are marvelous, and *He* is glorious in His holiness'" (James Hervey, Vol. 4, 1750, A. D.).

"Think not that I am come to destroy the law, or the prophets: I am not come to destroy, but to fulfil" (Matt. 5:17). As in Romans 8:3, 4, here again we are informed concerning the great objective before the Son of God in coming into this world. Having been, by His own free consent, "made under the law" (Gal. 4:4) not only to undergo its penalty and bear its curse, but also to keep its precepts (which is the principal part of it), Christ Himself here announces that He came to "fulfil" it. But the enemies of the truth have struggled hard, though quite unsuccessfully, to evacuate the meaning of that important word. They have affirmed that this term "fulfil" simply means Christ "filled out," or brought to light the hidden depths of the law's meaning, and revealed its searching holiness. But let it be duly noted that Christ here spoke of both the "law" and the "prophets"—did He "fill out" them? No, He *"fulfilled"* them!

Others say that Christ "fulfilled" the law in that He *expounded* it, which is contradicted by the whole tenor of His ministry: see particularily John 1:17. No, "fulfil" is here to be taken in its strict and obvious sense: just as "he that loveth another has *fulfilled* the law" (Rom. 13:8) means, he has met its requirements, he has kept its precepts. It is to be noted that Christ did not say, "Think not I am come to destroy the law *and* the prophets," but "the law *or* the prophets . . . but to fulfill." Two separate and distinct things were here predicated by Christ. Its obvious meaning was, the Old Testament, in all its parts and elements, *referred to* Himself and was *accomplished by* and in Himself. Thus, "the law" here stands for the whole Jewish law (including its types — the sacrifices of the law), though having primary reference to the *moral* law, as is unmistakably clear from the next twenty-seven verses. To obey its commands, to keep them in thought, word and deed, was the great end for which Christ became incarnate. This was man's duty, our duty; but we had failed to perform it, therefore did Christ come and discharge it for us.

In Matthew 5:20-42 Christ's main purpose was not to teach His people "Christian ethics" (*that* we have in the Epistles), but to arouse the consciences of His legalistic hearers. In this section of the Sermon on the Mount, our Lord expounded the law with the object of making men to see their *need* of a perfect righteousness (cf. Matt. 19:17), a righteousness which would fully meet the requirements of the thrice holy God, a righteousness in which *His* piercing eye could discern no flaw or blemish. It was *ignorance* of the law which was the real source of Phariseeism, for they claimed to fulfil it in the outward letter; therefore would Christ awaken their conscience by pressing its true inner import and exacting holy demands. It will be found that the "Sermon" perpetually returns to one main thought, applied with various modifications and peculiar terms; to awaken in men a sense of their depravity, to shut them up to the righteousness *of God*: see especially verses 28, 44!

Matthew 5:20 is the sum and substance of all that follows to the end of that chapter. What then is the "righteousness" there spoken of? It is that justifying righteousness of God which fully meets the need of a divinely-convicted sinner. Its opening "for" plainly points back to verse 17. That "righteousness" which *exceeded* the punctillious outward performances of the scribes and Pharisees is what the incarnate Son of God, acting as the Surety of His people, vicariously wrought out for them, and which upon their believing, is imputed to them; so that the flawless obedience of Christ to the whole will of God is reckoned to their account in such a way that *they* are legally regarded as having perfectly fulfilled the law in their own persons. God did not recede from His rights, but enforced them. The law *has been* fulfilled, by our Sponsor, and the transcendent merits of "the just" (Acts 3:14) are transferred to each of those for whom He acted. *This* is the "best robe" with which the returning prodigal is clothed! *This* is the "Court-dress" which fits for the King's palace. Thus can every true Christian not only say, "the blood of Christ has cleansed me from all sin," but also "*in the Lord* have I *righteousness*" (Isa. 45:24). Hallelujah! Much more remains yet to be said, but we must leave it for the next chapter.

CHAPTER SEVENTEEN

THE ATONEMENT — ITS RESULTS (RIGHTEOUSNESS CONTINUED)

In our last chapter we sought to show that in order to the justification of His people God required from Christ something more than a sacrifice which would blot out their sins. It has been rightly said that, "There are few questions of more importance than the one which has reference to the way in which a sinner becomes perfectly righteous before God. If he be not completely righteous, he cannot enter heaven" (J. C. Carson). When man fell from his sinless condition he was no more able to procure for himself a righteousness which would meet the inflexible demands of God's justice and holiness, than he could eradicate the sinful nature which now vitiates all his faculties. His only hope lay in a substitution who was able both to keep the law for him and to suffer the penalty for his breach of it. Both of these were indispensable if sinners were to be saved from hell and given a valid title to heaven. "If thou wilt enter into life, keep the commandments" (Matt. 19:17). Life is not to be obtained unless all is done that the law requires: it *must* be kept either by us or a surety.

"There is the same need of Christ's obeying the law in our stead, in order to the reward, as of His suffering the penalty of the law in our stead to our escaping the penalty; and the same reason why one should be accepted on our account, as the other. This is certain, that that was the reason why there was need that Christ should suffer the penalty for us, even that the law might be answered; for this the Scripture plainly teaches. This is given as the reason why Christ was made a curse for us, that the law's threatening a curse to us: Galatians 3:10, 13. But the same law that fixes the curse of God as the consequence of not continuing in all things written in the law to do them (v. 10), has as much fixed *doing* those things *as an antecedent of living in them* (v. 12). There is as much of a connection established in one place as in the other . . . We have not eternal life merely on the account of being void of guilt, but on the account of Christ's activeness in obedience and doing well" (Jonathan Edwards, Vol. 4, p. 92).

"I am not ashamed of the Gospel of Christ for it is the power of God unto salvation to every one that believeth . . . *For* therein is *the righteousness of God* revealed" (Rom. 1:16, 17). It is indeed pitiable to discover the evasive subterfuges to which men have resorted in their unworthy efforts to rob the Gospel of its distinguishing glory. Many who ought to have known better (some we fear, did) defined this expression as "God's *method* of justifying sinners." That the Gospel reveals the consummate wisdom of God in devising a way whereby *all* His attributes are illustriously displayed in the saving of His people, is perfectly true. That the Gospel exhibits the perfect consistency between the grace and righteousness of God, His mercy and justice, is a most blessed fact. Yet, *this* is not at all the meaning of that expression "the righteousness of God." Let such a definition be applied to II Corinthians 5:21 and its fallacy is at once exposed: "He hath made him to be sin for us, who knew no sin; that we might be made God's method of justification in him!"

"The righteousness of God. This is one of the most important expressions in the Scriptures. It frequently occurs both in the Old Testament and in the New; it stands connected with the argument of the first five chapters of the Roman epistle, and signifies that fulfilment of the law which God has provided, by the imputation of which sinners are saved" (Robt. Haldane). We are bold to affirm that the competency or incompetency of a man to expound the epistle to the Romans largely turns upon his understanding of this key expression. If he errs in his apprehension of "the righteousness of God," his whole scheme of interpretation is bound to be faulty and erroneous. Nor can any man fully preach the Gospel, so as to exalt Christ as He ought to be exalted, while he fails to unfold the blessedness of this vitally important term. Nor can any believer be fully established in the faith, nor is he capable of rendering to God that praise which is His due, while he remains ignorant of what is meant by "even the righteousness of God by faith of Jesus Christ unto all and upon all them that believe" (Rom. 3:22). What then, is meant by this expression?

The "righteousness of God" is that perfect conformity to the Divine law in heart and life which the holiness of God requires, which the grace of God has provided, which the incarnate Son of God has wrought out, and which the justice of God imputes to every one that believes. Let us enlarge upon this statement. First, the "righteousness of God" is that perfect conformity to the law in heart and life which the holiness of God requires. God cannot relinquish His rights, nor recede from His just claims. For Him to set aside the demands of the law for full obedience to it, would be as much as saying He had given a law which was *not* "holy and just and good" (Rom. 7:12). This could never be. Divine love gave the law; Divine wisdom drew it up; Divine justice requires the perfect performance of it. Therefore, second, Divine grace *provided* a satisfaction unto its righteous claims. Unfallen man failed to keep it; fallen man cannot keep it; so the God-man — forever be His name praised — came here to keep it in the stead of and in the behalf of His people.

It was by a *special* Divine constitution that Christ became subject to the law. Men are born under the law as the *natural* descendants of Adam. But not so the Lord Jesus Christ. As His humanity was produced in a supernatural manner (that is, not according to the settled order of nature, but by the intervention and power of the Holy Spirit), so He was "made under the law" (Gal. 4:4) by a special Divine appointment. Christ, as Man, by virtue of the personal union of His manhood with the second person of the Godhead, was raised high above the condition and state of a mere creature. "Being found in fashion as a man, He *humbled Himself* and became obedient unto death" (Phil. 2:8). He was under no *personal* obligation to the law, but voluntarily placed Himself under it, that He might work out for His people a perfect and vicarious righteousness. May our hearts truly be drawn out to Him in profoundest admiration and adoration for such an amazing condescension.

The unremitting and perfect obedience which Christ rendered unto the law proceeded from supreme love to God and unfeigned affection to men. "His delight in *God* was conspicuous even from His early years. The sacred solemnities of a sanctuary were more engaging to His youthful mind than all the entertainment of a festival. When He entered upon His ministry, *whole nights* were not too long for His copious devotions. The lonely retirements of the desert, as affording undisturbed communion with God, were more desirable to Christ than the applauses of an admiring world. So ceaseless and transcendent was His love to God, that He *never* sought any separate pleasure of His own, but *always* did those things which were pleasing in His Father's sight. 'Wist ye not that I must be about my Father's business?' was the rule of His childhood and the leading maxim of His whole life. In doing this, He was absolutely indefatigable. It was His 'meat and drink,' refreshing as the richest food, delightful as royal dainties, to finish the work that was given Him to do (John 4:34).

"How wakeful and jealous was His concern for the divine honor! I hear the vilest reproaches cast upon His own character. I see the most horrible indignities possible to His own person. Yet no resentful emotion reddened in His cheek; nor one angry syllable starts from His mouth. But when mercenary wretches profaned the Temple, and turned His 'Father's house' into a den of thieves, then His bosom throbs with zeal, then He makes His tongue like a sharp sword, and having first severely rebuked, afterwards resolutely expels, the sacriligious intruders. Indeed, His zeal for the house of *the Lord* and for the purity of His ordinances, is represented by the evangelical historian as *eating Him up* (John 2:17). Like a heavenly flame glowing in His breast, it sometimes fired Him with a graceful indignation, sometimes melted Him to godly sorrow, always broke forth and exerted itself in a variety of vigorous efforts, till it even consumed His vital spirit . . .

"Who can declare the *charity of Jesus Christ?* It was ardent, it was unintermitted, it was unbounded. Though always serene and serious, He was never sullenly grave. His conversation was affability itself, and the law of kindness dwelt on His lips. What fretted and chagrined the disciples, made not the least ruffling impression on their *Lord.* The rude and troublesome behavior of some, the weak and impertinent talk of others, served only to display the unalterable mildness of His temper. Nothing could embitter His spirit. Even the wicked and unthankful were partakers, ample partakers of His benevolence. Whoever applied to Him in vain? When did He dismiss any needy petitioner without the desired blessing? What heavy burden did He not unloose? What afflictive evil did He not relieve? He even 'took our infirmities and bare our sicknesses' (Matt. 8:17). In all their afflictions He was afflicted.

"He not only relieved when His aid was implored, but anticipated the expectations of the distressed. He 'went about doing good' (Acts 10:38), seeking the afflicted and offering His assistance. With great fatigue (John 4:6) He traveled to remote cities; with no less condescension, He visited the meanest villages, that all might have the honour and benefit of His healing Presence and heavenly instructions. He gave sight to the blind, health to the diseased. He delivered the wretched soul from the dominion of darkness and from the tyranny of sin. He made His followers partakers of a divine nature, and prepared them for a state of never-ending bliss. Nor were these righteous acts His 'strange work,' but His repeated, His hourly, His almost incessant employ. When ridiculed and affronted, He kindly bore and kindly overlooked the insult. When contradicted by petulant and presumptuous sinners, He endured, with the utmost serenity of temper, their unreasonable cavils and their obstinate perverseness.

"When His bloody sweat tinged the stones, when His bitter cries pierced the clouds, and were enough to awaken the very rocks into compassion, His disciples slept, stupidly and repeatedly slept. But did their Divine but slighted Master resent the unkindness? Did He refuse to *admit* an excuse for their disobedience and neglect? Nay; He *made* their excuse, and that the most tender and gracious imaginable: 'The spirit indeed is willing, but the flesh is weak' (Matt. 26:41). When His *enemies* had nailed Him to the cross, as the basest slave and most flagitious malefactor, when they were glutting their malice with His sorrows, His torments, and His blood: nay, when they spared not to insult and revile Him, even in His last expiring agonies; far, very far from being exasperated, this *Hero of heaven* repaid all their contempt and barbarity with the most fervent supplications in their behalf: 'Father, *forgive* them, for they know not what they do' (Luke 23:34) was His plea. Divine, adorable compassion" (Jas. Hervey).

Now as the Christian bows in admiration and adoration before the Holy Spirit's description of the exquisitely lovely ways of our Lord, let him not miss that which is most evangelical of all in the four Evangelists, namely, that the perfect life of Christ was not only, nor even primarily, a pattern for our *imitation,* but was also, and supremely, in order to our *justification.* To present to a ruined and impotent creature the flawless life of the Holy One of God, is *no* "glad tidings," but as another has said, "only a consummate Copy for a *withered* hand to transcribe." But O my brethren, when our faith is enabled to lay hold of the blissful fact that, from Bethlehem to Calvary, Christ acted as our Surety and Representative, that by *all* He did He wrought out for us a perfect righteousness, which in the construction and judgment of the law is *really ours;* that God Himself imputes that righteousness to us, and will forever deal with us according to its deserts, *then* we behold the light of the *glorious* Gospel and enter into the "unsearchable riches of Christ."

"And is this righteousness designed for *us?* Is this to be our wedding-dress, this our beautiful array, when we enter the regions of eternity? Unspeakable privilege! Is this what *God* has provided, to more than supply our loss in Adam? Boundless benignity! Shall *we* be treated by the Judge of the world as if *we* had performed all this unsinning and perfect obedience? Well might the prophet cry out, like one in astonishment, '*How great* is His goodness!' How great indeed! Since all that *the Lord Jesus* did and suffered, was doing and suffering for us men and our salvation, is imputed to us for righteousness, and is the sole and infinitely sufficient cause of our justification; is not your heart enamoured with a view of this incomprehensibly rich grace? What so excellent, what so comfortable, what so desirable, as this gift of a *Saviour's* righteousness? Though delineated by this feeble pen, methinks it has dignity and glory enough to captivate our hearts and fire our affections: fire them with ardent and inextinguishable desire after a personal interest and propriety in it? O may the eternal Spirit reveal our Redeemer's righteousness in all its heavenly beauty and divine lustre. Then, I am persuaded, we shall esteem it *above everything*. We shall regard it as the 'one thing needful.' We shall count *all* things in comparison of it, worthless as the chaff, empty as the wind" (Jas. Hervey).

It is that perfect obedience which Christ rendered to God, His absolute conformity to the law, which makes Him competent to save. Thus saith the Lord God, He *shall* "justify many." On what consideration? Why this: because He is "My *righteous* Servant" (Isa. 53:11). It is because of His perfect obedience in life and in death that "Judah shall be saved" from eternal damnation, and "Israel shall dwell safely," having been given an indefeasible title to life and glory; for it is on this very account, namely, that God raised unto David "a *righteous* Branch" and that He is owned as "the Lord our righteousness" (Jer. 23:5, 6). It is this which renders His intercession so prevalent. He is an Advocate, a successful Advocate, with the Father. Why? Because He is "Jesus Christ *the righteous*" (I John 2:1)! Has the Lord Jesus risen on His people with "healing in his wings"? It is because He is "the Sun *of righteousness*" (Mal. 4:2). So various, so efficacious, so extensive, are His beneficent influences, that like a "sun" (the monarch of the material creation), He enlightens and enlivens; like "wings," He cherishes and protects; like an all powerful remedy, He "heals" and restores. And all this by virtue of His *righteousness*.

Pitiable indeed, though perhaps needful it is, that we should now turn away from this glorious object, and briefly look at some of the objections which a carping unbelief has brought against it. Not a few who have been looked upon as exceptionably able students of the Word, have dogmatically affirmed that "the righteousness of Christ" is an expression of human invention, and is nowhere to be found in Holy Scriptures. It is sufficient refutation to quote II Peter 1:1 — "to those who have obtained like precious faith with us in the righteousness of our God and Saviour Jesus Christ" (R. V. and also margin of A. V.)! This inspired sentence is the key to all those texts in the New Testament and many in the Old, which mention the "righteousness *of God.*" It is not the essential righteousness of an absolute God, but the *vicarious* righteousness of an *incarnate* God! Just as "the Church *of God* which He hath purchased with His own blood" (Acts 20:28) means, and can only mean, that the church of God who became incarnate, the church of Christ.

It has been objected that God would have been unjust to require Christ to perfectly obey the law, and after having done so, inflict upon Him the penalty which the law enforces upon the *dis*obedient. Such an objection had held good if Christ acted only in the capacity of a *private* person, that is, as a single or isolated individual. But He did not. He came here as the federal Head of His people (Rom. 5:14 last clause; I Cor. 15:45, 47), made one with them (Heb. 2:11, 14). To say that the law requires no man to obey and die too, is specious reasoning, quite beside the point at issue. The real question is, Did the law require a *transgressor* to obey and die? There is a *twofold* debt which sinners owe to God: as *creatures,* perfect obedience to the law; as *criminals,* liability to suffer its punishment. The claims of the law cannot be relaxed at either point. In coming here as the Sponsor of His people, Christ assumed *all* their debts, and discharged their full responsibilities both as creatures and criminals. It needs to be steadily borne in mind that Christ was "made under" (Gal. 4:4) a *broken* law, and consequently, under its curse: therefore justice required that He should not only fulfill its precepts, but suffer its penalty.

Had the Surety died only, He had delivered us from punishment, but that would have afforded no claim to "life," no title to the "reward" (Rom. 10:5). Scripture declares of the Divine commands that "in *keeping* of them there is great *reward*" (Psa. 19:11), but it nowhere affirms that in undergoing their curse there is the same reward. God's elect, fallen in Adam, not only needed to be made negatively guiltless, but positively righteous. To "reign in life" (Rom. 5:15), to be entitled to the "crown" (II Tim. 4:8), required the *obedience* of Christ to be imputed to us. Just as in sanctification there is *both* the putting off the "old man" and the putting on of the "new man" (Eph. 4:22-24), so the Divine sentence of justification proceeds on the *double* basis that there is "no condemnation" resting upon those in Christ, and *also* that His righteousness has been "imputed" to their account (Rom. 4:11). Romans 4:25 unites the two: Christ was "delivered [to death] for our *offences* [remission] *and* was raised again for our *justification*"— righteousness. "This is the heritage of the servants of the Lord, and *their* righteousness is *of me*, saith the Lord" (Isa. 54:17).

John Bunyan, in the account which he gave of the Lord's dealings with him, recorded with artless simplicity the establishment of his soul in this most glorious truth. "Now I saw that Christ Jesus was looked upon by God, and should be looked upon by us, as the common or *public* person, in whom all the whole body of His elect are always to be considered and reckoned: that *we fulfilled the law by Him,* died by Him, rose from the dead by Him, got the victory over sin, death, the devil, and hell, by Him; when He died we died; and so of His resurrection," etc. (*Grace Abounding*). May it please the Lord to grant a like precious faith unto many readers of this book. To have the heart established in this blessed truth is worth infinitely more than the riches, honors, pleasures of this perishing world.

Let us return now to the objections which Satan has moved men to make against this precious truth. One of the favorite "arguments" of the Romanists against the teachings of the Reformers upon this subject was: If God has transferred the righteousness of Christ to believers then they are sinless, holy, righteous in their own persons, as righteous as Christ is righteous. But this is a confounding of things that differ. The saints of God may be considered either as to what they still are *in themselves* or as justified *in Christ.* That this distinction is not of human invention, is capable of being established from many scriptures. Take one passage only from either Testament: "I am black, but comely" (Song of Sol. 1:5). Yes, "black" in myself, as a fallen descendant of Adam, and such

I continue to the end of my earthly course; but "comely," as I am in Christ (Col. 2:10). "Purge out therefore the old leaven, that ye *may be* [experimentally] a new lump, as ye *are* [judicially, in Christ] *un*-leavened" (I Cor. 5:7). They who make not this distinction are ignorant of "the *mystery* of the Gospel" (Eph. 6:19).

Others have objected—though it is not likely many will echo it in these days of lawlessness—that if Christ has fully kept the law for His people, then *they* are freed from all obligation to personally keep it. The answer is, True, God does not require His people to keep the law for the *same* ends and upon the same accounts that Christ fulfilled it, namely, to satisfy Divine justice and purchase a title to everlasting life and an inheritance in heaven. But for *other* ends, God *does* require His people to obey the law, namely, as creatures in subjection to His holy will, and out of loving gratitude for all He has done for them. Christ kept the law to earn eternal life for us—carefully ponder Romans 5:21; I John 4:9; Christians are to keep it from a desire to please Christ: "If ye love me, *keep* my commandments" (John 14:15). Nor do we have to keep the law by our own power: "In the Lord have I righteousness *and* strength" (Isa. 45:24).

Again, it has been objected that such a thing as *vicarious obedience,* the transferring of moral merits from one to another, is quite unknown in human history. What of that? That only goes to prove the *uniqueness* of Christ's work. Many things which are impossible to man *are* possible to God. Those who refuse to believe in the vicarious obedience of Christ (most probably to their own eternal damnation) because of its unprecedented character, have the same ground for rejecting His miraculous birth, His impeccability (incapableness of yielding to temptation), His unique life, His raising Himself from the dead; for none of these have any parallel in human history either! But this particular objection overlooks entirely the unique *relation* which existed between Christ and His people, namely, their federal union: in the eyes of God's law, what Christ did His people did.

"For as by one man's disobedience, many were made [legally constituted, as in II Corinthians 5:21] sinners, so by the obedience of One shall many be made [legally constituted] righteous" (Rom. 5:19). One had thought this was plain enough for any who profess to bow to Scripture, yet there have been those who, doing manifest violence to the Greek (see Bagster's Interlinear), have insisted it should be rendered "one obedience," which they limit to Christ's willingness to be crucified. As though anticipating this very perversion, in Philippians 2:8 the Spirit has expressly declared that, Christ "became obedient *unto* death," not merely "*in* death." Death was the final act of His obedience, referring us back to all the previous virtues and duties of His righteous walk. Just as Jehovah's promise "and even *to* hoar hairs will I carry you" (Isa. 46:4) does not exclude God's sustaining grace in youth and manhood, so "obedient unto death" does not exclude the vicarious obedience of Christ's *life*. In like manner, "justified by His blood" (Rom. 5:9) was the climax or consummation of the complete satisfaction which Christ offered to God. Let us now briefly consider –

D. *Its Typification*

The double value of Christ's Word was shadowed forth as soon as sin entered the world: See Genesis 3:21. Two things are to be noted there. To procure those "skins" blood must be shed, life must have been taken. Very, very striking was this. The first blood ever spilt on this earth, was shed not by the hand of man, but by the hand of God! The first life taken in this world was not Abel's (as many suppose), but that of sinless sacrifices. Their blood pointed forward to that of Christ's which cleanseth the believer from all sin. But more: the skins taken from those slain animals "*clothed*" Adam and Eve, thereby foreshadowing that "robe of righteousness" (Isa. 61:10) with which the believer is covered.

"The name of Christ not only cancels the sin; it supplies in the place of that which it has cancelled, its own everlasting excellency. We cannot have its nullifying power only: the other is the sure concomitant. So was it with every typical sacrifice in the law. It was striken; but as being spotless it was also burned on the altar for a sweet-smelling savour. That savour ascended as a memorial before God: it was accepted for, and its value was attributed or imputed to, him who had brought the vicarious victim. If, therefore, we reject the imputation of righteousness, we reject sacrifice as revealed in Scripture; for Scripture knows of no sacrifice whose efficacy is so exhausted in the removal of guilt, as to leave nothing to be presented in acceptableness before God" (B. W. Newton).

How beautifully was the imputation of the perfect righteousness of Christ to all whom He represented typified by what is recorded in Psalm 132:2. The costly and fragrant ungent which was poured upon Aaron's head and which ran down his beard, descended to the very skirts of his clothes. So the merits of our great High Priest have passed to and upon all who are members of His mystical Body. Again; when Aaron (as the representative) presented the names of the children of Israel before God, he did not *barely* present them, but he bore their names on his breastplate, engraved on *precious* stones (Ex. 28:17-20), thereby adumbrating, as far as earthly things can, the splendid and exalted nature of the Redeemer's righteousness *in which* we are presented to God.

Let the reader carefully and prayerfully ponder the wonderful incident portrayed in Zechariah 3:1-5. There we behold a "brand plucked out of the fire" (v. 2). Observe particularly the *two* things done for and to him. First the command is, "*Take away* the filthy garments from him" (v. 4), figuring the removal of our sins. Second, "they set a *fair* mitre upon his head and clothed him with garments" (v. 5), emblemizing that vicarious and immaculate righteousness of Christ, which is not only "unto" but also "*upon* all them that believe" (Rom. 3:22).

E. *Its Imputation*

"To him that worketh not, but believeth on him that justifieth the ungodly, his faith is counted for righteousness" (Rom. 4:5). Here again the enemies of the truth have fought hard to rob God's children of the comfort and assurance which the blessed teaching of this chapter is designed to give them. Many have argued that God imputes to faith itself an intrinsic value which He accepts *in lieu of* perfect obedience to His law. But this is a most horrible perversion. Faith is an emptying thing, which causes the pauper to gladly receive God's gracious gift, and possesses no more merit than does the appeal of a beggar for charity. The "his faith is counted *for* righteousness" does *not* mean "in the stead of" for the Greek preposition is "eis" and not "anti," and signifies "unto" as in Romans 10:10: "with the heart man believeth *unto* righteousness."

Our Surety gave full satisfaction to the law, but we are not credited with this by God's gracious imputation until we have faith in Christ. "The righteousness of God by faith of Jesus Christ unto all and upon all *them that believe*" (Rom. 3:22). "For Christ is the end of the law for righteousness to everyone *that believeth*" (Rom. 10:4). Therefore is this righteousness also called "the righteousness of faith" (Rom. 4:13). It is denominated the "righteousness of God" because God required, ordained, provided, accepted and imputed it. It is a righteousness which exalts God's justice, magnifies His law, manifests His grace, and displays *all* His awful and lovely attributes in their full lustre. It is designated the "righteousness of Christ" (II Pet. 1:1), because He wrought it out without the co-operation of His creatures. It is the "righteousness of faith" because faith apprehends it.

From the way in which certain men have spoken of "the imputation of righteousness" many have deemed them orthodox on this vital subject, but their blank denial of the imputation of *Christ's* righteousness thoroughly exposes their heterodoxy, to all who bow to the authority of Holy Writ. "That righteousness might be imputed to them" (Rom. 4:11). *What* righteousness? *Whose* righteousness? The only possible Scriptural answer is: that perfect satisfaction which Christ rendered to *all* the demands of the law, and which God places to the credit of every true believer in Him. So truly is Christ's righteousness placed to their account, it is said to be "*upon* all them that believe" (Rom. 3:22). Such persons actually *possess* it. They *wear* it as their "robe" (Isa. 61:10).

"That we might be made the righteousness of God in Him" (II Cor. 5:21). Yes, *in Him,* as our Proxy and Head, and this because He wrought out a justifying-righteousness not only in our nature, but in our name, not only as our Benefactor, but as our Representative. "*In the Lord* [not in themselves] shall all the seed of Israel be justified" (Isa. 45:25). In the Lord Jesus, believers have a righteousness without spot or blemish, perfect and all glorious; a righteousness which has not only expiated all their sins, but satisfied every requirement of the law's precepts. "That I may win Christ, and be found in him, *not* having *mine own* righteousness which is of the law, but that which is through the faith of Christ, the righteousness which is *of God* by faith" (Phil. 3:9, 10).

God's imputation of Christ's righteousness to the believer, is not in esteeming him to be righteous when really he is not so. Nor is it a naked pronunciation of any one to be righteous *without* a just and sufficient foundation for the judgment of God declared therein. God pronounces none righteous who are not so. Nor is it a *transfusion* of Christ's righteousness unto those who are to be justified, so that they should be inherently righteous thereby. No; it is a Divine and legal grant whereby God, out of His mere love and grace, on the simple consideration of the whole mediation of Christ, makes an effectual donation of a real and true righteousness, even that of Christ Himself, unto all who believe; and so accounting it as *theirs,* on His own gracious act, as not only to absolve them from all sin, but granting them the right to eternal life and the title to an everlasting inheritance in heaven. The meritorious obedience of Christ is so truly transferred to believers that they are called "the righteous" (Matt. 25:40). Surely the Christian has cause to say, "my mouth shall show forth *thy* righteousness, thy salvation all the day" (Psa. 71:15) – the one being founded upon the other, the latter deriving its origin from the former; there could be no "salvation" without a proper, real, law-*fulfilling* righteousness.

CHAPTER EIGHTEEN

The Atonement—Its Effects

Having dwelt at length upon the principle "results" which the Satisfaction of the Mediator has secured, we turn now to look at some of its leading "effects." The distinction we have in mind is not very clearly intimated by these two terms, so we must define what we intend by their use. In treating of the "results" we have almost (though not quite) confined our attention to the objective or external benefits which Christians derive from the work of their great High Priest. Here, we desire to point out the subjective or internal blessings which accrue to us from it. In this chapter we shall endeavor to take up and follow out in fuller detail what was briefly touched upon in Chapter 12, division 2, where, under the "Application" of the Atonement we mentioned, The Spirit Regenerating.

That aspect of Truth which is now to be before us has received but scant notice even by many who wrote most helpfully upon the true nature and character of the Satisfaction of Christ. There has been a sad failure to duly hold the balance of Truth. Not a few have so stressed the *legal* results secured by our Saviour's sacrifice, and have so failed to proportionately emphasize the *experimental* effects which it purchased, that it is greatly to be feared multitudes have been deceived into supposing that *they* had a saving interest therein, when, in fact, they lacked the Scriptural marks of those who have passed from death unto life. Christ died to "save his people from their sins" (Matt. 1:21): not only from the guilt and penalty of them, but also from their pollution and power.

It is because there has been such a onesided calling unto faith without an equal insistence for repentance, and because there has been such an emphasis laid upon the Grace which is revealed in the Gospel without a proportionate exposition of its Holiness, that ground has been given for the enemies of the Truth to charge the Gospel with immoral tendencies, to affirm that it encourages careless living and releases men from the due performance of their duties, that it is unfriendly to the producing of good works. And the deplorable thing is that the lives of many who profess to have been saved by grace through the righteousness of Christ, have tended to confirm their contentions, until not a few who have had dealings with professing Christians, have said (and with much cause), "If that is what Christianity produces I want nothing to do with it!"

It needs to be loudly affirmed, trumpeted forth from every "orthodox" pulpit in the land, that the mediatorial work and sufferings of the Lord Jesus not only obtained for God's people redemption from the penal consequences of their sins, but has also secured *their personal sanctification.* Well did Thomas J. Crawford say, in his splendid work *The Doctrine of Holy Scripture Respecting the Atonement* (1874), "In speaking or thinking of the 'salvation' which Christ has purchased, there are many who seem to attach to it no farther idea than that of mere *deliverance from condemnation.* They forget that *deliverance from sin* – the cause of condemnation – is a no less important blessing comprehended in it. Assuredly it is just as necessary for fallen creatures to be delivered from the pollution and moral impotency which they have contracted, as it is to be exempted from the penalties which they have incurred; so that, when reinstated in the favor of God, they may at the same time be made capable of loving, serving, and enjoying Him forever. And in this respect the remedy which the Gospel reveals is fully suited to the exigencies of our sinful state, providing for our complete redemption from sin itself, as well as from the penal liabilities it has brought upon us.

"Nay, it would seem as if the former of these deliverances – that is to say, our deliverance from sin itself – were represented in some passages of Scripture as the grand and ultimate consummation of redeeming grace, to which the latter, though in itself inestimably precious and important, is preparatory. Witness these plain and forcible declarations: 'He died for all, *that* they who live should not henceforth live unto themselves, *but unto him* who died for them and rose again' (II Cor. 5:15). 'Christ also loved the Church, and gave himself for it, that he might *sanctify it and cleanse it* with the washing of water by the Word, and that he might present it to himself a glorious Church not having spot or wrinkle or any such thing; but that it should be holy and without blemish' (Eph. 5:25-27). 'He gave himself for us, that he might redeem us from all iniquity, and purify unto himself a peculiar people, *zealous of good works*' (Titus 2:14). 'The blood of Jesus, who through the eternal Spirit offered himself without spot unto God, should purge your conscience from dead works, *to serve the living God*' (Heb. 9:14). These statements seem to indicate that our redemption from the guilt and penal consequences of sin was intended to be the means to an ulterior end — that end being our personal sanctification."

Certain it is that the inestimable blessings of justification and sanctification are represented in the Word of God as *inseparable* results of the Saviour's mediation. Nor ought we to have any difficulty in apprehending how the Satisfaction of Christ, in obtaining for us the former blessing, should thereby secure our attainment of the latter. For our redemption by the blood of Christ binds us to His service as a purchased or peculiar people: "Ye are not your own, for ye are bought with a price; therefore glorify God in your body and in your spirit, which *are* God's" (I Cor. 6:19,20). Furthermore, it has (as we have shown in Chapter 12) procured for the redeemed the grace of the Holy Spirit "which he shed on us abundantly" (Titus 3:6), and by which His purchased people are renewed in the whole man after the image of God, and are enabled more and more to *die* unto sin and to live *unto righteousness*.

The sanctifying power of "the redemption that is in Christ Jesus" is practically displayed in and by the character and conduct of true believers. There is as marked a difference between the children of God and the children of this world, as there is between light and darkness. There is as real a distinction, *outwardly manifested,* between the blood-bought and the blood-washed people of Christ and those whose iniquities are not purged, as there is between life and death. Even in this life, according to the measure of their growth in grace, those who have been born again are witnesses to the present efficacy of Christ's Satisfaction. Still more so will they be in the life to come, when they are freed from all those infirmities and blemishes which now cleave to them.

"Never, then," (to quote again from T. Crawford) "was there a more unfounded calumny than the assertion that personal holiness is disparaged or dispensed with in the scheme of our redemption. So far from being so, it is magnified and honored. True, it is not the *foundation* on which we are called to build; but it is a prominent part of the *stately edifice,* for the erection of which that foundation has been laid. It is not our *remedy,* but it is the completion of *the actual cure* which that remedy is designed to accomplish. It is not in any respect or in any degree *the means of salvation,* but it is one of the most essential and most precious elements of *salvation itself.*"

What is that salvation which Christ has purchased for His people? Of what does it consist? What are its prime elements? Someone answers, Deliverance from the everlasting burnings, which our sins justly deserved. True, yet that is only one part of the answer. A valid title to everlasting bliss in Heaven, says another. Equally true, yet that answer also fails to cover all the ground. What about the *present!* What is the precious portion which the redeemed enjoy even now? Or, suppose we put it another way. Many profess to have been saved by Christ, yet, though quite sincere in their profession, when measured by the Scriptures, it is evident that they are mistaken. How, then, may the writer and the reader be sure that he is not mistaken? Who are the *legitimate* claimants of this privileged state? Salvation is an experience, a personal experience, which is begun in this life. And it is this we shall now seek to describe.

1. EMANCIPATION

"If the Son therefore shall make you free, ye shall be free indeed" (John 8:36). Free *from what?* First, from the power of *indwelling sin.* Not that the sinful nature is eradicated or even slain, but that the *heart* is delivered from its dominion. "Being now made free from sin" (Rom. 6:22). That which was once loved, is now hated. Those solicitations which were gladly heeded, are now resisted. "The fear of the Lord is the *beginning* of wisdom" (Prov. 9:10). None have been made wise unto salvation (II Tim. 3:15) unless there has been implanted in their hearts a filial respect for God. And, "the fear of the Lord is to *hate* evil" (Prov. 8:13), and "by the fear of the Lord men *depart from* evil" (Prov. 16:6). The heart of a saved person is set upon pleasing God.

Second, the Christian is delivered from the power of *the world.* "The friendship of the world is enmity with God, whosoever therefore will be a friend of the world is the enemy of God" (James 4:4). The friendship of the world consists of indulging worldly lusts, following worldly vanities, fellowshiping with worldlings. It is for the heart to find its satisfaction in the perishing things of time and sense. From this the grace of God delivers its favored subjects, by fixing their heart upon One who is "altogether lovely." Before Christ saves him, a man seeks happiness in the pleasures, honors, or riches of this world; but when He delivers *"from* this present evil world" (Gal. 1:4), his affections are drawn unto things above. "For whatsoever is born of God *overcometh* the world" (I John 5:4). The heart of a saved person finds its delight in God.

Third, the Christian is delivered from the power of *the Devil.* For this purpose did Christ leave Heaven: "to proclaim liberty to the captives and the opening of the prison to them that are bound" (Isa. 60:1), and when the Spirit of God applies the Gospel in power to the heart, then is that individual "delivered from the power of darkness and translated into the kingdom of His dear Son" (Col. 1:13). It was "in *time past*" that Christians "walked according to the course of this world, according to the prince of the power of the air" (Eph. 2:2). When Christ saves a soul, He breaks Satan's chains, delivers his captive, and brings him into the place of liberty. True, the Devil still tempts, harasses and wounds the Christian, but destroy him or take him prisoner again he cannot. Concerning all God's children it is written, "they *overcame* him [the Devil] by the blood of the Lamb" (Rev. 12:11). The heart of a saved person is occupied with serving God.

"That the righteousness of the law might be fulfilled in us, who walk not after the flesh, but after the spirit" (Rom. 8:4). The first part of this verse has been before us in previous chapters, the second half is what we will now consider. There we have described those unto whom God imputed the righteousness of Christ. It is by these marks they may be clearly identified: they walk not after the flesh, they walk after the spirit. A course of godly living, of spiritual behavior, is both the inseparable concomitant of union with Christ and an infallible evidence thereof. The "walk" is that which is open to the observation of others, and is plainly seen by them. It is not any particular act which is here specified, but the general course and uniform tenor of the life that is referred to.

"Who walk not after the flesh." The principle of evil is still within, active, powerfully opposing (Gal. 5:17); nevertheless, the Christian has been freed from its dominion, so that it is no longer the controlling power in his heart and life. The best of God's children offend in many things (James 3:2), yet the prayer of their heart is, "Order my steps in thy Word: and let not any iniquity have dominion over me" (Psa. 119:133). Sometimes real saints have sad falls into outward and open sins, yet they do not continue therein, but are brought to repent of and forsake them. To walk after the flesh is to follow a course of self-will, self-pleasing, self-gratification (Isa. 53:6), and this no *saved* person does or can do.

They walk "after the spirit." This gives us the positive side, for when grace works within the heart its subject is enabled to "overcome evil with good." When God saves a sinner he is not only so far delivered from the power of indwelling sin that his walk—his regular course of conduct—is no longer controlled by fleshly principles and lustings, but he is also enabled to live a spiritual and godly life. Christians are not only effectually taught to deny "ungodliness and worldly lusts" but also to "live soberly, righteously, and godly, in this *present* world" (Titus 2:12). To "walk after the spirit" is to respond unto the promptings of that new nature received at regeneration; it is to be controlled by new and unworldly principles; it is for a person to be dominated by the Holy Spirit, so that he loves God, serves God, and glorifies God. How this is brought about we shall now see under—

2. Regeneration

As we wish to be as concise as possible we shall here limit ourselves to one aspect of this miracle of grace, namely, the Holy Spirit reversing that depraved state of soul spoken of in Romans 8:7, "The carnal mind is enmity against God: for it is not subject to the law of God, neither indeed can be." When God renews His people He deals directly with the will, powerfully bringing it into a conscious subjection to *His* will. There is what may be called a transfer of the moral law from the tables of stone to the fleshly tables of the heart: "I will put my laws into their mind, and write them in their hearts" (Heb. 8:10). God secures the intelligent acquaintance of the Christain with His law and a cordial acquiescence in it. But let it be emphatically affirmed that this transfer is *not* of such a nature that the law of God is no more to be found outside and above the will of the Christian.

At regeneration the law of God does not disappear as an authoritative code of duty, because it has become the desire of the Christian's heart and the purpose of his will to please God. Not so: that which the Holy Spirit has secured is a changed heart, which lives in the recognition of God's authority, and is able to say, "I delight in the law of God after the inward man" (Rom. 7:22). Instead of salvation having freed its subjects from subjection to God, from obedience to Him, from obligation to keep His law, it has subdued his enmity against God's law and bestowed a love for it — a love that finds expression not only in endearing words, but in practical submission to the authority of the Ruler of heaven and earth.

It is at this very point that the modern Antinomians have erred. Infected by that spirit of lawlessness which is so rife in the world, and misled by an erroneous conception of the *nature* of spiritual "liberty," they have insisted that Christians are entirely delivered from the claims of God's law. They suppose that an inward consent to the holiness of His commands presents a higher ideal of spiritual freedom, than subjection to an external code. But the reverse is the fact. The withdrawal of objective law is really the denial of responsibility, and *liberty* is infringed, when responsibility is infringed. Spiritual liberty is not the power to do as we please (*that* is licentiousness), but the power to do as we *ought;* it is the being delivered from the bondage of sin which prevented us from serving God. The true nature of spiritual liberty is clearly enough defined in Psalm 119:45: "I will walk at liberty: *for* I seek thy precepts."

When a sinner is regenerated, he is made "willing" (Psa. 110: 3) to be under the law of God, to be in subjection to his Maker. The obedience of the Christian is not that of a slave, for the law of God is within his heart in the character of a holy tendency, as well as standing over him with its commandments. Nor is his obedience the operation of a *mere* mental tendency or spiritual mechanism working out its own bias—as of a vessel languidly drifting with the stream. No, it is the obedience of a loving and loyal *subject,* adoring his King and saying, "Lord, what wilt thou have me to do?" It is the renewed heart gladly *owning* the rightful authority and supremacy of its Maker. And *this* is the highest ideal of *liberty* that can be framed. It is the liberty of Heaven itself, for there God does not abdicate His *throne,* nor cease to issue His *commands* (Psa. 103:20).

It is equally vain to assert that a subjective view of the Law—love in the heart dispensing with the need of external commands—presents a higher ideal of Grace. Grace is not a species of lawlessness, or mercy dispensed by ignoring the claims of justice. Grace reigns through righteousness (Rom. 5:21), and that at *every* stage. Not only has Christ met every claim of the law against His people, but, by the workings of His Spirit, He places in their hearts a new principle, which causes them to cry, "O how *love* I thy law" (Psa. 119:97). The triumph of Grace is that it effects a *reconciliation* between the blatant rebel and the righteous Governor of all, and makes an insurrectionist a loyal subject. Well might the apostle say, "Do we then make void the law through faith? God forbid: yea, we *establish* the law" (Rom. 3:31).

3. SANCTIFICATION

This is another fruit of the Cross of Christ. The Lord Jesus not only rendered a perfect obedience unto the law for the justification of His people, but He also merited and procured for them those supplies of His Spirit which were essential unto their sanctification. To deliver us from the guilt of sin is an unspeakable mercy, yet would it not be a perfect favor unless He also purged us from the venom of sin which has infected our nature. Had the believer been pardoned without being "purified" (I Pet. 1:22), he had still been unfit for converse with God. But God not only satisfied His *justice* in the sacrifice of Christ, but also magnified His *holiness* by providing for the renewing of His people in His own image. Personal holiness is just as essential a part of "salvation" as is forgiveness. Therefore did the sanctification of our Surety not only secure for His people a perfect legal standing before God, but also provided for their perfect experimental fitness for His presence.

To "sanctify" is to set apart unto, to dedicate or devote to, God. Where polluted man is concerned, he must be *purified* (both judicially and experimentally) before he is meet for the Lord's use (II Tim. 2:21): note how in Ephesians 5:26 "sanctify" is defined by "cleanse." Now there is a double sanctification pertaining to the Christian: judicial and experimental. *Christ* is the believer's sanctification as truly as He is his righteousness, see I Corinthians 1:30; but unless such a bare statement be defined and amplified, it conveys no definite concept to us. The satisfaction of Christ is the *meritorious* cause of the Christian's sanctification, but the work of the Spirit is the *efficacious* cause thereof, hence we read of the "sanctification of the Spirit" (II Thess. 2:13). That takes place at the new birth, when the regenerated soul is set apart unto God, separated from those dead in sin. That aspect of our experimental sanctification is absolute and complete. But there is another side to the Christian's experimental sanctification which is relative or progressive, and which, because of sin indwelling us, is never perfected in this life.

This practical (in contrast from positional) and progressive (in contrast from absolute) sanctification consists of two branches: mortification and renovation. A complete summary of these is given to us in Titus 2:12. There, mortification is comprehended under two words, answering to the two tables of the law: *denying* "ungodliness," which comprehends the first four commandments; denying "worldly lusts" which covers the last six commandments. Then, that renovation which the grace of God produces is to "*live* soberly," which respects ourselves;

"righteously" or "justly" in all our dealings with our neighbors; and "godly" in connection with God. When Divine grace "brings" *salvation* to a person, his heart is inclined unto obedience, and he is made fruitful in his life unto the glory of God.

Now the heart of the Christian is made holy by regenerating grace purifying it from the pollution (*not* presence) of sin, implanting a hatred of and a striving against it; and by renewing us after God's image. In that spiritual life which was communicated at the new birth, there is contained in embryonic form all spiritual graces and fruits which, by the operations of the Spirit through the Word, are developed and matured. By the Spirit, the renewed heart is kept under the influence of efficacious grace, and it is disposed and enabled to fear the Lord, walk in His statutes, and be conformed to His law. The more the Christian *feels* his own utter inability to serve God acceptably, and the more earnestly and constantly he beseeches Him to work in him "both to will and to do of his good pleasure," the clearer evidence has he of his experimental and progressive sanctification, and in *this* way is he assured of his justification.

As the Christian finds that he is becoming less and less disposed to confer with flesh and blood (either his own wisdom or that of others), and more and more consults the Holy Scriptures, because he is desirous of learning his duty; as he denies self, takes up his cross, and seeks to follow Christ; as every fresh discovery of God's will commands his attention and fills him with holy reverence; as he is more ready, more cheerful, more determined in his obedience; as his supreme desire is really to glorify God, and this becomes the *prevailing* state of his heart and mind; then, though he is increasingly conscious of the plague of his own heart, and mourns more deeply and frequently than ever his *many* failures, both of omission and commission; nevertheless, it is evident that the work of sanctification is advancing in his soul.

The *rule* of our sanctification is God's written Word (John 17:17), for by it alone does the Spirit work, forming in the saint those dispositions which it both promises and requires. The Holy Scriptures are the one rule by which all of our conduct is to be regulated. Practical holiness is a personal conformity of heart and life to what God's Word enjoins. The "commandments of men" (Matt. 15:9) are of no weight or value whatsoever. *Their* "touch not, taste not, handle not" (Col. 2:21) are to be resolutely refused. No creature is to be allowed to dictate unto the Lord's freeman. Our one concern must be to obey, serve and please *God*.

To sum up this division. Sanctification may be considered, *first*, as an *act* of God the Spirit (I Pet. 1:2) already completed, when the Christian is set apart unto God by His life-giving operation, by His begetting us with the Word of truth (James 1:18), from which root the fruits of practical holiness grow. *Second*, as the *state* of acceptance with God, into which salvation brings us: I Corinthians 6:11. *Third*, as a *growth*, an increasing conformity to God in heart, mind, and life: II Corinthians 7:1. *Fourth*, as a *longing*, an (as yet) unrealized desire, a panting after and praying for complete conformity to the image of God's son: I Thessalonians 5:23; which desire is realized at the moment of the soul's entrance into Heaven, and consummated at the resurrection of his glorified body. Each and all of these four aspects of one sanctification are the *fruits* of Christ's satisfaction—purchased for His people. By that perfect sacrifice which He offered unto God, the Lord Jesus procured for us all that we need for time and eternity, and *He* is only fully honored when we perceive that every gift, operation, blessing and fruit of the Holy Spirit comes to us on the ground of the Redeemer's merits.

4. Preservation

This too is another of the precious fruits produced by the tree of Calvary. "By one offering he hath perfected *forever* them that are sanctified" (Heb. 10:14). Herein lies one of the main differences between the perfect satisfaction of Christ and the typical offerings under the law. The atonement made by Israel's high priests availed only for one year: twelve months later it must needs be repeated. But the sacrifice of Christ was once for all: its virtue and efficacy is eternal. "There is therefore now no condemnation to them which are in Christ Jesus" (Rom. 8:1), nor can anything ever separate His people from the love of God (Rom. 8:35-39). "Wherefore he is able also to save them *to the uttermost* that come unto God by him, seeing he ever liveth to make intercession for them" (Heb. 7:25). A perfect, unforfeitable, eternal salvation has Christ procured for His own.

Yet on this point also we need to carefully remember that the Lord does not deal with us as sticks and stones, but as rational creatures; not as irresponsible automatons, but as accountable beings. He preserves His people through means which He inspires them to use. He preserves in the path of practical godliness, not in a course of carnal carelessness. The hearts of believers are like gardens, wherein there are not only flowers, but weeds also; and as the former must be watered and cherished, so the latter must be curbed and nipped. If nothing but the dews and showers of God's promises fell on our hearts, though they tend to the nourishing of our graces, yet the weeds of corruption would grow with them, and in the end choke them, unless they be nipped by the severity of the Divine threatenings.

Although God has pledged Himself to secure those for whom Christ died, and that in the use of means, therefore they cannot apostatize; nevertheless, He has plainly warned us that there is an infallible connection between sin and destruction (I Cor. 6:9), and that the one must be avoided, if the other is to be escaped. We *must* "watch and pray" if temptations are to be escaped from. We are "kept by the power of God *through faith*" (I Pet. 1:5). We are not only saved by faith at the outset of our spiritual career, but we are supported and sustained by it through all our consequent experience: "the just shall *live* by faith" (Heb. 10:38). As it is by faith we enter that narrow way which leadeth unto life, so it must be by faith we walk all the journey through, for it is only "through faith and perseverance" that we "inherit the promises" (Heb. 6:12).

The life of the Christian, between his being delivered from Hell and his actual entrance into Heaven, is not a picnic, but a warfare. There is armor to be put on, weapons to be used, enemies to be vanquished, if the fight is to be won. Therefore are we bidden to make our "calling and election *sure*" (II Pet. 1:10), and that, by *adding* to our faith, virtue, knowledge, temperance, perseverance, godliness, brotherly-kindness and love. Therefore are we required to "show the same diligence to the full assurance of hope *unto the end*" (Heb. 6:11). God calls His people unto glory and eternal bliss via a path of self-denial and holy obedience. If we *neglect* our duties, there is no promise that God will perfect that which concerneth us. They who deny not the flesh, who refuse not the friendship of the world, who press not forward along the highway of practical holiness, evidence that they have *no* spiritual life, no matter what their profession may be. But they who deny self, take up their cross, and follow Christ, no matter how weak and unprofitable they may feel, are assured that He who has begun a good work in them "*will* finish it" (Phil. 1:6).

CHAPTER NINETEEN

The Atonement — Its Extent

Considering all the ground which has already been carefully gone over, there really ought to be no need for a separate discussion of this phase of our subject. The question, *For whom* did Christ make satisfaction — for whose sins did He atone? has been clearly anticipated and definitely answered in almost every aspect of our theme which has been before us. If we go back to the very foundation, namely, the everlasting covenant, there we find that the Father promised the Son a specific reward (Isa. 53:10-12) upon His performance of the work assigned Him. The Son perfectly accomplished that work (John 17:4), therefore He *must* "see of the travail of his soul and be satisfied." If a single one of those for whom He died be not regenerated, justified, sanctified and glorified by God, then the Father's promise to His Son would be nullified.

The *nature* of Christ's satisfaction determines to a demonstration those who are the beneficiaries of it. First, it was a *federal* work. There was a legal oneness between Christ and those for whom He acted. The Saviour stood as the Surety, and if a single one whose debts He paid receive not a full discharge from the law, then Divine justice would be reduced to a farce. Second, it was a *substitutionary* work. Christ acted not only on the behalf of, but in the stead of, those who had been given to Him by the Father; hence all whose sins He bore *must of necessity* have their sins remitted — God cannot punish twice, once the Substitute and then again the subject. Third, it was a *penal* work: every requirement of the law, both preceptive and punitive, was fulfilled by Christ, therefore all for whom He acted *must* receive the reward of His obedience, which is everlasting life. Fourth, it was a *priestly* work: His sacrifice being accepted by God, its efficacy and merits *must* be imputed to all those for whom He offered it.

The *design* of Christ's satisfaction as made known in Scripture reveals its scope. To suppose that the greatest and grandest of all God's works was without design would be to be guilty of blasphemous thoughts. That design was framed by infinite wisdom, so that there can be no flaw or failure in it. That design is executed by omnipotence, so that it is impossible to thwart it. What that design was, has been shown (in part) in the 9th chapter of this series. It was not an indefinite and undefined one. Scripture has made known in plain and unmistakable terms that the mediatorial work of Christ was in order to God's being magnified, the God-man glorified, and God's elect saved. The eternal Son of God became incarnate in order to "*save* His people from their sins" (Matt. 1:21).

But without reviewing any further the preceding chapters, let us now say why we deem it expedient to devote a separate chapter to the more specific stating and proving of what has come before us previously in only a more or less incidental or subordinate way. It is because a right (Scriptural) view of *this* point is absolutely essential, if God is to be honored and Christ is to be glorified by us therein. The enmity of the Serpent against the Seed of the woman has been inveterate throughout the ages, and perhaps at no other one point has he so persistently attacked the glory of Christ. While it is impossible for Satan to either undo the finished work of the Saviour, or to destroy any of its fruits, yet he is permitted to *misrepresent* it, and nowhere has his subtlety been more exercised and manifested than in the means employed here. He has indeed appeared as an "angel of light." His very attempts to *discredit* the satisfaction of Christ have been made under the guise of *magnifying* it, and that is why he has succeeded in getting many men reputed as "orthodox" to do some of his foul work for him.

Perhaps it will enable most of our readers to grasp more readily what we have just referred to in the above paragraph, if we frame the following questions. Which seems to have the greater tendency to *exalt* Christ: to say that He died because He desired and sought to make possible the salvation of all mankind or to say that He died only for God's elect, the "little flock"? Which seems to display the more His compassion for sinners? Which seems to bring out the more the value of His blood: to say that it avails only for the "few"? or to say that its merits are so infinite that every member of Adam's race would be redeemed did he or she put their trust in it? The very fact that every one of us would answer the question in the *wrong* way until we are taught aright from Scripture, not only evidences the worthlessness of carnal reasoning upon spiritual things, but also shows to what a terrible extent our minds have been poisoned by the venom of the Serpent. If it can yet be clearly shown that, in *reality,* the wider view actually *dishonors* Christ, then the consummate guile and malice of the Devil therein should be plainly apparent.

Before exposing the futility of the above reasoning, let us prepare the way by giving other illustrations or examples of our inability to think aright where spiritual things are concerned. Does it not seem to us that a greater revenue of glory had accrued to God had sin never invaded His dominions and corrupted His creatures? Yet *He* deemed otherwise, or else He had not suffered it so to be. Again; does it not seem to the Christian, *every* Christian, that he could glorify God more in this present life if the sinful nature were eradicated from his being? Yet if this were so, God *would* take the "flesh" completely out of our beings when He regenerated us. And does it not seem to many a reader that he or she could accomplish more for Christ, if better health, different circumstances and surroundings, or more money, were given to them by God? And so we might continue. The fact is that the wisest Christian is utterly incapable of thinking rightly about Divine things until his thoughts are formed by Scripture.

But coming now to a closer answering of the questions raised above. First, many imagine the glory of God is exceedingly exalted by affirming that He truly desires the salvation of every member of Adam's fallen race, and that they who teach that His free grace is restricted to the elect, grievously dishonor His benevolence. Now to maintain aright the glory *of* God we must speak in the language of His Word. Only that is glorious in God which He ascribes unto Himself. "Our inventions, though ever so splendid in our own eyes, are unto Him an abomination, a striving to pull Him down from His eternal excellency, to make Him altogether like unto us" (J. Owen). "God is dishonoured by that honour which is ascribed to Him beyond His own prescription" (Jerome). To assign unto God any thing which He has not assumed, is only to deify our own imaginations.

Many objects present a fair appearance when viewed at a distance, but their defects become apparent when examined at close quarters. So it is here. The assertion that God's design in sending His Son to this earth was that every sinner might be saved by Him, may at first glance seem to conduce unto the magnifying of His goodness and grace, but a little reflection thereon should quickly show the contrary. It certainly is not to the glory of God to suppose that the success of Christ's costly undertaking should be left contingent on the creature's will—*that* can never be the measure of *His* honor. And it certainly is not to the glory of God to suppose that He designed to save any that perish, for that would show His benevolent purpose was frustrated and would proclaim a disappointed and defeated Deity. The truth is that they glory of God's grace consists not in the number of objects to whom it is shown, but in its being *free* and *undeserved,* thus tending to lay the highest of all obligations on those who are concerned therein.

The fact is that those who advocate the scheme of a general redemption, are so far from magnifying the grace of God, that they, really, degrade both Divine grace and Christ's sacrifice. For according to their theory God has only provided a precarious salvation, which is offered to the caprice of man's acceptance, a mere possibility, which can only become actual through the sinner's compliance with certain conditions; a possibility, which when properly examined, is seen to be an impossibility. How vast the difference between a precarious salvation, and an infallible one! How immeasurably superior a redemption which secures the certain salvation of every one for whom it was made, and a suppositionary redemption which *guarantees* the salvation of *none,* leaving everything uncertain, dependent upon fickle man! How infinitely greater the glory which comes to God by that plan, through which grace *efficaciously* works in and applies the saving benefits to all for whom Christ died, than a method which would exalt the power of the creature and set the crown upon his free-will!

If it be still contended that we magnify the grace of God far more by proclaiming its universality rather than by insisting upon its particularity, by affirming that it extends to all mankind rather than to an elect remnant, then to carry out such an argument to its logical conclusion, we should be obliged to believe that God *will save all,* for He certainly will do that which is for His highest glory—*this* being the paramount consideration before Him in *all* that He does: see Psalm 29:9; Proverbs 16:4; Revelation 4:11. Moreover, such an argument would require, yea demand, that Divine grace be extended unto the fallen angels as well as to all mankind. Will men pretend to reflect on God's goodness because He has not extended His grace to all who might have been the objects of it had He so pleased? Has He not a right to do what He wills with His own?

Which exalts Christ the more? which demonstrates the more the value and efficacy of His atonement: that which effectually secures the actual salvation of every one for whom it was made? or that which ends in the great majority of those for whom He shed His precious blood being eternally punished in hell? Surely none with any spiritual discernment can fail to see which view is more glorifying to the Redeemer. And if we call to mind the *nature* of His satisfaction, that it was a specific bearing of the sins of definite persons, that it was a paying of their debts, a suffering the law's curse in their stead, in order that they might go free; and when we remember that the Judge of all *accepted* this atonement, was satisfied with the price the Sponsor paid —then, where would be God's honor, His justice, His faithfulness, were He, notwithstanding, to yet punish millions of those for whom His Son bled and died? If Christ died for all men universally, then all men universally *must be saved.* There is not other possible alternative, except to say that God will punish *twice,* first in the person of the Surety, and then in the persons of many in whose place He is supposed to have stood.

We sincerely trust that neither writer no reader is lacking in compassion to his fellow-creatures, yet we must not allow our pity for men to lead us to adopt any principle which is dishonoring to the Divine perfections and subversive of Christ's satisfaction. Others may speak for themselves, but the writer would not dare to trust his salvation to a Saviour who was unable to save those for whom He died. If it were true that Christ shed His blood for those who are now in hell, what guarantee would be left me that I shall not go there? An atonement, that *fails* to atone, a sacrifice which fails to deliver, is worthless. To say that salvation is possible to all, *if* all would receive Christ, is to ignore those unequivocal words of the Saviour in John 6:44, "No man *can* come to me, *except* the Father which hath sent me *draw* him." To say that salvation turns upon the sinner's own acceptance of Christ would be like offering a sum of money to a blind man upon the condition that he would see, or offering to ransom a prisoner on the proviso that he burst his way out of his steel-walled cell.

"Many divines say that Christ did something when He died that enabled God to be just, and yet the Justifier of the ungodly. What that *something* is they do not tell us. They believe in an atonement made for everybody; but then, *their* atonement is just this; that Judas was atoned for as much as Peter, that the damned in hell were as much an object of Jesus Christ's satisfaction as the saved in heaven. Though they do not say it in proper words they must mean that, in the case of multitudes, Christ died in vain, for they say He died for all, and yet so ineffectual was His dying for them, that many are damned afterwards. Now, such an atonement I *despise* — I reject it. I had rather believe a limited atonement that is *efficacious* for all for whom it was intended, than an universal atonement that is not efficacious for anybody, except the will of man be joined with it. Why, my brethren, if we were only so far atoned for by the death of Christ that any one of us might afterwards save himself, Christ's atonement were not worth a farthing, for there is no man of us can save himself — no, not under the Gospel" (C. H. Spurgeon on Isaiah 53:10).

But is not a true believing on the Lord Jesus Christ required *in order to* a receiving of God's great salvation? Certainly it is, but it is the office of the Holy Spirit to *give* saving faith to *every one* of those for whose sins Christ atoned. There is an infallible connection insured between the one and the other. The costly price of redemption was far too precious in the sight of God for it to be cast away on souls that perish. Therefore did He predestinate that the Spirit should communicate life to all for whom Christ died. "Who was delivered for our offences, and was raised again for our justification" (Rom. 4:25): that is clear enough—all whose "offences" Christ bore, *must be* "justified"! There are inseparable and saving benefits bestowed upon all them whom Christ loved and gave Himself for. "For if, when we were enemies, we were reconciled to God by the death of his Son, much more, being reconciled, we *shall be* saved by his life" (Rom. 5:10): these go together, hence, as the greater part of men are *not* "saved" by His life, that is proof positive that they were *not* "reconciled by His death."

"Christ hath redeemed us from the curse of the law . . . That we might receive the promise of the Spirit through faith" (Gal. 3:13, 14): to each of those whom He redeemed, Christ gives His Spirit. "For he hath made him to be sin for us, who knew no sin; that we might be made the righteousness of God in him" (II Cor. 5:21): as inevitably as Christ was "made sin" for those for whom He died, so inevitably must those for whom He was made sin be "made the righteousness of God in him"! "He that spared not his own Son, but delivered him up for *us* all, how shall he not with him *also* freely give us all things?" (Rom. 8:32): if God delivered up Christ for all mankind, then He will, He *must* to make good His word here, freely bestow (not "offer," but actually *"give"*) repentance, faith and every spiritual blessing to all mankind. It is this sure and certain connection between Christ's *purchase* of salvation and the actual *enjoyment thereof* by those for whom it was wrought, which the advocates of a universal redemption lose sight of. Hear that prince of the Puritans, John Owen:

"Redemption is the freeing of a man from misery by the intervention of a ransom. Now, when a ransom is paid for the liberty of a prisoner, does not justice *demand* that he should have and enjoy the liberty so purchased for him by a valuable consideration? If I should pay a thousand pounds for a man's deliverance from bondage to him that detains him, who hath power to set him free, and is contented with the price I give, were it not injurious to me and the poor prisoner that his deliverance be not accomplished? Can it possibly be conceived that there should be a redemption of men, and those men not redeemed? that a price should be paid, and the purchase not consummated? Yet all this must be made true, and innumerable other absurdities, if universal redemption be asserted. A price would be paid for all, yet few delivered; the redemption of all consummated, yet few of them redeemed; the judge satisfied, the jailer conquered, and yet the prisoners inthralled!"

The difference then, between truth and error on this vital subject, lies in the returning of scriptural answers to these questions: What was the purpose of God in the mission of Christ? Was it to make the salvation of all Adam's race possible? or was it to make the salvation of His own people certain? Was it simply to remove those "obstacles" which stood in the way of the Divine righteousness pardoning any one? or was it to remove the *sins* of those whom God had predestinated unto eternal glory? Was it simply to "open a way" whereby sinners *may* approach unto the Holy One? or did Christ die the Just for the unjust that "He might *bring us to God*" (I Pet. 3:18)? That the second of each of these alternatives is the true one, consider:

1. THE PURCHASE OF CHRIST

By the term "purchase" Scripture signifies that Christ meritoriously procured for His people the actual bestowment upon them of all those good things which He earned for them, which may be summed up under "life," "salvation," and an "eternal inheritance." Now these blessings were not purchased for His people "conditionally," but *absolutely*, just as when a surety pays a debt, the debtor is necessarily discharged, or as when a ransom is given for the redeeming of a captive, the captive must be freed. Christ's work was not of such a nature that the will of God is still *conditional* as to whether or not the reward of His satisfaction should be bestowed upon certain ones. No, He has *absolutely* obtained for His people peace with God and the remission of their sins, and that by purchasing for them that very faith with which they believe, appropriate and enjoy the salvation which He wrought out for them.

Scripture is most explicit in demonstrating that Christ's purchase and the Spirit's application of the purchased blessings have for their objects the *same* individuals: that for whomsoever Christ obtained any spiritual blessings by His death, unto them it shall most certainly be communicated. For whomsoever He wrought reconciliation *with* God, in them doth He (by His Spirit) work reconciliation *unto* God. The one is not extended to any to whom the other does not reach. It is true that no sinner obtains any of the saving benefits of Christ's satisfaction until he repents and believes, but it is equally true that Christ has purchased these very graces for His people, and is now exalted on High to administer them: Acts 5:31, etc. The Scriptures perpetually conjoin together the benefits *purchased* by Christ and the benefits *bestowed* on those for whom they were purchased, so that we cannot sever the one from the other. "The chastisement of *our* peace was upon him, and with his stripes *we* are healed" (Isa. 53:5): His chastisement and our peace, His wounding and our healing, are inseparably associated.

Thus the *design* of Christ's satisfaction is infallibly made known by the *results* of it. The intendment of God *in* the atonement is plainly evident through what is accomplished *by* it, for whatsoever He has purposed must be effected (Isa. 46:10); hence, what *is* secured by the sacrifice of Christ makes manifest what God planned it *should* procure. "If there be anything plainly taught in Scripture, it is that the sacrifice of Christ was made for those only who shall eventually be saved by it. If the wisdom of men cannot reconcile this with *their* views of what is right, let them be prepared to dispute the matter with the Almighty in the day of Judgment" (Alex. Carson).

2. THE RECTITUDE OF THE DIVINE CHARACTER

God's justice indispensably requires that all the benefits of Christ's sacrifice should be imputed and imparted to every one for whom it was offered and accepted. "Shall not the Judge of all the earth do right?" A God of truth, and without iniquity, just and right is He. The Supreme Being gives to every one his due. This principle cannot be violated in a single instance. He cannot, according to this, either remit sin without satisfaction, or punish sin where satisfaction for it has been received. The one is as inconsistent with perfect equity as the other. If the punishment for sin has been borne, the remission of the offence follows of course. The principles of rectitude suppose this, nay peremptorily demand it: justice could not be satisfied without it. Agreeably to this it follows that, the death of Christ being a legal satisfaction for sin, *all* for whom He died *must* enjoy the remission of their offences.

"It is as much at variance with strict justice or equity that any for whom Christ has given satisfaction should continue under condemnation, as that they should have been delivered from guilt without satisfaction being given for them at all. But it is admitted that all are not delivered from the punishment of sin, that there are many who perish in final condemnation. We are therefore compelled to infer, that for such no satisfaction has been given to the claims of infinite justice — no atonement has been made. If this is denied, the monstrous impossibility must be maintained, that the infallible Judge refuses to remit the punishment of some for whose offences He has received a full compensation; that He finally condemns some, the price of whose deliverance from condemnation has been paid to Him; that, with regard to the sins of some of mankind, He seeks satisfaction in their personal punishment after having obtained satisfaction for them in the sufferings of Christ; that is to say, that an infinitely righteous God takes double payment for the same debt, double satisfaction for the same offence, first from the Surety, and then from those for whom the Surety stood. It is needless to add that these conclusions are revolting to every right feeling of equity, and must be totally inapplicable to the procedure of Him who 'loveth righteousness and hateth wickedness'" (W. Symington).

Christ made full satisfaction unto the law of God (Matt. 5:17; Gal. 4:4, 5), but how could He have made satisfaction for the sins of those on whom the law will take satisfaction for ever? How can the justice of God have been appeased in the case of those against whom its flaming sword will awake to all eternity? Christ expiated offences (Rom. 4:25), but how can those offences for which the guilty perpetrators shall suffer endlessly, have been expiated? How did Christ redeem from the curse of the law (Gal. 3:13) those who are to be kept in everlasting thraldom and misery? This scheme postulates a Saviour of those who are never saved, a Redeemer of those who are never redeemed, a Deliverer of millions who are never delivered.

To reply to the above by saying that, Christ made a sufficient atonement for the sins of all men universally, but that many are not saved by it because they *trust not* in it, is to lose sight of the fact that half of the human race have never heard the Gospel, and so *could not* believe it! Whatever blame may rest upon Christians for their dilatoriness and selfishness, the Holy Spirit would most certainly have stirred up some to carry the glad tidings to those who have perished in heathen darkness *had* Christ purchased their salvation. To say otherwise would be rank blasphemy. The special mission *of* the Spirit is *to* apply the saving benefits of Christ's salvation to *all* for whom it was made. The One who is able to "raise up children" out of "stones" (Matt. 3:9) *cannot* be checkmated by the coldheartedness of His people.

3. THE DECLARATIONS OF HOLY WRIT

As we have shown in previous chapters, the Satisfaction of Christ had its origin in the sovereign will of God, hence His mere good pleasure decided and determined *who* should be saved by it. A favored section of Adam's race were chosen to be its beneficiaries: herein, we behold the "goodness" of God. Fallen angels and the remainder of Adam's family were not to be redeemed by it, but were predestinated to suffer the due reward of their iniquity: therein we behold the "severity of God" (Rom. 11:22)! The same contrastive principles are adumbrated in the material creation: nature, no more than Scripture, knows anything of a God who is mighty to save and yet not mighty also to destroy—witness tidal waves, tornadoes, earthquakes, famines and pestilences.

In keeping with what has just been said, we find that Scripture divides mankind into two classes: the Church and the world, the "friends" of God and His "enemies," the "sheep" and the "goats." And let it be properly noted that whatever is affirmed distinctly of the one class, is implicitly denied of the other. Every assertion that Christ died for "His people," is a repudiation of the theory that He died for all mankind. Just as when it is said that a certain man toils to provide food for his family, no one is foolish enough to conclude that he is *also* laboring to provide food for all mankind; so when the Word declares that Christ "loved the Church and gave himself for it" (Eph. 5:25), all should see that such discriminative language is meaningless, if He also loved and gave Himself for the entire human race.

"Not every one that saith unto me, Lord, Lord, shall enter into the kingdom of heaven; but he that doeth the will of my Father which is in heaven. Many will say to me in that day, Lord, Lord, have we not prophesied in thy name? and in thy name have cast out demons? and in thy name done many wonderful works? And then will I profess unto them, I never knew you: depart from me, ye that work iniquity" (Matt. 7: 21-23). Here a broad line of distinction is drawn between two classes of the human family, with respect to one of which the Saviour makes the solemn affirmation, "I *never knew* you." The import of those words, according to Scripture usage, is too plain to be misunderstood; the antithetical "The Lord *knoweth them that are his*" (II Tim. 2:19), shows that He *never* had a *saving cognizance* of those to whom He shall say "depart from me."

"Our Lord speaking of those for whom He died, calls them sheep: 'I lay down my life for the sheep' (John 10:15). He explains who His sheep are by saying that they are such persons as 'hear his voice and follow him' (vv. 3, 4), and He adds, 'I give unto them eternal life, and they shall never perish.' Does it not plainly follow from His words that those for whom He died *shall be* saved, that He died for none but those upon whom the gift of faith should be bestowed? And does He not signify, by particularizing them as the persons for whom He laid down His life, that He did *not die* for others of an opposite character? If He died for all, there would be no meaning in saying that He died for His 'sheep,' because in this case there would be nothing *peculiar to them,* nothing by which they were distinguished from any other description of men" (J. Dick, 1850). To this we may add, the name "sheep" is synonymous with "elect," for such are "sheep" *before* they believe, yea, before they are born (see John 10:16); and that in this very same passage Christ affirmed there were some who are *not* His "sheep"—*see* 10:26.

"*All* that the Father giveth me *shall* come to me" (John 6:37): but this would not be true if the enmity of the carnal mind, the stubbornness of the unrenewed will, or the oppositions of Satan, were able successfully to resist the "drawing" (John 6:44) of the Father! Christ expressly said, "I pray *not* for the world" (John 17:9), therefore He *died not* for the world, for His sacrifice and His intercession have *the same* objects: (Rom. 8:34). "Feed *the Church* of God which He hath purchased with His own blood" (Acts 20:28): if the atonement be of universal extent, if Christ's blood be shed for all, then such discriminating language would not only be unnecessary, but altogether misleading. "The Son of man came not to be ministered unto, but to minister, and to give His life a ransom for *many*" (Matt. 20:28): *no* satisfactory reason can be given why Christ should say only "many" if all mankind were also included: cf. Hebrews 9:28. "Who gave himself *for us,* that he might redeem us from all iniquity and purify unto himself a peculiar people, zealous of good works" (Titus 2:14): those for whom Christ died are "a *peculiar people,*" and not the whole Adamic race indiscriminately.

Those passages which are appealed to by those who advocate the doctrine of universal redemption will be carefully considered in the next chapter.

CHAPTER TWENTY

THE ATONEMENT—ITS EXTENT (CONCLUDED)

That aspect of our subject which is now before us has been a vexing question among theologians, especially so during the last century, for Christ's death for God's people only was never denied till the basic truth of Election was rejected; and that rejection only became common about one hundred and fifty years ago. Were it not so vitally important that we should be quite clear about this branch of our theme, we should avoid the discussion of it as too controversial. But inasmuch as the extent of the Atonement depends upon its *nature,* and directly concerns the honor of God and the glory of His Son, we feel called upon to give our best attention to the same.

In our last chapter we endeavored to present some of the evidences which prove that the atonement of Christ was a *real* one, a *definite* one, an *efficacious* one, that whatsoever it was designed to effect must be accomplished. Appeal too was made to some of those Scriptures which expressly make known for *whom* Christ died, namely, His "Church," His "people," the "sheep." Yet clear and plain, full and frequent, as are the declarations of Holy Writ concerning the purpose and design of God in the death of Christ, so that he who runs ought to be able to read, yet, scarcely any truth of Scripture is now more frequently called into question than is this one. A theory diametrically opposed thereto has been advanced by the enemies of the Truth, and, sad to say, is now being promulgated by many who imagine they are the friends of Christ—as to whether or not they are, God alone can infallibly determine.

On practically every side where there is any pretense of honoring Christ today, it is taught that the love of God extends to all mankind, that Christ gave Himself a ransom for the whole human race, and that the Holy Spirit is now seeking to woo and win every sinner to Him. So uniform has this preaching become, so fervently has it been advocated, so widely has it been accepted, that for any one to affirm the contrary, is to be looked upon as a setter forth of "novelties," and for him to *press* the same, is to invite his being denounced as a narrow-minded and harsh-hearted bigot, a heretic of the worst sort. Yet such an one can always console himself with, "If I yet pleased men, I should not be the servant of Christ" (Gal. 1:10).

Ere we turn and examine those passages which are appealed to by those who proclaim a universal redemption, three things should be carefully considered. First, since all of Adam's race are not pardoned and saved, and never will be, then Christ cannot have made an atonement for their sins: this was shown at length in our last chapter. Second, the Holy Scriptures cannot contradict themselves. Being the inspired Word of God, there cannot be any inconsistencies in them: they cannot teach that Christ died for God's elect only, and also affirm that He died for all mankind as well: one or the other is an erroneous deduction which men have drawn from them. Third, seeing they explicitly teach the former, then there must be some honest and legitimate way of interpreting those passages which may, at first glance, seem to teach the latter.

Now the Word of God does not yield up its meaning to lazy people. Salvation is free; but "Truth" has to be "bought" (Prov. 23:23); yet few indeed are willing to pay its stipulated price. Not only do the Scriptures have to be "searched" (John 5:39), and searched "daily" (Acts 17:11); not only does passage have to be carefully compared with passage (I Cor. 2:13); not only must all this be done in meekness (Psa. 25:9) and complete dependency upon God (Prov. 3:6); but there must be a fervent crying "after knowledge" and an importunate "lifting up of the voice for understanding," and seeking her "as silver" (which entails hard labour and diligent perseverance), yea, a searching for her as for "hid treasure" (Prov. 2:1-5).

It is at the above point that so many have failed. The meaning of God's Word cannot be ascertained as easily as can that of a newspaper article, nor can any enter into the "*mystery* of the Gospel" (Eph. 6:19) as readily as one may solve a problem in mathematics. If a person approaches Holy Writ with prejudice, his mind is closed against *its* teachings. If he regards any passage as plain and simple and is satisfied that he already understands it, he is not likely to cry unto God for or receive light from it. If he assumes that he is now in possession of practically all that the Bible teaches on a subject (contrary to I Cor. 8:2), or blindly follows some man unto whom he credits the same thing, then God will take the wise in their own craftiness (I Cor. 3:19) and suffer them to remain in darkness. It is because of this that so many are misled by the mere *sound* of certain words.

Our last statement has received many a solemn illustration. Take the controversy which has been waged in certain quarters as to whether or not man remains in a state of consciousness after he passes out of this world. How many who deny that he *does* so, have appealed to such passages as "the dead praise not the Lord" (Psa. 115:17), "the dead know not any thing" (Eccl. 9:5). But the matter cannot be settled so easily. Those passages must be studied in the light of their contexts, the dispensation under which they were given, and then interpreted in harmony with other passages of a different, but not conflicting, nature. Take again the great controversy between the Reformers on transubstantiation: how easy it was to be deceived by the mere *sound* of those words, "This *is* my body!" The same principle applies to our present subject. This issue cannot be settled by an appeal to such words as "God so loved *the world*" and Christ "died for *all*" (II Cor. 5:15). Such expressions need to be *studied* and interpreted in keeping with the Analogy of Faith.

Incalculable damage has been wrought by unequipped men undertaking to preach the "simple (?) Gospel" and expound the Holy Scripture. There has been a zeal which was not proportioned with spiritual knowledge. Men with the merest smattering of Scripture consider themselves qualified to pass judgment on the teachings and writings of those who have devoted a lifetime to the continuous and concentrated study of God's Word. To a multitude of evangelists and preachers of today, we would say, "O that ye would altogether hold your peace! and it should be your wisdom" (Job 13:5). Rightly has it been said, "Modern theology is largely based upon the sound rather than the sense of Scripture. And it is an everyday practice for men to expound texts who cannot even quote—much less expound—the contexts" (J. M. Sangar). "Not a novice" (I Tim. 3:6) has been deliberately ignored, and "Be not many of you teachers" (James 3:1, R. V.) has been defiantly disobeyed.

When men say that God has provided an atonement which is designed for all mankind, they need to be asked, Do you mean that Christ's sacrifice procured for all sinners that quickening grace of the Holy Spirit which is indispensably needed to bring men to a cordial and saving reception of the atonement? Do you mean that an atonement has been made by Christ so as to infallibly secure that all shall be saved by it? If so, be honest, and declare yourself a "Universalist." But if you do not mean this, then cease using empty words which can only deceive souls and dishonor Christ. The real issue is not so much upon the scope of the atonement, as it is upon the *efficacy* of it!

Let us now briefly set forth that position which is popularly maintained in these degenerate times. We are told that there is such a *fulness* in the atonement, that the value of Christ's sacrifice is *sufficient* for the salvation of the entire race, were all men to believe in Him. But this means that the sufficiency of the atonement is a *conditional* one—conditional upon the whole world believing. But that "condition" is not so easily performed. Almost all preachers today speak of faith in Christ as a comparatively easy matter, but the Scriptures teach quite otherwise: *see* Matthew 19:25, 26; John 5:44; 6:44; Ephesians 1:19; I Peter 4:18. The Word of God represents the fallen children of Adam as being spiritually bound with chains, shut up in death, securely held in prison, so that nothing short of a *miracle* of grace, the putting forth of Divine omnipotence can free them. In his masterly treatise on "Particular Redemption" W. Rushton (1831) illustrated this *conditional* sufficiency of the atonement thus:

"A wealthy and philanthropic individual visits Algiers and approaches a dungeon in which a wretched captive lies bound with chains and fetters, and strongly secured within walls and doors and bars. He proclaims aloud to the captive that he has brought gold *sufficient* for a ransom, on condition that the captive will liberate himself from his chains, burst open his prison doors and come forth. Alas, exclaims the wretched man, your kindness *does not reach* my case. Unless your gold can *effect* my deliverance, it can be of no service to me. To *offer* it on *such* terms can do me no good. Now man by nature is *spiritually* as unable to believe in Christ, as the Algerian captive is *physically* unable to break his chains and the prison doors; so that all this boasted sufficiency of the atonement is only an empty offer of salvation on certain terms and conditions; and *such* an atonement would be much too weak to meet the desperate case of a *lost* sinner.

"But how different is *the salvation of God!* 'By the blood of thy covenant, I have *sent forth* thy prisoners out of the pit wherein is no water' (Zech. 9:11). The Lord Jesus, by His death, hath paid the ransom, and made the captive His own. Therefore He has a *legal right* to their persons, and with His own right arm He brings them forth. It is His glory 'to *bring out* the prisoners from the prison, and them that sit in darkness *out of* the prison house' (Isa. 42:6, 7)." Yes, Scripture affirms that "He *sent* [not 'offered!'] redemption unto his people" (Psa. 111:9).

Turning now to the principal passages to which holders of this view, appeal, let us begin with John 3:16: "For God so loved the world that he gave his only begotten Son," etc. To a superficial mind this declaration appears to settle the controversy once for all. We do not use that term "superficial" in any invidious sense, but common honesty will not allow us to substitute another for it. Anyone who has examined a concordance and looked up the passages where "world" occurs, soon discovers that this word is used in the New Testament in quite a number of ways and with widely different latitudes, so that nothing can be determined for certain by the occurrence of this term in John 3:16. Sometimes the "world" signifies the unbelieving as in John 15:18, in others it includes none but believers as in Romans 11:12, etc. Sometimes the "world" denotes the material system, created by Christ (John 1:10), in others it is applied to a mere handful of people as in John 7:4 and 12:19. In the great majority of instances it is a general and indefinite expression which has reference to *the Gentiles* in contradistinction from Israel after the flesh.

Now it is a fundamental and unvarying rule of interpretation that both definite and indefinite phrases or terms must be understood and defined in strict accordance with *the subject* about which they are employed. So it is with John 3:16. The subject of that verse is *the love of God*, to which the indefinite expressions "world" and "whosoever" are joined. Therefore, if we would discover to a certainty *who* are the objects of God's love, we have to diligently compare and examine other passages where the love of God is mentioned. Then we learn that His love is *eternal*: Jeremiah 31:3; Ephesians 1:4, 5. That it is *uninfluenced*. Nothing in its object calls it into exercise, prompts or attracts it (Deut. 7:7, 8): it proceeds simply from the spontaneous will of God. It is *immutable* or unchanging (Song of Sol. 8:6, 7). Those whom God loves, He loves forever (John 13:1), *nothing* can ever separate from it, nothing can ever cause God to cease loving those on whom He set His love (Rom. 8:35-38). It is *sovereign* (Rom. 9:13): there was no more cause in Jacob why *he* should be the object of the Divine love, than there was in Esau.

The love of God is known by its *manifested* effects. There is an infallible connection (as there is between cause and effect) between the *love* of God and His *ordination* of its objects to life and salvation: hence we read, "We are bound to give thanks always to God for you, brethren *beloved of the Lord,* because God hath from the beginning *chosen you to salvation*" (II Thess. 2:13). So also, those whom God loves, He regenerates. "Behold, what manner of *love* the Father hath bestowed upon us, that we should be called the *sons* of God" (I John 3:1)—making them "sons" is the certain effect of His having loved them from all eternity. Those whom God loves, He "draws" to Himself (Jer. 31:3). Those whom God loves, He "chastens" (disciplines) so that they become actual "*partakers* of his holiness" (Heb. 12:6, 10). It therefore follows that those who are *not* made His "sons," who are not made "partakers of his holiness," were never the objects of His love.

The same love of God which was the cause of sending Christ to die for the salvation of His people, is *also* the same cause which "freely gives" all things *with* Christ (Rom. 8:32), i.e., the Spirit to regenerate, faith to receive Him, love to be devoted to Him: compare II Peter 1:3. Were it otherwise, God's love would be incomplete, inadequate, deficient, unefficacious. God's love for me would be vain, if it did not actually save me, deliver me, and win my heart to Him. John 3:16 simply states that *design* of God's love, and that is, that all who *believe* in Christ should be saved by Him, which believers, in their unbelieving state, are found "scattered abroad" (John 11:52) throughout the earth, among the Gentiles as well as the Jews.

The popular interpretation of John 3:16 is repudiated by all the *facts* of history. First, take the history of the human race *before* Christ was born. Unnumbered millions lived and died "*without* God and without hope" (Psa. 9:17). If God "loved" *them,* where is the least evidence of it? He "suffered all nations to walk in *their own* ways" (Acts 14:16). He "gave them over to a reprobate mind" (Rom. 1:28). He announced to Israel "you *only* have I known of all the families of the earth" (Amos 3:2). Second, take the history of the race *since* Christ was born. Remember the "dark ages" which lasted not for a few days, but for a thousand years, when the Papacy dominated almost all Christendom and the Bible was withheld from the peoples. And since the great Reformation, what untold millions have died in heathendom without ever hearing of Christ! It would be inexplicably strange if God should "love" multitudes to whom He never so much as *signified* His love — leaving them in entire ignorance of the Son of His love! Third, take the coming Day of Judgment. To whom will God's *love* then be exercised?

To sum up our comments on John 3:16. We understand "the world" here to mean men of *all nations,* with an especial reference to the Gentiles, whom Nicodemus (as all Jews) considered to be accursed. To those who reject this explanation, and say, We keep by the plain declaration "God so loved the world," we ask them to apply the same principle to the following passages: "on *the Gentiles* also was poured out the gift of the Holy Spirit" (Acts 10:45), "God also *to the Gentiles* granted repentance unto life" (Acts 11:18), "declaring the conversion of *the Gentiles*" (Acts 15:3). Is that expression "the

Gentiles" in these passages a general and indefinite one, or a universal and specific one? is it a relative or an absolute one? That is, does it take in *all*, or refer only to *some?* Acts 15:44 answers the question: "God has visited the Gentiles to *take out of them* a people for his name!"

The last clause of II Peter 3:9 is frequently quoted, but without any attention being given to the first part of it. Is that honest? The "*any*" whom the Lord is "not willing" should perish, is clearly defined: verse 8 shows that it is God's "beloved" who are here addressed and referred to. The "promise" which He is "*not* slack" in fulfilling, has reference to the return of Christ (v. 4), which "scoffers" (v. 3) suppose will never be fulfilled. The great reason why God has not yet sent back His Son is because the last of His elect have not been regenerated: all of *them* shall come to repentance before human history can be wound up and verse 10 fulfilled. Thus, the "any" looks back to the "us-ward" in the previous part of the verse!

"Behold the Lamb of God, which taketh away the sin of the world" (John 1:29). John the Baptist was the herald of a new dispensation. One of the leading distinctions between the Old and New Testament dispensations was with regard to its *scope*. The former was greatly restricted, being, for two thousand years, almost exclusively confined to a single nation; and to that limitation the members of the Church had become thoroughly accustomed. But the new dispensation possessed an opposite character. At the cross, the "middle wall of partition," by which the Jews were kept separate from all other nations, was broken down, so that henceforth there should be no difference between Jew and Gentile, bond and free. But the previous regime had given rise to a deeply-seated prejudice in favor of exclusive privilege, which it was no easy matter to uproot.

Although the Saviour had manifested a regard for a Roman centurion, a woman of Samaria, and had even plainly declared "other sheep I have which are not of this fold" (John 10:16), still the exclusive sentiment retained a firm hold even upon the minds of His disciples. They were Jews, and were manifestly reluctant to descend to a common level with others, in regard to the enjoyment of religious privilege. Clear proof of this is seen in the case of Peter (Acts 10:14): God had to work a miracle before he was willing to preach the Gospel to Cornelius. The jealous antipathy of the Jews comes out even more noticeably in I Thessalonians 2:15, 16. This one consideration accounts for and throws much light upon the use of terms of an *extensive* import when speaking of the *new* economy. To mark the contrast from Judaism, the strongest language that could be used became necessary: hence the employment of "the world" and "all men" to denote men in general without regard to national distinction.

From what has been said above, it is not to be surmised that the Holy Spirit moved men to employ language which was *not* strictly true or accurate. Far from it. Nothing is more common, either in the writings of men or in the Word of God, than to use a *general* designation when it is intended to express a general principle, but which does *not* include *every* individual comprehended in the general designation employed. When we read that a certain city is smitten with a small-pox epidemic, no one concludes that *every* individual in it has contracted that disease. So when we read in Exodus 9:6 that "*all* the cattle of Egypt died," we must not take those words absolutely, as Exodus 9:9, 19, 25 plainly show.

A critical examination of the terms of John 1:29 obliges us to take into account the undeniable fact that a very considerable portion of the human race was already in hell when the Son of God became incarnate. This one consideration is sufficient to show that we are *compelled* to understand that the "world" here is far less extensive in its scope than the whole human family. Again, that Christ *did not* "take away the sin of," bear the guilt of, suffer for, the iniquities of all alive on earth in His own day, is abundantly clear from His own words to the Pharisees, "Ye shall die in your sins" (John 8:24 and cf. 9:41). The best commentary upon John 1:29 is the song of the redeemed, "Thou wast slain, and hast redeemed us to God by thy blood *out of every* kindred, and tongue, and people, and nation" (Rev. 5:9)!

"Who gave himself a ransom for all, to be testified in due time" (I Tim. 2:6). What has been said above concerning the signification of the term "world" when used in connection with the objects of God's love or the subjects of Christ's redemption, applies with equal force and pertinency to the word "all." That Christ gave Himself a ransom for "all" *without distinction* of nationality, social status, age or sex, is blessedly true; but to say that He died in the stead of "all" *without exception* cannot be maintained without involving the most palpable absurdities and contradictions. Nor is there anything elsewhere in Scripture which *obliges* us to give to "all" in this and similar verses an absolute and unlimited meaning.

The word "all" is employed in Scripture with considerable latitude and variety of meaning; very rarely indeed is it used without limitation. Mark 1:5 says that "*all* the land of Judea and they of Jerusalem were all baptized" of John, yet Luke 7:30 shows the Pharisees and lawyers were "not baptized of him." When the Saviour told His disciples that "ye shall be hated of *all* men for my name's sake" (Matt. 10:22), it is obvious that those who believed on Him must be excluded. When we read that "*all* men came unto" Christ (John 3:26), we can only understand that many of the Jews attended upon His ministry. When Christ declared He would "draw all unto" Himself (John 12:32), He had in mind the "all that the Father giveth me" of John 6:37. So here in I Timothy 2:6 the "ransom for all" is defined by the "ransom for many" of Matthew 20:28. The "all" of I Timothy 2:4 and 6 is simply emphasizing the *contrast from* the Jewish nation only.

I John 2:2. Here again many have been deceived by the mere sound of terms. The very first word of this verse shows that Christ is the "propitiation" of those *only* for whom He is an "Advocate with the Father," and John 17:9 proves that He prays for none but the elect. Again, if the closing words of this verse expressed an unlimited universality, then the previous clause would be quite superfluous: if the "whole world" takes in all the race, then it would be meaningless to say that Christ is the propitiation "for *our* sins" and *also* for every body's – the "our" would be included. Instead, the "our" refers to *Jewish* Christians, for John was an apostle to the "circumcision" (Gal. 2:9) and his epistle was written (first) to such (see 2:7); the "whole world" signifies God's elect scattered among the Gentiles. Romans 3:25 shows that Christ's "propitiation" is *limited to* those who put their faith in it.

Scripture always interprets Scripture: if the reader really desires to know the meaning of I John 2:2 let him compare John 11:51, 52 and 17:20, carefully noting the "also." That this expression the "whole world" is *not* an unlimited one, is clear from the last clause of Revelation 13:3, compared with Revelation 20:4; or Revelation 12:9 with Matthew 24:24. To affirm that Christ shed His blood for the sins of all mankind, is to be guilty of charging Him with rebellion against the sovereign will of God. But how far from the truth is such a concept! "Every part of our Lord's conduct on earth was an act of *obedience to* the Father's will (John 6:38). How then could He lay down His life for any but those who were given Him of the Father to be redeemed from among men? Had He laid down His life for all mankind, He would have *gone beyond* His commission" (James Haldane).

It remains to be pointed out that there is a (relative) universality to Christ's sacrifice in three respects. First, in *time*: its efficacy was not limited to one generation or dispensation. Being "foreordained before the foundation of the world" (I Pet. 1:20), His merits extended to *all* believers from Abel onwards. Second, in *place*: the efficacy of Christ's death was not to be limited to any one nation: Revelation 5:9. Third, in *virtue*: "The blood of Jesus Christ his Son cleanseth us from *all* sin" (I John 1:7). Christ's sacrifice made atonement for Noah's drunkenness, Lot's incest, David's murder, Peter's denial, Paul's persecution of the Church. In *these* three respects there is *no* limitation to His sacrifice.

Luke 19:41-44. Christ's weeping over Jerusalem is often regarded as His lamentation over lost sinners. Such was not the case. Verses 43, 44 show plainly that He had before Him the destruction of the city. As He foresaw the awful siege and contemplated the unparalelled temporal calamities, He was deeply moved. As a nation, the doom of the Jews was sealed: the things belonging to their civic peace were now hid from their eyes. But so far from their spiritual state being hopeless, or Christ bewailing *that*, He knew full well that in a few weeks at most thousands of them would believe to the saving of their souls!

Space will only allow us to notice briefly a few more texts.

The "all men" of Romans 5:18 is explained by I Corinthians 15:22. I Corinthians 8:11 asks a question, not states a fact: it warns against the evil *tendency* of uncharitable conduct. The "all" for whom Christ died (II Cor. 5:15) are in that same verse said to "live unto . . . him which died for them." The "world" of II Corinthians 5:19 are those unto whom God is "not imputing their trespasses," and that is certainly *not* the "world of the ungodly" (II Pet. 2:5). The "living God" of I Timothy 4:10 is the Father (see Matt. 16:16), and "Saviour" there means Preserver—in a temporal way. Christ "tasted death for every" (Heb. 2:9): there is *no* word for "man" in the Greek, and the next verse shows it is "every" *son*. That some whom the Lord "bought" (II Pet. 2:1) shall be damned, presents no difficulty: He *bought* "the field" (Matt. 13:43, 44), but "redeemed" only His people; as Man (Acts 17:31) He has acquired the *right* to judge and dispose of all.

To reason as some have done from the second half of Hebrews 9:26 that Christ made atonement for no man's sins in particular, but only for sin in general, is really too purile for serious consideration. Yet this is what is being taught in many places today. The Cross is looked upon as little more than an honoring of the moral government of God, a satisfying of His justice abstractly considered. Such a theory involves this absurdity: that Christ died not for *sinners,* but for *sin.* Sufficient to point out in refutation that "sin" has no existence apart from *sinners!* Sin is not a mere non-entity, or metaphysical abstraction, but a moral agent to which it belongs. Separate sin from sinners and it ceases to be. Surely the Son of God died for something else than a mere abstraction!

To say that in the atonement of Christ God has laid a sufficient and suitable basis for the salvation of all men, *if so be* they would avail themselves of it, may sound very plausible, yet is it, in reality, meaningless jargon. Such an assertion ignores the eternal and sovereign *election* of the Father. It *dissevers* the work of the Spirit from the work of Christ. It repudiates the lost condition of man. While professing to widen the extent of the atonement, it compromises its reality and efficacy. To say that everything turns on the sinner's acceptance, is to affirm that Christ did nothing more for those who are saved than He did for those who are lost. It is not faith which gives Divine efficacy to the blood; it was the blood which efficaciously purchased faith. To make the eternal salvation of sinners turn upon an act of their own wills, would not only be leaving the success of the redemptive work of Christ, contingent upon the fickle caprice of men, but would allow them to divide the honors with Christ!

To talk of God's "offering assistance to sinners" while He leaves them in a state of *un*-regeneracy, is the veriest trifling. To say that Christ died for all the sins of all who hear the Gospel, and that the *only* thing which can now damn them is their unbelief, is to fly in the face of Ephesians 5:5, 6, etc. Moreover, such a statement is, really, a contradiction in terms. Either their unbelief is a *sin,* or it is not. If *not,* then why are they punished for it? If it *be,* then, according to their own affirmation, Christ atoned for it, and there is nothing more in their unbelief than there is in their other sins to hinder them from partaking of the fruits of Christ's sacrifice. Let such choose which horn of the dilemma they please.

Seeing that Christ died for the elect only, *how* is the Gospel to be preached to sinners indiscriminately? This question will be carefully considered and answered at length in a following chapter.

CHAPTER TWENTY-ONE

The Atonement – Its Typification

Christ has been greatly dishonored and His atonement grievously misrepresented by the attempts which have often been made to illustrate it from supposed analogies in human relations. Rightly has it been said that, "The plan of redemption, the office of our Surety, and the satisfaction which He rendered to the claims of justice against us, have no parallel in the relations of men to one another. We are carried above the sphere of the highest relations of created beings into the august counsels of the eternal and independent God. Shall we bring *our* own line to measure *them?* We are in the presence of Father, Son and Holy Spirit; one in perfections, will and purpose. If the righteousness of the Father demands a sacrifice, the love of the Father provides it. But the Love of the Son runs parallel with that of the Father; and not only in the general undertaking, but in every act of it we see the Son's full and free consent" (*Waymarks in the Wilderness*, Vol. 6).

But while no parallel to the Great Transaction, or to the relation of the Father, Son and Holy Spirit to its accomplishment, can be found in any of the relations of mere creatures to one another, God has graciously adapted a series of *types,* historical and ceremonial, to the illustration of His wondrous plan, and especially to portray the various aspects of the office and work of Christ. In them the Divine wisdom is signally displayed, and it is the part of human wisdom to devote our closest attention to the same. By the typical system, God was not only educating His people for the "good things to come," but was also preparing human language to be a fit medium for the revelation of His grace in Christ. It is to the types we must turn if we would define aright the sacrificial terms of the New Testament.

But an impression obtains in some quarters that instruction by the types belongs to an inferior dispensation, and was only designed for the Church in the days of its infancy. Scripture teaches otherwise. It is true that "the typology of the Pentateuch is the Divine kindergarten," yet it is also true that "Whatsoever things were written aforetime were written for *our* learning" (Rom. 15:4), and that God's dealings with Israel were "*our* types" (I Cor. 10:6 margin). Yea, so far from the study of the types being an elementary one, Hebrews 5:10-12 shows that they furnish our "strong meat."

While it is true that the "typology of the Pentateuch is the Divine kindergarten," this does not mean either that the teaching of the types is to be lightly esteemed, or that the instruction which they furnish is inferior in quality to that which is given in the Epistles. No schoolchild is really qualified to take in the teaching of the higher grades until he is thoroughly familiar with and has more or less mastered the lessons of the lower grades. So none are fully equipped to receive the evangelical teachings of the New Testament, if the key-phrases of the Old Testament types are neglected. Not only has the sacrificial work of Christ as many aspects as there are great sacrifices in the Pentateuch, but the doctrinal statements of the Epistles are frequently couched in the language of the types, and can only be rightly interpreted in the light which they furnish.

"A type is something emblematic or symbolic, used to express, embody, represent or forecast, some person, truth or event. It is an image or similitude of something else, sustaining to doctrinal teaching some such relation as a picture does to a precept or promise, representing to the eye or imagination a concept addressed to the ear or understanding. It is one of the most frequent forms of figurative teaching in Scripture, but being sometimes more obscure than obvious demands keener insight and closer study" (A. T. Pierson). The types were prophecies, forecasts of things to come, and therefore do they furnish one of the most striking and conclusive proofs of the Divine inspiration of the Scriptures, for only He who knew the end from the beginning could have so accurately, so fully, and so marvelously anticipated and adumbrated Calvary thousands of years before Christ died.

"The Old Testament types were a mode of instruction of the way in which God was to be approached, and were peculiarly suited to the human mind struggling with a sense of guilt; and they have furnished to the Church of all times, a vocabulary or nomenclature, without which men could not with sufficient precision have been able to hold intercourse with each other on the subject of the Atonement. It deserves special notice that prophecy and the sacrifices are always found together, and throw light upon each other; and that they run in parallel lines through the entire Old Testament economy. Nay, the sacrifices may be regarded as a sort of prophecy, or a guarantee to which the veracity of God was pledged, for the shadow must one day be a reality" (Geo. Smeaton). "A type is a *prophetic symbol,* and since prophecy is the prerogative of Him who sees the end from the beginning, a real type, implying as it does a knowledge of the Reality, can only proceed from God" (Liddon's Bampton Lectures).

The Old Testament types supply incontrovertible evidence that the Gospel was no novel invention of New Testament times. When the risen Saviour would make known to His disciples the meaning of His death, we read that, "Beginning at Moses and all the prophets, he expounded unto them in all the scriptures the things concerning himself" (Luke 24:27). So far from the evangel of the apostle's being any (absolutely) new thing, every element in it was revealed long centuries before their birth, not only in words, but in visible representations: there was both a wondrous anticipation of and preparation for the Gospel. Thus a reverent contemplation of the types supplies a blessed confirmation of faith, for they attest the Divine authorship of both Testaments. Moreover, they stimulate adoration; even when we know a person, we enjoy looking at his picture; so here. It is *Christ* that is before us in them.

The *Divine* origin of sacrifice is self-evident. Whoever would have dreamed of the device of offering animal sacrifices to God as a method of acceptable worship? That Abel should have "brought of the firstlings of his flock and of the fat thereof" (Gen. 4:4), can only be satisfactorily accounted for on the ground that he knew this was what God required from him. And this is precisely what the New Testament affirms: Hebrews

11:4 declares that it was "by faith" that Abel offered his sacrifice, and Romans 10:17 says "faith cometh by hearing, and hearing by the word of God." Thus, Abel had received a revelation from God, and *believing* what he had "heard," acted accordingly. Moreover, the acceptance of Abel's sacrifice by a Divine testimony of approval (Gen. 4:4), which, no doubt, was given by the descent of consuming fire from heaven — Leviticus 9:24; Judges 6:21; I Kings 18:38 — intimate the same thing. *That* solemn testimony of reception would only have terrified the offerer, had he himself *invented* this mode of worship! "The lightning shooting round the altar, and consuming the victim, would have conveyed the impression of an angry God: how, then, could they have apprehended by this means that they were reconciled? How could they have known without a Divine revelation that this consuming fire was a token of Divine *acceptance*?" (G. Smeaton).

The great sacrifice of Christ was foreshadowed from the beginning. He who predestinated the salvation of His elect, did also appoint the means thereto: the Lamb was "foreordained before the foundation of the world" (I Pet. 1:20). Then what memorial could be devised more opposite than that of animal sacrifices? By such a means was exemplified the *death* which had been denounced upon man's disobedience, and in the shedding of the victim's blood and the violent character of its death, was portrayed something of the awfulness of that death which was the "wages of sin." At the same time a fit representation was also made of that death that was to be undergone by the Redeemer, and thus there was connected in one view the two cardinal facts in the history of men — the *fall* and *recovery* from it. The Old Testament sacrifices were a "showing forth of the Lord's death" till He came.

It is both important and blessed to note that the Gospel-covenant was revealed by God immediately after the Fall. The promise that the woman's Seed should bruise the serpent's head (Gen. 3:15) and the institution of the types (Gen. 3:21), were to the very end that faith and hope might be preserved in what God had so graciously purposed. God did not leave even our first parents in ignorance of His merciful designs, but made known the nature of His eternal counsels. Soon after, a further revelation was made unto Cain and Abel, and still later to others. The infinite wisdom of God so contrived the types that they might in the most intelligible manner (that material things can describe spiritual) signify the Redeemer, and life and salvation through Him. "From the time of the Fall, there has been but one way open to Heaven, and that was through Christ; and all believers, before and under the law, hoped for pardon of sin and salvation through Him. In hopes of that pardon and salvation they observed the typical services" (W. Romaine).

That the Old Testament saints perceived something at least of the mystical and spiritual meaning of the types is clear from a number of passages; that they had a much clearer and fuller apprehension of them than is commonly supposed, is the writer's firm conviction. The Lord Jesus declared that "Abraham rejoiced to see my day: and he saw, and was glad" (John 8:56). Hebrews 11:13 tells us that the patriarchs confessed themselves to be "strangers and pilgrims on the earth," which shows they knew that their true "inheritance" was in Heaven; while Hebrews 11:14, 16 expressly states they sought and desired "an heavenly" country. Job said, "I know that my Redeemer liveth" (19:25), and the Hebrew word there for "Redeemer" signifies one who is a redeemer by right of affinity or kinship—not only a Redeemer in act, but in office. So also David acknowledged, "my flesh longeth for thee . . . to see thy power and thy glory, so as I *have seen* thee in the sanctuary" (Psa. 63:2), that is, by means of the figures and shadows of the vessels of the tabernacle and the Levitical services and sacrifices.

"First the blade, then the ear and then the full corn in the ear" enunciates one of the principles of Divine work in everything, the types not excepted. The further we proceed, the profounder their meaning, and the fuller their detail. In the Divine clothing of our first parents with "coats of skins" (Gen. 3:21), there were illustrated the facts that: fallen man needed an external covering to fit him to stand before God; that he could not produce this by his own labors; that the life of an innocent victim must be taken, in order to provide a suitable covering for him; that God Himself must provide it. In the offering of Abel and God's acceptance of the same (Gen. 4:4), we learn that God can only regard any sinner with favor by virtue of his acceptance in Christ. The *Divine* origin of sacrifices is again intimated in that before flesh was eaten by man, the distinction between clean and unclean animals was quite familiar (Gen. 8:20). The power of an accepted sacrifice to remove the Divine curse was plainly signified in Genesis 8:21. The principle of substitution was strikingly manifested in Genesis 22:13.

What may be termed the first *great* sacrifice was the "Passover," recorded in Exodus 12. There we behold the efficacy of the Lamb's precious blood to deliver those sheltering beneath it from that judgment of God which their sins deserved. What virtue, an infidel might ask, had the blood of a poor animal to secure the life of Israel's first-born from the sword of a mighty and invisible angel? Was the blood on the door a necessary mark for the angel, because he had not understanding enough to distinguish between the houses of Egyptians and Israelites? Could not God have signified His pleasure to the angel without such a mark as that? The answer to these, and all such questions is, God's design was to furnish a type of *Christ,* and instruct the faith of His people in things to come.

The following is a bare outline of the point in the Passover-type which may be profitably studied by the reader. First, Divine judgment was pronounced: "*all* the firstborn [the representative of the family] *in* [not 'of'] the land of Egypt shall die" (Ex. 11:5). Second, God "put a difference between the Egyptians and Israel" so that not one of His own people were hurt (Ex. 11:7). Third, not by Israel's choice or Moses' recommendation, but by Divine appointment every Israelitish household was to take an unblemished lamb, kill it, and apply its blood to the outside of his house (Ex. 12:3-7). Fourth, the Divine promise was, "when I see the blood, I will pass over you" (Ex. 12:13). Fifth, the angel entered not such houses, for death had *already* done its work there — a substitute had been slain. Here is *redemption;* deliverance from judgment.

At Sinai God made known His will much more fully respecting the sacrifices which He required. A great deal of instruction therein is to be found in the first seven chapters of Leviticus, into most of which we cannot now enter: much deeply important teaching is to be found therein in a typical form. The Levitical sacrifices emphasized the enormity of sin and the punishment which must be visited upon it, as well as set forth the dependence of the forgiving grace of God on an expiatory offering. Under the Mosaic economy an elaborate system was developed to show that in many ways man offends God and is worthy of death. The sacrifices vividly evidenced the fact that the Divine punishment incurred was inevitable, yet that that punishment could be borne by a substitute, and on that ground the offender could be restored to favor. The principal thing they were designed to exhibit was the indispensable necessity of atonement by vicarious expiation: the one great truth they illustrated was that God could not sacrifice His holiness to His love.

That the Mosaic sacrifices all pointed forward to Christ and had their end in Him, was evidenced by the fact that very soon after He had come and shed His blood, God caused the shadows to pass away. Within a very few years the temple was destroyed, and with it all the Jewish sacrifices ceased. And though a century or two later Julian the Apostate gave the Jews permission to rebuild their temple, and that for the very purpose of restoring the ancient rites, yet God from Heaven blasted all their attempts in a miraculous and extraordinary manner.

The Levitical sacrifices made clear to men the ground on which the Divine pardon could be obtained. It was not an act of absolute mercy, nor was it bestowed on the sole condition of penitence, but on the consideration of something quite distinct from both. "And it shall be, when he shall be guilty in one of these things, that he shall confess that he hath sinned in that thing. And he shall bring his trespass offering unto the Lord for his sin . . . and the priest shall make an atonement for him concerning his sin . . . and it shall be forgiven him" (Lev. 5:5, 6, 10). If we compare these verses with Leviticus 17:11, which informs us that "it is the blood which maketh an atonement for the soul", then the proof is conclusive that the sacrifice presented by the offender was the appointed means of obtaining forgiveness for his transgression.

The burnt offering (Lev. 1) and the sin offering (Lev. 4) claim particular attention, for not only were *they* the most important sacrifices of the Levitical dispensation (as Psa. 40:6 intimates), but they represented the sufferings of our great High Priest under two distinct aspects. The burnt offering principally shows Christ as He was to God, the sin offering as He is to men. In both He was represented as a sin-bearer, for in both of these sacrifices transfer was made of sin by the priest laying his hand on the head of the victim (Lev. 1:4; 4:4); in both the victim's blood was shed and sprinkled (Lev. 1:5; 4:4-6); in both atonement was made for sin (1:4; 4:20); and both were burnt, either wholly or in part upon the altar (1:9; 4:9, 10). These points of union were sufficiently close to show that they corresponded in representing the sacrifice offered by our High Priest on the cross.

But there were also distinctive differences between them of a character sufficiently marked to show that they represented Christ's sacrifice under *different* aspects. Thus, the burnt offering was voluntary (Lev. 1:2, 3), the sin offering compulsory (Lev. 4:2, 3). The burnt offering was flayed, cut into pieces, and the inwards and legs washed in water; but none of these three things were required of the sin offering. The blood of the burnt offering was merely sprinkled round about upon the altar (1:11), but the blood of the sin offering was put upon the horns of the altar, sprinkled seven times before the Lord, before the veil of the sanctuary, and poured out at the bottom of the altar of burnt offering (4:6, 7). Other differences we now pass over, desiring to direct attention merely to the first one mentioned.

The *voluntariness* of Christ's death is clearly brought out in Psalm 40:7, 8 and Ephesians 5:25; John 10:17, 18 also shows He freely laid down His life for His sheep. But, when in the councils of eternity, ratified by the everlasting covenant "ordered in all things and sure," Christ had undertaken to be our Surety, *then* what was before purely free and voluntary became in a sense *compulsory*. Just as when God binds Himself by oath, He is obliged to fulfil His word, so Christ once He had bound Himself to stand in His peoples' place and stead, was no longer free — though, not that He wished to be free. Just as the type was bound with cords "unto the horns of the altar" (Psa. 118:27). so Christ was held fast to the Cross not only by love to His people, which floods could not quench, but by His own eternal covenant-engagement.

The substitution of Christ in the sinner's place was most distinctly shown in the types, particularly in the sin offering. Before the animal was slaughtered, the sacrificing priest laid his hand upon its head (Lev. 4:3, 4). That act represented the transferring of sin from the transgressor to the victim (Lev. 16:21): it identified the one with the other. It showed the substitution of the victim for the offender, and declared by a visible sign that it bare his sins and endured his death-penalty. In this way was the solemn yet blessed truth of *imputation* foreshadowed. It was because God transferred to Christ the guilt of His elect, constituting Him "sin for us," that the sword of Divine justice smote Him as He bare our sins in His own body on (or "to") the tree.

The most important of all the types is that which is found in Leviticus 16: the appointed ritual for the great day of atonement. The type of Leviticus 16 goes much farther than does the one in Exodus 12: the Passover illustrated the *redemptive* character of Christ's sacrifice; that of Leviticus 16 its *propitiatory* nature. In Exodus 12 we see the blood sheltering from judgment those who are under it; in the early chapters of Leviticus, we see the power of the blood restoring to communion the penitent transgressor; but in Leviticus 16 we behold the blood opening a way into the very presence of God, entitling the penitent and believing worshipper to come with boldness unto His very throne.

By a careful comparison of Deuteronomy 27 and Leviticus 16 we may discover how the law was, and still is, a "schoolmaster" unto Christ (Gal. 3:24). In the former chapter, we see that the law demanded implicit and complete obedience to its demands (v. 10); and how that the Levites pronounced with "a loud voice" a *curse* on the transgressor of it (vv. 14, 15). That curse was repeated twelve times, according to the number of Israel's tribes, and on each pronouncement thereof "all the people" were required to say "Amen": the final word being "Cursed be he that confirmeth not all the words of this law to do them" (v. 26)—cf. Galatians 3:10. The law required sinless perfection under the penalty of eternal damnation, and thus it revealed the imperative need of an *atonement*. While in

Leviticus 16 we see how that law by its great sin-offering, with its blood of atonement, pointed forward to Christ.

The sacrificial system of Judaism reached its climax on the great day of atonement. As the ark was the chief object in the tabernacle, so the annual Day of propitiation was the chief one in Israel's religious calendar. On that auspicious occasion the high priest divested himself of his robes of "glory and beauty" (Ex. 28), and put on "the holy linen" garments (Lev. 16:4). The spotless white in which he was clothed spoke of the perfect *righteousness* of Christ, which, tested as it was both by man (John 8:46) and Satan (John 14:30), and then passing through the infinitely searching scrutiny of God under the fiery trial of the cross, insured the Divine acceptance of that satisfaction which He made to God on behalf of His people.

Two young goats were selected "for a sin-offering"; though there were two animals, it was but one offering. Two goats were selected in order that a fuller representation might be given: the one being designed more expressly to exhibit the *means*, the other the *effect* of the atonement. They were brought and presented together before the Lord (v. 7), the Lord determining by lot which of them was to be slain. The other animal stood by and was atoned for (Hebrew of verse 10) by the dying victim, and then bore away the sins laid upon it into the land of eternal forgetfulness (vv. 21, 22): a blessed figure of that *remission* of our sins when we believe on the Lord Jesus Christ unto salvation.

Passing by what was done with the bullock, we confine our attention unto the two goats. After the one had been killed, the high priest took its blood within the veil and sprinkled it upon the mercy-seat not once, but seven times "before" Him to provide a *perfect* standing ground for His people. The antitype of this is seen in Hebrews 9:12, "But by his own blood he entered in once into the holy place, having obtained eternal redemption" (Heb. 9:12). The consequence of this is that "Having therefore, brethren, boldness to enter into the holiest by the blood of Jesus, by a new and living way which he hath consecrated for us" (Heb. 10:19, 20).

After the high priest had finished his work inside the sanctuary, we are told, "he shall bring the live goat, and Aaron shall lay both his hands upon the head of the live goat and confess over him all the iniquities of the children of Israel . . . and shall send him away by the hand of a fit man into the wilderness: and the goat shall bear upon him all their iniquities into a land not inhabited" (vv. 20-22). That was a continuation and completion of the ceremony concerning the sin-offering, so that this symbolic transfer of their sins to the head of the scapegoat, which bore them away, plainly signified that the atonement effected by the sacrifice of the first goat was the complete removal of all their transgressions from before the face of God.

"And Aaron shall come into the tabernacle of the congregation, and shall put off the linen garments, which he put on when he went into the holy place, and shall *leave* them there" (Lev. 16:23). Why? To denote that his work was *finished*. The blessed antitype of this we see in Luke 24:12: on the resurrection morning, those who came to Christ's empty sepulchre "beheld the *linen clothes*" lying there, a token that He was risen from the dead, and so of atonement completed, and accepted by God.

One other important feature in the types, often overlooked, claims our notice, namely, the *burning* of the victim's body on the altar (Lev. 1:10 etc.). The animal was first slain as a just judgment for the sin which had been transferred to it by the laying on its head of the hand of the offerer; and then, after guilt had been borne, its flesh was laid on the altar and burned, and went up with acceptance unto God, a "sweet-smelling savour." In this was represented the glorious truth that, not only was Christ our sin-bearer, but that He is also our *righteousness* before God (Jer. 23:6; II Cor. 5:21). We are identified with Him not only in His *death* for us, but also in the *fragrance* of it before God.

In Numbers 19 there is yet another most important type upon which we can only now say a few words. In it we see how the death of Christ has made full provision for those defilements which His people contract while passing through this evil world. In it too we behold again the steady progress in the types, and the deeper instruction which God gave to Israel from time to time. They were yet in the land of Pharaoh when the passover was instituted: the doom of Egypt and their own deliverance therefrom were the thoughts then presented to their souls. Later, they were brought nigh to God, Himself tabernacling in their midst, and in Leviticus 16 they are shown the high demands of His holiness. Now in Numbers 19, they are taught that even the unavoidable contact with death (the world lying in the Wicked one) defiles. But God has provided cleansing from it.

In closing, we call attention to one other deeply important value of the types and the use to which they may be put: they furnish an infallible rule by which can be *tested* any man's (our own included) *interpretation* of the New Testament Scriptures concerning the Atonement! He who denies the penal and vicarious nature of Christ's death, repudiates the clear testimony of the types; he who sets aside the efficacy of His sacrifice by reducing it to a merely "making possible" the salvation of men does likewise, for the types know nothing of an ineffectual sacrifice. So too in them we see plainly the *limitation* of God's love to His elect people, for no lamb was provided for the Egyptians, nor did Aaron make any atonement for the sins of the Midianites and Ammonites!

CHAPTER TWENTY-TWO

The Atonement — Its Proclamation

We have now arrived at what is, from some standpoints, the most difficult aspect of our subject. Exactly what is it which the servant of God ought to preach? Or, more specifically, what constitutes the main item in his message to the unsaved, and in what is he to instruct the saints? To many it appears that he who clearly apprehends the limitation of God's love to His elect, and the satisfaction of Christ being made for them only, is to be fettered in the preaching of the Gospel; yea, not a few suppose that if a preacher really believes such doctrines as these, he will have no message at all for the unsaved. But such is far from being the case: those who draw such conclusions err grievously. No honest mind can ponder the epistles of Paul without seeing that he believed firmly in the sovereign love and discriminating grace of God, and the restricted design of the atonement; yet none can read through the Acts without discovering that the same Paul was a most zealous evangelist and preached a Gospel which was as free as the air we breathe.

That Christ died only for those who shall be infallibly saved, is a doctrine which seems to have an adverse bearing towards the world at large, and to embarrass the free proclamation of the Gospel. A feeling arises that there is something very much like an inconsistency or incompatibility between the restricted design and efficacy of the Great Propitiation to a predetermined and limited number of the race, and the commission which Christ has given to His servants. In seeking to grapple with this difficulty, let us begin by inquiring, Is an *un*-limited atonement necessary in order to warrant ministers of the Gospel tendering Divine pardon to all men without exception, and inviting and exhorting them to come to Christ? In seeking answer to this question, it should be evident that our conduct in preaching the

Gospel and addressing our fellowmen with a view to their salvation, should not be regulated by any *inferences* of *our own* from the nature and extent of the provision actually made for saving them, but is to be governed solely by the instructions which *God has given.* It is not for us to reason and argue, but to *obey.*

The commission which Christ has given to His servants is too plain to be misunderstood. They are commanded to "preach the Gospel to every creature" (Mark 16:15). They are required to proclaim to their fellow-men, of whatever character, and in all variety of circumstances, glad tidings of great joy. They are bidden to preach "repentance and remission of sins" in His name "among all nations" (Luke 24:47). They are enjoined to say, "All things are ready, come unto the marriage," and to go forth into the very highways, and as many as they shall find "bid to the marriage" (Matt. 22:4, 9). They are to invite men to come to Christ, and beseech their hearers to be "reconciled to God" (II Cor. 5:20). They are to freely announce that, "The Gospel of Christ is the power of God unto salvation *to every one that believeth*" (Rom. 1:16), and that "*whosoever* shall call upon the name of the Lord shall be saved" (Rom. 10:13). Nothing could be clearer than this, and no philosophical reasonings or theological sophistries must be allowed to negative their marching-orders.

God's *revealed* will is our only rule to walk by, and must ever be held as sufficient warrant for all that we do. In seeking to know our duty as to whom we should preach and as to what we are to say unto our fellow-men, Holy Writ is to be our sole guide and authority. Denominational customs, creedal prejudices, the example of eminent preachers, are no criterion at all. "To the Law and to the Testimony" (Isa. 8:20), must be our one and only recourse. Our business is to "preach the Word" (II Tim. 4:2), leaving God to apply it according to His eternal purpose. We are to "sow beside *all* waters" (Isa. 32:20). Thus our duty is clearly defined. Like the Sower in the parable (Matt. 13), we are to scatter the Seed on the stony as well as on the good ground.

The servants of God are to "preach the Gospel" (Mark 16:15), which is a proclamation of mercy through Christ. The

Gospel is a Divine revelation of the way of salvation by free grace through the Lord Jesus. It announces deliverance from condemnation and the bestowment of eternal life upon all who comply with its terms. The Gospel presents not a system of philosophy, but the person of the God-man as the Object *of faith.* It makes known how the thrice holy God may be just and yet the Justifier of lawbreaking sinners. The things of our eternal concernment are therein proposed to us. A compliance with this Divine revelation is made of "repentance toward God and faith toward our Lord Jesus Christ" (Acts 20:21). Remission of sins is freely promised to *all* who thus comply with it. But it also implies and denounces tidings of the very opposite nature to all who neglect it: "he that believeth not shall be damned" (Mark 16:16); "the Lord Jesus shall be revealed from heaven with His mighty angels, in flaming fire taking vengeance on them that know not God, and that *obey not the Gospel*" (II Thess. 1:7, 8).

Now in preaching the Gospel to a single individual (which is, usually, more difficult than preaching to a crowd) it is in nowise necessary to say to him, Christ died for *you,* He bore *your* sins on the Cross. Neither the Lord Jesus nor the apostles adopted such a mode of procedure. Take one pertinent illustration from each of them. In His discourse to Nicodemus, Christ did not say, "As Moses lifted up the serpent in the wilderness even so shall the Son of man be lifted up *for you,*" but "even so shall the Son of man be lifted up that whosoever *believeth in him* should not perish" (John 3:14), thus pressing the responsibility of His hearer. So too when the Philippian jailer cried, "What must I do to be saved?" Paul said, "Believe on the Lord Jesus Christ," but he did *not* add "who died for *you.*" It is not until *after* we have truly believed, that we learn we are among that favored company for whom the incarnate Son shed His precious blood.

The Gospel declares that "Christ died for the ungodly" (Rom. 5:6), and that the most ungodly wretch there is out of Hell who repents and believes shall be saved. "This is a faithful saying, and worthy of all acceptation, that Christ Jesus came into the world to save *sinners*" (I Tim. 1:15), yea, even the "chief" of sinners. That great fact supplies a *warrant* to preach the Gospel unto all men, but it is only as the individual sinner *believes* on Christ it becomes known that Christ died for *him*. Thus, to preach the Gospel to every creature and call on them to believe and be saved, is quite consistent, for it is a Divinely-revealed truth that "whosoever believeth" *shall be* saved! Any man who experiences a difficulty in freely preaching the Gospel because he cannot announce that Christ died for every individual of the human race, does not clearly understand what the "Gospel" is. The Gospel message is that Christ died for the most guilty who repent and believe.

Nor is God guilty of the slightest deception in sending forth His servants to tender salvation to *all* sinners on the terms that they repent and believe, for He *is* true to His Word. He *does* save *every* sinner who complies with His terms; nor does He withhold His Spirit from any who truly desire Him to work in them a saving repentance and faith.

The ground on which a sinner is bidden to believe unto the saving of his soul is neither God's decree of election, nor that Christ died for him in particular, but the plain declaration of the Gospel itself, namely, "he that believeth and is baptized shall be saved" (Mark 16:16). It cannot be said too emphatically that the *only* warrant for personal faith in Christ which *any* man has, is that which the indiscriminate commands, invitations and promises of the *Gospel* hold forth. If we were assured of the absolute universality of redemption, or if we were permitted to read every name recorded in the Lamb's book of life, the case would be no plainer and more certain than it now is. The One who "cannot lie" most solemnly declares that "*whosoever* believeth" in His Son shall not perish, but have everlasting life. Christ Himself expressly announces, "him that cometh unto me I will in no wise cast out" (John 6:37). Any other warrant than this would be entirely inconsistent with the nature of *faith*: to demand it is sheer rebellion.

Neither God's sovereign foreordination of an elect company unto salvation, nor the limitation of Christ's atonement to that company, in anywise alters the fact or militates against the truth of the indiscriminate tender of pardon which is made by and through the Gospel. It is *every* man's duty *to* "repent and believe the Gospel." It is God's gracious purpose to receive and save *all* who do thus repent and believe. The proclamation which God is making through the Gospel is real and sincere. The reason why so many do not benefit from that proclamation and avail themselves of its proffered mercy, is their own wilful refusal of it. The door of Divine mercy stands *wide* open: over its portals stands written "whosoever will may come." If those invited insist upon making "excuse" then their blood is upon their own heads. Their very refusal to come to Christ that they "might have life" (John 5:40) only makes manifest the inveteracy of their sin, and will yet most fully justify the righteous judgment of God in the day to come—Psalm 51:4; Matthew 22:12; Romans 3:19.

"An indiscriminate offer of an interest in the Atonement has been made for two thousand years since Christ died. But remember that the same indiscriminate offer was made for four thousand years *before* He died! The offer then was that *if* men would 'believe' upon a Christ to be sacrificed hereafter they *should be* saved. Now, is it sense or nonsense to believe that at the end of those four thousand years Christ died for the purpose of saving those who had *already rejected* Him, and who had consequently gone to their own place? Would it not have met the precise case of all who lived on earth before His advent if He had promised them that at the end of time He would die to save all those who had previously believed? Would there have been any propriety in His promising to die also for those who had previously *rejected* His kind offers and been lost? As far as the design of the Atonement, the purpose to be attained by His death, is concerned, what conceivable difference does it make whether the sacrifice of Christ be offered at the beginning, the middle, or the end of human history? If He had died at the end, He certainly could not die for those who had previously rejected His offers and perished therefor. And since He did die in the middle, why may not the Gospel be offered on the same terms to all men, as well after as before His death?

"The only difficulty lies in the fact that finite creatures are utterly unable to comprehend the sovereign will and the unchangeable all-knowledge of God, which absolutely shuts out all contingency in relation to the hopes, the fears, the doubts, the responsibilities, the struggles, of human beings. Events are contingent in themselves. But there is no contingency in relation to the Divine purpose. One event is conditioned in the Divine decree. God's purpose, His design of redemption, like every other Divine purpose, is timeless. What has been and what will be, who have believed and who will believe, are all the same to Him. To Him the believers and the elect are identical. His design in the Atonement may with absolute indifference be stated either as a design to save the elect, or as a design to save all who have believed or who would believe on His Son" (A. A. Hodge).

"The preachers of the Gospel in their particular congregations, being utterly unacquainted with the purpose and secret counsel of God, being also forbidden to pry or search into it (Deut. 29:29) may from hence justifiably call upon every man to believe, with assurance of salvation to every one in particular upon his so doing, knowing and being fully persuaded of this, that there is enough in the death of Christ to save every one that shall so do; leaving the purpose and counsel of God, on whom He will bestow faith, and for whom in particular Christ died (even as they are commanded), to Himself" (J. Owen).

Nothing but confusion can disturb our minds if we fail to distinguish sharply between God's eternal purpose and man's present duty: the two things are quite distinct, and have *no* connection between them. The purpose or decree of God is *not* the rule of our duty, nor is the performance of our duty in doing what we are commanded any declaration of God's eternal counsels that it should be done. There is no sequel between the universal precepts of the Word and God's purpose in Himself concerning specific persons. The business of the preacher is to urge the fact that God "now commandeth all men every where to repent" (Acts 17:30), leaving it with the Spirit to work a saving repentance in whom He pleases. When I tell an individual sinner, "This is His command, that we should believe on the name of His Son Jesus Christ" (I John 3:23), I know not whether God has decreed to work a saving faith in him, nor is that any of my business; my duty is to discharge the commission Christ has given me, and the duty of my hearers is to comply with God's demands. God Himself will see to the accomplishment of His foreordination.

Coming now to a closer answer to the questions raised at the beginning of this chapter: the supreme business of God's servants is to preach *Christ*. Now to do this there must be a Scriptural setting forth of His glorious person, as the eternal Son, the Maker of heaven and earth. There must be an exposition of His two natures: His absolute Deity, His holy humanity. There must be an explanation of His offices: a Prophet to reveal the will of God, a Priest to offer Himself a sacrifice to God, a King to rule over the people of God. There must be a declaration of the two states in which He exercises His offices. First of humiliation: His condescension in becoming flesh, the reasons for this, and the glorious consequences of it. Second, His glorification: His exaltation to the right hand of God, His headship over the Church, His intercessory ministry. But supremely, there must be the preaching of His obedience to the law, His perfect righteousness, His vicarious death, the all-sufficiency of His merits to those who trust in Him.

"I determined not to know any thing among you, save Jesus Christ, and him crucified" (I Cor. 2:2). We are not only to open up the mystery of His person, the manifold glories of His many offices, the perfections of His character, but, above all, we are to expound the meaning of the Cross. It is only by dwelling much on the varied significations of Calvary that the truth can be fully told out, whether the sinfulness of man's sin, or the greatness of God's love. To illustrate the various aspects of the sacrificial work of the Redeemer, a close study needs to be given to and then a free use made of the Old Testament types.

But it is not sufficient to barely "preach" Christ, there must also be an *application* made of what is revealed in Scripture concerning Him to the use of God's people, that their hearts may be drawn out to Him, and that they may see their interest in Him. To "preach" is to *woo*. The servant of God is not only an advocate pleading his Master's cause, refuting the objections of opposers, but he also is a witness, telling out of his own experience the preciousness of Christ. Thus he is to attract, allure and win souls to Him. That which best fits any minister to "preach" Christ is to himself *walk* and commune *with Him!* A part of some of the typical sacrifices was reserved as a feast for the offerer and his friends. So we must teach the saints to look away from self to Christ, to *feed on* Him, to live by Him, to be occupied with His perfections.

Because men are by nature *opposed to* Christ, the servant of God must needs begin with *the Law,* so as to discover to them the dreadful state they are in. The claims of God upon us as His creatures must be pressed. The perfect and constant obedience which He requires from man must be clearly set forth. Then the utter failure of man to meet God's righteous claims upon him, and the exceeding sinfulness of his disobedience. A way must be made *for* the Gospel, by showing and convincing people that they are out of Christ, under the condemnation of a holy God, and of themselves utterly unable to liquidate their debts. The ministry of John the Baptist must precede that of Christ! The contents of Romans 1:18 to 3:20 must be stressed before the good news of Romans 3:21-26 is proclaimed. What need of a physician till we know we are sick? What need of a Saviour till we know we are lost? What need of Christ to cleanse till we see our filthy defilement?

At the outset, the preacher needs to recognize and realize that "The carnal mind is enmity against God" (Rom. 8:7). No arguments of his can overcome, no inducements melt the heart of stone. Paul may plant, and Apollos may water, but God only can give the "increase." Nothing short of the supernatural working of the Spirit can bring a sinner to Christ. Therefore both the preacher and his Christian hearers need to be much in prayer, *seeking* the Holy Spirit's grace and power to quicken, convict and convert the lost. We are fully assured that one principal reason why there are so few genuine conversions today, is because there is so little real and importunate praying unto God.

"We are to dwell largely on the being and perfections of God, and our original obligations to Him, who is by nature our Creator. We are particularly to explain the nature and reasonableness of the Divine law, and to answer the sinner's objections against it. We are to exhibit to his view the sin which he stands charged with in the Divine law, and the curse he is under for it, and the only way of obtaining pardon through the blood of Christ. In a word, we are to open to his view the whole plan of the Gospel, the infinite riches of God's grace, the nature and sufficiency of Christ's atonement, the readiness of God to forgive repenting sinners who come to Him in the name of Christ, the calls and invitations of the Gospel, the dreadfulness of eternal misery in the lake of fire and brimstone; the glory and blessedness of the heavenly state, the shortness and uncertainty of time, the worth of his soul, the dangers which attend him, from the world, the flesh and the devil, the inexcusable guilt of final impenitence," etc. (Jos. Bellamy, 1759).

It is most important for us to recognize and constantly bear in mind the fact that the Gospel is *addressed to* the sinner's *responsibility*. It is true from one viewpoint that the Gospel comes to men who are not on probation, but under God's condemnation, yet from another viewpoint (equally true) it is delivered to their accountability. It bids men to be reconciled to God (II Cor. 5:20), by which is meant, the throwing down of the weapons of their warfare against Him. It calls upon them to "forsake" their way and thoughts and return unto the Lord, and announces to all who do so that He will "have mercy upon" them (Isa. 55:7). It bids them "Repent and be converted," which means a right-about-face, a turning from sin and self-pleasing unto God, and this, in order that their "sins may be blotted out" (Acts 3:19). It commands all men to believe in Christ and receive Him as their Lord. It announces that failure to believe is adding sin to sin and increasing their condemnation (John 3:18).

The preaching of the Gospel is both a declaration of God's revealed will to pardon all who comply with its terms, and an insistence upon the duty devolving on all who hear it. The business of Christ's servants is to present what Scripture teaches concerning the salvation of men and the way which God has ordained in order to their obtaining of it. We are constantly to press the fact that God has inseparably connected salvation with repentance and faith. Many today are laboring under the delusion that the *only* relation between God and men is that of Creditor and debtors, and that Christ paid the whole debt, and therefore none are under any obligations of *duty*, and that *all* God now requires from any sinner is for him to believe that Christ *has* done all, and that faith is merely and simply a resting and relying in that fact. But such a concept is a fatal delusion, and grossly dishonoring to God.

The God of the New Testament is *not* another God from Him who is revealed in the Old Testament! God is there set forth as the Lawgiver, as the Ruler over all, requiring perfect conformity to His demands. Now those requirements of God were neither unjust nor tyrannical, but instead, righteous and merciful. Nor did Christ come here to abrogate the law, but rather to "magnify the law, and make it honorable" (Isa. 42: 21). And when the Holy Spirit begins a saving work in the soul, He presses the requirements of God's law, convicts of failure to meet those requirements, and produces a deep and lasting sorrow for such failure. Further, He creates in the heart which He renews a *love* for the law (Rom. 7:22) and a holy longing and determination to please and serve God. Thus, the work of the Spirit in those who are truly saved is *not* to the setting aside of that *duty* which every man owes to God — his Maker, Sustainer, and Governor — but is the imparting of a delight unto and power for the performance of that duty!

Thus the *first* duty of the evangelist is to call upon all men to *repent*: see Mark 1:15. This is his very commission from Christ: see Luke 24:47. It was thus that Peter (Acts 2:38; 3:19) and Paul evangelized: see Acts 17:30; 20:21. Our business is to show *why* God requires this repentance, namely, for us to acknowledge the righteousness of His claims upon us. Our business is to show *what* repentance consists of: see Proverbs 28:13; Acts 3:19; I Thessalonians 1:9; etc. Our business is to emphasize the fact that God never has and never will pardon any sinner until he *does* repent: see Leviticus 23:29; 26:40-42; I Kings 8:46-50; Psalm 32:3-5; Jeremiah 4:4; Ezekiel 18:30-32; Luke 5:32; 13:3; Acts 3:19; 11:18; II Corinthians 7:10.

The next great duty of the evangelist is to call on his hearers to "believe on the Lord Jesus Christ." That this call may be something much more than a mere *uttering* of the *word* "Believe"!, "Believe"! we must carefully define and explain *what* saving faith consists of. That it is, first, a sincere renunciation of all other ways and means of salvation: Acts 4:12. Second, that it is the free and full consent of the heart *to* God's way of salvation: Romans 10:9. Third, that it is a personal trusting in Christ and relying upon the sufficiency of His satisfaction unto God: Acts 16:31. Saving faith is more than a bare belief of the Truth. The dying Israelites might have been fully assured that a look at the brazen serpent would give healing, but until they *actually* "looked," in full confidence in God's promise, they had not benefited one whit!

None receive a soul-freeing discharge from the power and penalty of sin till they believe in Christ. Though the law of God has been satisfied and every demand of His justice met as to the sins of the elect, yet this has not hindered God from ascribing such a *way* for their coming to Him as is suited to the exalting of His glory and the honor of Christ. This the Spirit accomplishes by preparing the soul of the sinner for the enjoyment of God, and that, by the "law of faith." The *benefits* of Christ's death are only *applied* when we believe. The personal state of those for whom He shed His blood is not actually changed by His death itself, for they still lie under the curse whilst they are unregenerate (Eph. 2:3). That which Christ has procured for His own is left in the hands of the Father, for Him to bestow when He sees fit. Repentance and faith are necessary not to add anything to Christ's atonement, nor to merit forgiveness, but only to the actual *receiving* of it.

That which God calls the sinner to "believe" is *the Gospel*. The first act of faith does not consist in believing that Christ died for me, but that He died for *sinners*. Christ is presented as an Object of *faith*. The Gospel announces that the Lord Jesus stands ready to receive every sinner who will throw down the arms of his rebellion, and trust in Him alone for salvation. As I do this, and *am* saved by Him, I obtain clear evidence of my election unto salvation: John 6:37; II Thessalonians 2:13. The business of the preacher is *not* to "offer" Christ to sinners, but to "*preach*" Him, expounding the *doctrine* of the Gospel. Our duty is to give the general call; the Holy Spirit will see to its effectual application unto God's elect.

The Gospel is a Divine fan: by it the wheat is separated from the chaff. "The Gospel is addressed equally to the seed of the woman and the seed of the serpent. To the one it is the savor of life — to the other the savor of death; hence it is depicted as a two-edged sword, proceeding out of the Redeemer's mouth. It resembles the pillar interposed between the Egyptians and Israel: 'It was a cloud and darkness to them, but it gave light by night to these.' 'If our Gospel,' says the apostle, 'be hid, it is hidden to them that are lost'; if men receive not the atonement made upon Calvary, as the only ground of their hope — if they do not take shelter under the Saviour's wings, then 'there remaineth no more sacrifice for sins, but a certain fearful looking for of judgment and fiery indignation,' which shall devour them as the implacable enemies of God" (James Haldane).

While pressing on all their bounden *duty* to repent and believe, let not the servant of God be slack in plainly teaching that both repentance and faith are Divine *gifts*: Ephesians 2:8, 9; Acts 5:31. The natural man can no more savingly repent and believe than he can create a world: John 6:44. "We may as well melt a flint, or turn a stone to flesh, as repent in our own strength. It is far above the power of nature, nay, most contrary to it. How can we hate sin, which naturally we love above all? forsake that which is as dear as ourselves? it is the almighty power of Christ which only can do this: we must rely on, seek to Him for it: Jeremiah 31:18; Lamentations 5:21" (D. Clarkson, 1690).

Finally, let the servant of God see to it that his zeal in preaching the Gospel to the unsaved, does not cause him to withhold from "the children" their needed *bread*. The reprobate may vomit it out, but the regenerate will be nourished thereby. Every preacher is under bonds to see to it that, at the close of his pastorate he can say, "I have not shunned to declare unto you *all* the counsel of God" (Acts 20:27). Only by so doing will he fulfil his commission, preserve the balance of Truth, establish God's saints in the faith, and glorify his Master.

CHAPTER TWENTY-THREE

THE ATONEMENT — ITS RECEPTION

"What must I do to be saved?" is the earnest and urgent inquiry of one who has been truly awakened by the Holy Spirit and made to feel his lost condition and deserts of eternal punishment. Where such an inquiry is sincerely made, the comforting answer furnished by the Scripture is simple and plain: "Believe on the Lord Jesus Christ, and thou shalt be saved." Yet this does not mean that the preaching of the Gospel is an easy matter, for which every Christian is qualified. Far, far from it. From the Divine side, none but those called of God and supernaturally taught by Him are fitted for such a blessed and solemn task; from the human side, a life's constant study is required to prepare a servant of Christ for proclaiming His "unsearchable riches." Incalculable damage has been wrought by novices running into evangelical activities without being sent of God. To all such we would say, "O that ye would altogether hold your peace! and it should be your wisdom" (Job 13:5).

In the last chapter we sought to indicate, though in little more than outline form, something of what is comprehended by or included in the proclamation of the Atonement. Briefly stated it is this: an exposition and explanation of the teaching of Scripture concerning the wondrous person of the God-man, of His relation to the Church as Sponsor and Surety, of His varied offices, of His perfect work; freely setting Him forth as an all-sufficient Saviour, ready to receive any who truly feel their need of Him and who trust in Him. In this chapter our aim is to set forth how the virtue of His sacrifice actually becomes ours, in what way we are made the recipients of those priceless blessings which He purchased for His people. O may the Spirit so guide us into the Truth that we may be enabled to treat of this important section of our subject in such a way as to truly honor God, edify His people, and help exercise souls.

In taking up the *reception* of the Atonement two things need to be kept quite distinct and treated of separately, namely, the operation of the Spirit, and the act of the awakened sinner. Some of the older writers distinguished these two things by employing the terms, the *application* of the Atonement and the *appropriation* of it: probably we cannot improve upon them. The one speaks of the benefits of Christ's satisfaction being brought to those for whom it was made; the other, having reference to us laying hold of them and making them ours. It is much like the two-fold mention of the tabernacle's furniture in Exodus, or the order of the five great offerings in the opening chapter of Leviticus. God began with the "ark" (Ex. 25:10), then the "mercy-seat" (25:17), the "table" (25:23), the "candlestick" (25:31), and then the "brazen altar" (27:1); but it was the very opposite with Aaron (the representative of the people): he had to commence at the altar of sacrifice, and came last of all to the ark. So the *Divine* order of the offerings was the burnt, meat, peace, and the sin and trespass; but as *men* used them (according to their needs) they had to begin with the sin-offering.

The great Satisfaction or Atonement originated in the mind of God, and was formulated in the terms of the everlasting covenant, which was drawn up between the Father and the Mediator. It was accomplished here on earth by Christ, the incarnate Son, who by His perfect obedience and sufferings met every demand of the law and procured the eternal salvation for that people which had been given to Him and whose Sponsor He was. It is proclaimed and propounded in the Gospel, and is expounded by the true servants of the Lord Jesus. The particular aspect of this mighty theme which is now to engage our attention is, How is the Atonement made good to those for whom it was offered? Through what Divinely-appointed channel do the virtues of Christ's redemptive work actually reach the individual soul? In other words, what is required before a sinner today personally receives the saving benefits of that wondrous transaction which was consummated at the Cross almost two thousand years ago?

The answer which is now generally returned to this question is, that it is by means of *the Gospel* salvation is conveyed to the soul. But obviously *this* answer is quite inadequate, for the great majority of those who hear the glad tidings which are published by the servants of Christ, are not saved thereby. To some the Gospel is "a savour of life unto life," to others it is "a savour of death unto death." What, then, is it which makes the difference? To the Thessalonians Paul wrote, "For our Gospel came not unto you in word only, but also *in power,* and in the Holy Spirit, and in much assurance" (I Thess. 1:5). The reference here is to the gracious and invincible operations of the third Person of the Trinity. God the Father is the Author of our salvation; God the Son is the Purchaser of it; God the Spirit is the Conveyer.

The imperative need for the work of the Spirit in order to make effectual the Atonement unto the actual saving of sinners is little perceived in these degenerate times, even by professing Christians. That man is a fallen creature is still allowed in some circles, nor has the term "total depravity" entirely disappeared from present-day preaching; yet as to the terrible consequences which sin has wrought in the human constitution, scarcely any now have more than the vaguest conceptions. So long as a man obeys the laws of his country, discharges with measureable faithfulness his human obligations, and does not grossly defy the commandments of God, it is popularly assumed that there is little wrong with him. That his *heart* is desperately wicked, that his *mind* is filled with enmity against God, that his *will* is antagonistic to Him, that he is altogether unconscious of the deadly virus of sin which has corrupted every part of his inner being, and which has completely unfitted him for any communion with the thrice Holy One, is something which is altogether unknown to the vast majority of those now bearing the name of Christian.

The truth is that the natural man is *dead* in trespasses and sins. Because of this he is oblivious to the righteous claims of God upon him, and therefore knows not that in view of his failure to meet those claims the wrath of God abides upon him. Because there is no spiritual life within him, he has no *spiritual* relish of or appetite for Divine things, though he may (through religious education) have an intellectual and theoretical interest in them. Because the natural man is alienated from the life of God, he is completely under the dominion of sin, so that the pleasing of self (having his own way) is the governing principle of his whole life. Tell him that *he* is on his way to the everlasting burnings, and that they are his *just* due, and he believes it not. Either he thinks that he has done nothing which deserves such terrible punishment, or he supposes that he *has been* "delivered from the wrath to come." Having *no* spiritual perception, his understanding being "darkened" (Eph. 4:18), it is *impossible* that he *should* be conscious of his dreadful condition or see his dire need.

Only the Spirit of God can awaken any sinner from the sleep of death: only He can impart spiritual life to the soul, supernatural light to the understanding, and sight to the eyes of the heart. This is what He is sent to do. He is "the Servant" of the Godhead who is here *to bring in* "the poor, the maimed, the halt, and the blind." He is the One who has been given to "compel to come in" that the Father's House may be filled with the appointed guests (Luke 14:21,23). He compels by His sweet constraints, making the unwilling willing, creating in their heart a desire for the Feast, making them to be conscious of their deep need of the Bread of life. The Holy Spirit is the One who shines into the sin-darkened mind so that it is made conscious of its vileness. He is the One who so searches the conscience that the individual is made to feel he is the greatest sinner out of Hell. He is the One who subdues the principle of self-love and self-will, so that the soul is brought into subjection to God. He is the One who communicates faith, so that the heart is enabled to embrace Christ as a personal Lord and Saviour.

"The Holy Spirit is as indispensable to your believing, as is Christ in order to your being pardoned. The Holy Spirit's work is direct and powerful; and you will not rid yourself of your difficulties by trying to persuade yourself that His operations are all indirect, and merely those of a Teacher presenting truth to you. Salvation *for* the sinner is Christ's work; salvation *in* the sinner is the Spirit's work. Of this internal salvation He is the beginner and the ender. He works in you, in order to your believing, as truly as He works in you after you have believed.

"This doctrine, instead of being a discouragement, is one of unspeakable encouragement to the sinner; and he will acknowledge this, if he knows himself to be the thoroughly helpless being which the Bible says he is. If he is *not* totally depraved, he will feel the doctrine of the Spirit's work a hindrance, and an insult, no doubt, just as an able-bodied traveller would feel that you were both hindering and insulting him, if you told him that he cannot set out on his journey without taking your arm. But as, in that case, he will be able to save himself without much assistance, he might just set aside the Spirit altogether, and work his way to heaven alone! The truth is, that without the Spirit's direct and almighty help, there could be no hope for a totally depraved being at all . . .

"If you understand the genuine Gospel in all its freeness, you will feel that the man who tries to persuade you that you have strength enough left to do without the Spirit, is as great an enemy of the cross, and of your soul, as the man who wants to make you believe that you are not altogether guilty, but have some remaining goodness, and therefore do not need to be wholly indebted for pardon to the blood and righteousness of Immanuel. 'Without strength' is as literal a description of your state, as 'without goodness.' If you understand the Gospel, the consciousness of your total helplessness would just be the discovery that you are the very sinner to whom the great salvation is sent; that your inability was all foreseen and provided for, and that you are in the very position which needs, which calls for, and which shall receive, the aid of the Almighty Spirit.

"Till you feel yourself in this extremity of weakness, you are not in a condition (if I may say so) to receive the heavenly help. Your idea of remaining *ability* is the very thing that repels the help of the Spirit, just as any idea of remaining goodness thrusts away the propitiation of the Saviour. It is your *not seeing that you have no strength* that is keeping you from believing. So long as you think you have some strength, in *doing* something—and especially in performing, to your own and Satan's satisfaction, that great act or exercise of soul called 'faith.' But when you find out that you have no strength left you will, in blessed despair, cease to work—and (ere you are aware) — believe! For, if believing be not a ceasing from work, it is at least the necessary and immediate result of it. You expended your little stock of imagined strength in holding fast the ropes of self-righteousness, but now, when the conviction of having no strength at all is forced upon you, you drop into the arms of Jesus. But this you will never do so long as you fancy that you have strength to believe" (From *God's Way of Peace* by H. Bonar).

O that there were many preachers today honoring the third person of the Trinity by thus magnifying and emphasizing *His* part in the work of salvation. O that the modern evangelist would faithfully press upon his unsaved hearers their utter powerlessness to turn unto God of themselves, and their inability to receive Christ as their Lord and Saviour until a miracle of Divine grace has been wrought in them. The Lord Jesus (our Exemplar) did not hesitate to plainly say to a promiscuous crowd, "No man *can* come to me, except the Father which sent me draw him" (John 6:44). The Father draws to Christ by the operation of the Spirit. It is written, "Not by works of righteousness which we have done, but according to his mercy he saved us, *by* the washing of regeneration and renewing of *the Holy Spirit*" (Titus 3:5).

Believing is necessary, indispensably necessary, before any sinner receives Divine forgiveness. But Scripture is very emphatic in declaring that no sinner can savingly believe apart from the powerful operations of the Holy Spirit. A miracle of grace has to be wrought in his heart before he is capacitated to lay hold of Christ. This must be so, for the human heart is fast closed against Him and will not come to Him that it might have life (John 5:40). The eyes of our understanding are blind, so that we see in Christ no beauty that we should desire Him. It is with the heart that man believeth unto righteousness (Rom. 10:10), and the heart must first be wooed and won by Christ (through the Spirit's operations) before it will turn to Him. "The love of God is shed abroad in our hearts by the Holy Spirit" (Rom. 5:5). Until this takes place, the Lord has to say of us all, "I know you, that ye have not the love of God in you" (John 5:42).

In the application of the Atonement to the elect, each of

them is entirely passive. Until the Holy Spirit has performed His initial work of grace in the soul, not only is each individual utterly incapable of seeking after Christ (see Rom. 3:11), but he has no desire toward Him and no sense of his real need of Him. Not until he has been Divinely quickened and brought out of that grave into which the fall of Adam brought us all (Rom. 5:12), is any man capable of performing any spiritual actions. There cannot be the manifestations of life before life itself is imparted. A bitter fountain cannot send forth sweet waters, neither can a corrupt heart delight in a holy object. An evil tree cannot bring forth good fruit, neither can the unregenerate hate sin or love God. "It is the Spirit that quickeneth, the flesh profiteth nothing" (John 6:63).

For one who by sinful instinct loved and idolized self, making everything subservient to having his own way, to be brought to deny and loathe himself (Job 42:6), and to forsake his own ways (Isa. 55:7), is something which nothing short of Omnipotence can bring about. For one who naturally hates God (desiring rather to think about and be occupied with any one or any thing else) to be brought to love Him and delight in Him—love Him with all the heart and delight in Him supremely—is indeed a miracle of grace. Yet, let it be pointed out that true love to God is not begotten by fears of Hell nor by hopes of Heaven—the promptings of self-preservation will produce the one, as the workings of self-love will inspire the other. No, unless I love God for *what He is in Himself*, I do not love Him at all, but only lie to Him with my lips. Yet it is only the Spirit who can cause any soul to say from the heart, "Who is like unto thee, O Lord . . . glorious in holiness!" (Ex. 15:11)

Thus, each person of the Godhead is due His own particular praise. The Father for having chosen us in Christ before the foundation of the world, and predestinated us unto the adoption of children. The Son for having served as our Surety, fulfilled our obligations, and paid our debts. The Spirit for having brought us from death unto life, convicted us of our lost condition, awakened us to our need of Christ, and drawn us to Him. If the Father is to be adored because of His predestination, and the Son because of His propitiation, equally so is the Spirit for His regeneration. We are indebted to the One as much as to the Others. The work of Christ had been in vain, were it not for the work of the Spirit in us. "Thanks be unto God for his unspeakable gift" (II Cor. 9:15) applies as much to the Comforter as it does to the Redeemer.

The embracing of Christ by faith presupposes both a true knowledge of ourselves and of the Saviour Himself. There has to be a Divine conviction given to us of that sin and wretchedness, thraldom and bondage, unto which we are reduced by the Fall. The law must be our schoolmaster unto Christ. Without a discovery to us of sin and misery by the law, the sinner will never flee unto Him who is "the end of the law for righteousness" (Rom. 10:4). A man at sea sailing in a shattered boat close unto a great rock, will refuse to leave his boat and cast himself upon the rock for safety, so long as he believes his boat is strong enough to carry him to land. But when the winds and waves beat into his frail craft and break her in pieces, and not till then, will he be glad to avail himself of the rock. So while the poor sinner imagines that his own doings and good intentions are sufficient to carry him through to Heaven, he will never betake himself to the Rock of ages.

The powerful wind of the Spirit is needed to demolish that "refuge of lies" (Isa. 28:17) in which the sinner shelters, if ever he is to perceive that a continuing to rest upon his own fancied goodness and righteousness must inevitably sink him into Hell. Not until the Spirit strips him of his own worthless doings, and makes him to stand naked in all his shame and filthiness before God, will he truly cry, "What must I do to be saved?" As the apostle declared, "I was alive [in my own estimation] without the law once, but when the commandment came [when God applied it in power unto my understanding and conscience, and showed me how far short I came of its righteous demands] sin revived [I then had a real apprehension of the exceeding sinfulness of sin and of my utter unfitness to stand for a moment before the thrice holy God], and I died" — saw myself as utterly lost (Rom. 7:9).

Until the Spirit *does* press upon the soul the claims of God and its lifelong disregard of the same, until He applies to us that holy standard which bids us love God with all our heart, mind and strength, and our neighbor as ourself, and convicts us of the fact that not only have we made no honest attempt to do so, but have had no sincere *desire* to keep it, we are utterly blind to our dreadful sins of *omission*. Until the Spirit brings home to the heart our true state, notwithstanding all our selfish wishes to be delivered from Hell and taken to Heaven, yet the heart remains blind to the glory of God and what is due Him from us. So far from the unregenerate sinner being willing to repent of his sins, he knows nothing whatever about the worst of his sins. So far from desiring to humble himself before God, he is totally ignorant of the reason *why* he should humble himself. So far from being anxious to be made spiritually alive, he is quite oblivious to the fact that he is spiritually dead. And so far from seeking the gracious enablement of the Spirit to reconcile him to God, he is quite unaware that he is the enemy of God. But all of this is well-nigh wholly lost sight of today by preachers and evangelists. The general assumption is (even though it be not plainly formulated), there is so little wrong with the fallen descendants of Adam that all they need to do is read the Bible and hear the Gospel preached, and they will easily be turned to Christ. A little information, plus a little earnest persuasion, and almost anyone can be induced to sign a card and "accept Christ as his personal Saviour." Consequently, the humble, dependent, fervent, united and patient waiting upon God for the power of His Spirit is a thing of the past; and so too (with *very* rare exceptions) are *genuine* miracles of grace. This Laodicean age "has need of nothing" (Rev. 3:17), least of all does it feel its dire and desperate need of the Spirit of God to awaken the dead, to pull down strongholds and cast down every high thing that exalteth itself against the knowledge of God (II Cor. 10:4, 5).

Not until the sinner has been emptied of his self-sufficiency, convicted that he is an outlaw against God, and brought into the dust before Him, is he ready to appreciate Christ. Nor will he, nor can he, savingly embrace the Redeemer until the Spirit has revealed Christ *in* him. (Gal. 1:16). None can trust in a Saviour they know not; and to *know* Christ as a living reality is a vastly different thing from having heard about Him from the pulpit, or even to have read of Him through the

Scriptures. "For God who commanded the light to shine out of darkness hath shined in our hearts, to give the light of the knowledge of the glory of God in the face of Jesus Christ" (II Cor. 4:6): *this* is what *must* take place before any soul truly trusts Him. Have *you,* my reader, experienced this supernatural revelation of Christ to your *heart?* Once the Holy Spirit really reveals Christ to the soul, he needs no urging to receive Him: "They that *know* thy name *will* put their trust in thee" (Psa. 9:10).

Now it is not only the Spirit's province to apply the law, convict of sin, empty of pride, break down self-will, subdue self-love, but it is also His blessed office to take of the things of Christ and show them unto (John 16:14) those for whom He died. He is here to teach those whom He awakens from the sleep of spiritual death who the Redeemer is, the wondrous offices which He sustains, the great purpose for which He came into the world. He is here to slay their enmity against Christ, to destroy their unbelief, and to impart a saving faith. He is here to bring them into a saving knowledge of the truth: as the Lord Himself declared, "They shall be all taught of God. Every man therefore that hath heard, and *hath learned* of the Father [by the Spirit] cometh unto me" (John 6:45). The Spirit is here not to magnify Himself, but to glorify the Redeemer (John 16:14). He is here to reveal His lovely perfections unto God's elect, to win their hearts to Him, to conform them unto His blessed image.

Various motives have induced us to dwell at length upon the *application* of the Atonement as it is received by men. First, because *this* is the side of the Truth which most honors God, inasmuch as it gives to Him His proper place in the saving of sinners. Second, because of the appalling ignorance thereon which now so widely prevails. Third, so that the Christian reader may the better perceive *how much* he owes to the gracious operations of the Spirit. Fourth, to make clear to preachers and evangelists the urgent need of using the plough of the law *before* they attempt to sow the seed of the Gospel. It is of no avail to keep on saying to people "Believe on Christ" until you have employed that Scriptural material which the Spirit can use to convict souls of their *awful need of* Christ.

We turn now to consider, very briefly, the *appropriation* of the Atonement, or the sinner's own act in becoming a personal partaker of the saving virtues of Christ's satisfaction. As we showed in our last chapter, the Gospel is addressed to human responsibility: "This is a faithful saying, and worthy of all *acceptation,* that Christ Jesus came into the world to save sinners" (I Tim. 1:15). The business of God's servants is to preach and press the righteous demands of the Divine law, to call upon sinners to repent of their transgressions and turn from their wicked ways; to present Christ as a Saviour from the curse of the law, and bid their hearers lay down the weapons of their warfare against Him, and receive Him as their Lord and Saviour. Not until Christ is cordially received as Prophet, Priest and King, is forgiveness of sins to be obtained. As Prophet, to reveal to us the righteousness and grace of God. As Priest, who offered a sacrifice, the blood of which is sufficient to cleanse the foulest who trusts in it. As King, to rule over us.

The object or design in our first coming to Christ is to be saved by Him, to be saved *from self,* to be delivered from rebelling against God. He is the great Physician, and can allay the fever and cleanse the leprosy of sin. He who comes to Christ *without* a disposition to be *reconciled to* God, is only seeking deliverance from Hell, and does not desire that salvation which the Gospel proclaims, namely, deliverance from the power and condemnation of *sin.* Saving faith implies in its very nature both repentance and conversion, or a "turning to God from idols to serve the living and true God" (I Thess. 1:9).

A mediator must be accepted by *both* parties that are at variance, and each must stand to what He doth. God has declared Himself fully satisfied; it rests now with the individual sinner to also give the assent of *his* heart to Christ's dying in the stead of the ungodly and rest upon the sufficiency of His sacrifice. Saving faith is that act of the soul whereby one who is hopeless, helpless and lost in himself, does in a way of expectancy and trust seek for all help and relief in Christ alone. Faith is a going out of ourselves unto God in Christ, finding in Him all that we need for time and eternity. Faith is the one link between the sinner and the Sin-bearer. Faith is a receiving into our hearts the testimony of God concerning His Son, and a setting to our seal that He is true (John 3:33).

Should these lines be read by a sin-burdened soul, distressed by the plague of his own heart, and fearful that he or she has sinned beyond the hope of Divine pardon, we would point you to Him who is "mighty to save." Christ died not for righteous people, but for the ungodly (Rom. 5:6). He came here to save the *lost* (Luke 19:10). His promise is, "him that cometh to me I will in no wise cast out" (John 6:37). "He is able to save them to the uttermost that come unto God by him" (Heb. 7:25). Then look away from your ruined self, fly to Christ for refuge, trust in His precious blood and He will save you with an everlasting salvation.

CHAPTER TWENTY-FOUR

The Atonement — Its Rejection

All the race of Adam are guilty before God, and, consequently, none of them can by any works of their own find acceptance with Him. Almost every page of Scripture bears testimony to this truth. The whole scheme of revelation takes it for granted. The plan of salvation taught in the Word could have no place on any other supposition. The Son of man came here to save that which was *lost.* Were we not exposed to danger, there could be no salvation. When the Lord Jesus called Paul and sent him forth to preach to men, it was "to open their eyes," and "to turn them from darkness to light, and from the power of Satan unto God" (Acts 26:18). Here we have the character of the whole Gentile world: they are as ignorant of the true character of God and of the way of acceptance with Him, as blind men are ignorant of the real nature of the objects of sight. They walk, "In the vanity of their mind, having the understanding darkened, being alienated from the life of God through the ignorance that is in them, because of the blindness of their heart" (Eph. 4:17, 18).

That the world is guilty before God, is not only declared by Scripture, but is also to be seen by the present state of man with regard to happiness. It is obvious to any impartial observer that the human race is *miserable,* even amidst its mirth and dissipation. Men are *seeking* happiness (a proof that they do not *have* it) from the enjoyment of earthly things, according to their various tastes and appetites; but they find it not. From the highest to the lowest, there is that which *mars* their peace and enjoyment. The very things which the poor regard as evidences of the happiness of the rich, are but so many devices to drive away sorrow. If they would honestly express themselves, the millionaire in his mansion and the king on his throne would declare, "*all* is vanity and vexation of spirit." True happiness is to be found in God alone.

In such a state of guilt and misery is placed the whole human race. It is indeed a melancholy truth, but one which is altogether incontestible. Instead, then, of disputing the Divine testimony, let us inquire from the same authority, whether there be any way of escape. Is the fate of fallen men as hopeless as that of fallen angels? No, blessed be God, it is not. The same Word of Truth which tells of man's ruin, announces the Divine remedy; the same Book which describes human guilt and wretchedness, tells of a way of deliverance therefrom. The One, who, in the exercise of His high sovereignty, reserved the sinning angels in everlasting chains of darkness unto the judgment of the great day, has, in His abounding mercy, provided salvation for undone sinners of Adam's race.

The Divine way of salvation is the most stupendous monument of Divine wisdom and grace, of sovereignty and power, of justice and mercy, that ever was exhibited in this world. God has provided a Saviour, who, by His virtuous life and vicarious death, has made atonement for sin, by which all His people obtain eternal life. The whole scope of revelation, from the first intimation made in Eden (Gen. 3:15) to the end of the New Testament, bears witness to this marvelous and precious way of salvation. The Divine promises declared it, the types illustrated it, the prophets foretold it. When the Son of man was here, He announced that He "came to give His life a ransom for many" (Matt. 20:28): almost everyone knows that a "ransom" is a price paid for the recovery of anything that is lost to its original owner. The uniform teaching of the Epistles is, that "Christ Jesus came into this world to save sinners."

The Scriptures are both full and clear in making known the way in which guilty sinners are interested in the atonement of Christ. "Even the righteousness of God which is *by faith* of Jesus Christ unto all and upon all them that *believe*: for there is no difference; for all have sinned and come short of the glory of God; being justified freely by his grace through the redemption which is in Christ Jesus: whom God hath set forth to be a propitiation *through faith* in his blood, to declare his righteousness for the remission of sins that are past, through the forbearance of God; to declare at this time his righteousness: that he might be just, and the justifier of him which *believeth* in Jesus. Where is boasting then? It is excluded. By what law? of works? Nay: but by the law of *faith*" (Rom. 3: 22-27). In this passage the apostle not only establishes the guilt of man and the atonement of Christ, but also clearly asserts that *faith* is the medium through which sinners are interested in the work of Christ.

"But to him that *worketh not,* but believeth on him that justifieth the ungodly, his faith is counted for righteousness" (Rom. 4:5). Can any thing be more explicit? Can any thing be more directly to the point? Salvation must be given gratuitously, that no flesh may glory in God's presence. The "reward" of the man that "worketh," the apostle says, is *not* of "grace," but of "debt." It therefore follows that works of *no* kind whatever can give a title to the atonement of Christ or the favor of God.

But let it be said with emphasis that a saving reception of Christ's atonement is by *such* a faith which effectually changes the heart and the mind, so that the desires and pursuits of its recipient are entirely different than formerly. There has ever been a need to press this fact, for the enemies of the Gospel charge it as unfriendly to good works. But in these terrible days, when multitudes who profess to be saved by grace through the redemption of Christ, are giving the lie to their profession by continuing in a course of self-will and self-indulgence, the need for making clear this fact is doubly evident. Saving faith is that which "*purifieth* the heart" (Acts 15:9). "Therefore if any man be in Christ, he is a *new* creature: old things are passed away; behold, all things are become new" (II Cor. 5:17).

Formerly, the Christian sought for happiness in the pleasures, honors, or riches of this world; now he seeks it in those things which are above. He abhors the things in which he once delighted, and delights in what he once abhorred. "For I *delight* in the *law* of God" says the apostle, "after the inward man" (Rom. 7:22). Many things in the commandments of Jesus Christ are so disagreeable to flesh and blood, that they are (figuratively) called the cutting off of a right hand, or the plucking out of a right eye: yet the Christian not only acquiesces, but finds pleasure in yielding obedience to Christ in such things. True, he still has a corrupt nature to struggle against, yet his delight is decidedly in the law of his God. Saving faith is that which "overcometh the world" (I John 5:4). But we must now make a closer approach to our immediate theme.

The proclamation of mercy through the atonement of the incarnate Son of God is called the Gospel, or good news, because it announces deliverance from condemnation and eternal life to every believer. But it also necessarily implies and plainly denounces tidings of a very opposite nature to all who reject it, and in general to all the workers of iniquity. If it proclaims life to those who receive it, then death must be the portion of all who neglect it. This solemn fact is made prominent throughout the New Testament in the most awful and striking manner. Many are sheltering behind a profession of Christianity, and fondly hope that there is a sort of general impugnity in sin on account of the death of Christ; but all such are fatally deluded, for the Gospel denounces wrath against all who do not receive it, and against all evil-doers.

In the great commission which our Lord gave first to His apostles, He asserted as expressly that they who believed the Gospel shall be saved, as that they who believed it not shall be *damned* (Mark 16:16). What the Gospel is was shown in our last chapter, and Galatians 1:8 announces that any deviation from that Gospel, any substitution of another brings down the curse of Heaven upon the one who proclaims it, and by parity of reason, on those who accept it. What would be thought of this by those who pride themselves on their liberality of sentiment? who make the belief or rejection of the Truth a matter of trifling consideration? Here is the Truth, *God's* Truth: the rejection of the Gospel means the perdition in Hell of both soul and body forever.

"I am not ashamed of the gospel of Christ: for it is the power of God unto salvation to every one that believeth . . . for therein is the righteousness of God revealed from faith to faith . . . for the wrath of God is revealed from heaven against all ungodliness and unrighteousness of men" (Rom. 1:16-18). If the whole of these three verses be read attentively, it will be seen that the Gospel contains both a revelation of the "righteousness" of God and also of His "wrath." In like manner, the same chapter which tells us that "God so *loved* the world that he gave his only begotten Son, that whosoever believeth in him should not perish, but have everlasting life" (John 3:16), also declares, "He that believeth not the Son shall not see life, but the *wrath* of God abideth on him" (v. 36).

The condemnation of all who are ignorant of the true God and who reject the Gospel of Christ, is made known in II Thessalonians 1:7-9, "the Lord Jesus shall be revealed from heaven with his mighty angels, in flaming fire taking vengeance on them that know not God, and that obey not the Gospel of our Lord Jesus Christ: who shall be punished with everlasting destruction from the presence of the Lord, and from the glory of His power." This language is so terrible and decisive that nothing but the blindness and hardness of a depraved heart could defy it. To know God and receive His Son is "eternal life" (John 17:3), but to be ignorant of the true character of God and reject His Gospel entails eternal damnation.

"Therefore we ought to give the more earnest heed to the things which we have heard lest at any time we should let them slip. For if the word spoken by angels was stedfast, and every transgression and disobedience received a just recompense of reward: How shall we escape if we neglect so great salvation" (Heb. 2:1-3). Let those who trifle with their souls and refuse to seriously attend unto the Gospel, learn from this that God is in earnest in what He declares in the Scriptures. It seems incredible that people can hear and read unmoved the awful denunciations which the Word of Truth hurls against them. They surely cannot believe that such threatenings proceed from Him who cannot lie. Too late shall they discover that every word in them shall be faithfully executed.

Perhaps some are inclined to ask at this point, How can God justly punish men for rejecting a Saviour who never died *for them?* Many have regarded this as an insoluble problem; yet it is capable of a simple solution. First, let us duly attend to the plain and solemn declaration of Christ Himself: "He that believeth on him is not condemned; but he that believeth not is condemned already, because he hath not believed in the name of the only begotten Son of God" (John 3:18). Nothing could be plainer than that: if any find it difficult to fit that verse into their theology, then something is wrong with their theology — Christ is "despised *and rejected* of men."

It is quite true that every man lies under the condemnation of God before the Gospel first comes to him: the judgment for Adam's offense rests upon him (Rom. 5:12-19), to which is added the guilt of his own transgressions. But it is also true that *additional* guilt and condemnation comes to those who spurn the advances of Divine mercy made unto them through the Gospel. There are *degrees* of criminality, as there will be of punishment. Clear proof is furnished in those solemn words of Christ's: "And thou Capernaum, which art exalted unto heaven, shalt be brought down to hell . . . It shall be more tolerable for the land of Sodom in the day of judgment, than for thee" (Matt. 11:23, 24). So too, more tolerable shall it be in the Day of Judgment for the unevangelized section of Heathendom, than it will for multitudes in Christendom who refuse to obey the Gospel.

Christendom's sins are going to be punished (the more severely) for having scorned that glad tidings which was "worthy of (entitled to) all acceptation." And let us emphasize once more the fact that the Gospel message is *not* that Christ died for *me,* but that He died for *sinners.* The Gospel is addressed to human responsibility, and presents a Saviour who is ready to save all who will comply with its terms. If men will not come to Christ that they "might have life" (John 5:40), then their blood is upon their own heads. Therefore will God yet say to them, "Because I have called, and ye refused; I have stretched out my hand, and no man regarded; but ye have set at nought all my counsel, and would none of my reproof: I also will laugh at your calamity; I will mock when your fear cometh; when your fear cometh as desolation, and your destruction cometh as a whirlwind; when distress and anguish cometh upon you. Then they shall call upon me, but I will not answer; they shall seek me early, but they shall not find me: for that they hated knowledge, and *did not choose* the fear of the Lord" (Prov. 1:24-29).

The preaching of the Gospel unto men at large becomes a searching test of their state of heart. It *ought* to have a powerful influence upon them in breaking their hearts on account of sin. Why did the Son of God leave His heavenly glory and enter a life of unspeakable humiliation here on earth? Why did He suffer such frightful indignities at the hands of men, so that His face was spat upon, His hair plucked out, His back scourged? Why was He nailed to the Cross of woe, where His life's blood was poured out? The answer is, for *sin*. And can that be thought upon with any seriousness, and the heart not be broken before God? What will melt the hard heart of man and thaw it into godly sorrow for sin, if the contemplation of Christ's sacrifice will not do it?

O my readers, the shedding of the precious blood of Immanuel ought surely to melt the most adamant heart that is yet out of Hell. Would men but ponder the Saviour's passion, both in the character and degree of it, viewing its bitter ingredients and heightened circumstances, and then also consider that it was human transgressions which brought Him to Calvary, surely they would be far more deeply affected for sin than they now are. It is written, "they shall look upon me whom they have pierced" and *what* follows? This: "and they shall *mourn* for him as one mourneth for his only son, and shall be *in bitterness* for him" (Zech. 12:10). Ah, *that* is true penitence—a broken heart from viewing the broken body of Christ. What then must be the state, and what must be the punishment, of them concerning whom the Saviour has to ask, "Is it *nothing* to you, all ye that pass by? behold, and see if there be any sorrow like unto my sorrow" (Lam. 1:12).

Again; the proclamation of the Gospel and the serious consideration of the Saviour's sufferings ought to have a powerful effect in turning men *from sin.* Behold, my reader, the

Lord of glory dying as a sacrifice, making His soul "an offering for sin" (Isa. 53:10). Will you deliberately elect to continue living in that for which the Son of God died? Will you regard as a "sweet morsel" that which was more bitter than gall to the Beloved of the Father? God Himself *condemned* sin at the Cross (Rom. 8.3). Dare you, then, approve of it? O will you not condemn it too, repudiate it, turn from it in loathing, and seek grace from above to have nothing more to do with it? When you are tempted to sin, recall the bleeding wounds of the suffering Saviour. Nothing is more calculated to slay our love for sin than a contemplation of the awful wages which it paid to the Redeemer.

O what an indescribably dreadful state must they be in (as the writer and the Christian reader once were!) who turn a deaf ear to God's call through the Gospel, and in so doing "despise and reject" His Son! What a dreadful and unmistakable evidence is this that "the carnal mind *is* enmity against God" (Rom. 8:7)! Ah, that explains *why* it is that all men "make excuse" (Luke 14:18) when they are bid to come to the rich feast that Divine mercy has spread. It is not carelessness or indifference; no, the real root of the trouble lies much deeper: it is a desperately wicked heart (Jer. 17:9) which is opposed to the thrice holy God, that is the source of impenitence and unbelief. Men prefer material and temporal things to spiritual and eternal ones, the "pleasures of sin for a season" (Heb. 11:25), rather than those "pleasures for evermore" (Psa. 16:11) which are at God's right hand.

What has just been said above is no theoretical reasoning of ours, but the plain teaching of Christ Himself. After He had so solemnly declared, "he that believeth not is condemned already because he hath not believed in the name of the only begotten Son of God" (John 3:18), He at once (by way of explanation) added, "And this is the condemnation, that light is come into the world, and men loved darkness rather than light, because their deeds were evil. For every one that doeth evil hateth the light, neither cometh to the light, lest his deeds should be reproved" (vv. 19,20). No matter what (seemingly) plausible "excuses" men and women may make for their present rejection of the Gospel, He who cannot err insists that behind those excuses is a *love* of darkness (sin) and a *hatred* of the Light!

Let men say what they will with respect to their rejection of the Gospel, all their objections are founded in their disaffection to *truth and holiness*. They may claim to respect and believe God's Word, and that they want to be saved, or profess they *are* saved, but in truth they "hate the light because their deeds are evil." They will not part with their idols. They will not *forsake* that pleasant but Broad Road which leadeth to destruction. They will not *deny* "self," and submit to Christ as their *Lord*. They are willing to be saved their own way, but not God's. They wish to serve two masters, and make the best of both worlds. They may be good members of society, and be virtuous and pious, but the real language of their hearts is "we will *not* have this Man to *reign* over us" (Luke 19:14).

When people are told that they *despise* as well as "reject" Christ, they feel the charge is not true of them. When it is insisted upon that they *hate* Christ (John 15:18), they suppose the indictment is far too severe. Nay, they imagine they have a high estimate of Christ, that they sincerely own Him to be the most excellent One that has ever walked this earth, and that they are earnestly desirous of being saved by Him. But a "*deceived* heart has turned them aside" (Isa. 44:20). Had the Jewish nation been told one year before Christ began His public ministry that they would not only scorn Him, but put Him to death, would not *they* have indignantly denied such a charge? Most assuredly, they would. They would have answered: All our hopes center in Him, we are eagerly awaiting His promised advent, and shall gladly receive Him the moment He appears. And in so speaking, they would have been perfectly sincere. Yet God's infallible Word declares that Christ was the one "whom the nation *abhorreth*" (Isa. 49:7). And *why* did they? Because when He stood before them, He was *different* from what they expected.

Ah, my reader, in what has just been said above, we have the Divine explanation to the solemn situation which is confronting us today. History has repeated itself. The Jews would have willingly received a Messiah patterned after their own carnal desires. Had Christ presented Himself only as a Deliverer from their temporal troubles, gratified their fleshly lusts, and not interfered with *their* selfish plans, He had received a royal welcome from them. But for the *Holy* One of God they had no heart. For One who required repentance, for One who came to save them from the *present* dominion of sin, for One who demanded unqualified submission to God's will, for One who must be received as *Lord and Master,* they had no love. To forsake all and follow Him, suited them not. To abandon their idols, mortify the flesh, and enter the path of *obedience to* His commands and precepts, was altogether foreign to their every thought and desire.

And is it any different today? Not a whit. Present to men One who was filled with compassion for the suffering, who ministered to the needy, fed the poor, healed the sick, and, as a public Benefactor and Philanthropist, He is universally admired. Or, proclaim Him as a Deliverer from the wrath to come, as One who is willing to save from Hell and take to Heaven, and the movings of self-interest will induce multitudes to welcome Him as such. But, my reader, the Lord Jesus Christ cannot be *halved* in any such manner as this. He must be received just as He is, a *whole* Christ as the Scriptures present Him to us. As a Prophet to reveal God's will, and that, in order for us to walk therein. As a Priest to mediate, offering Himself as a sacrifice to God, presenting our sacrifices of praise to Him. As a King to occupy the throne of our hearts, to rule us by His precepts, to subdue our enemies. But *as such* the unregenerate see in Him no beauty that they should desire Him.

Thousands of professing Christians are willing to believe in Christ for salvation, but not to conform to Him in obedience. They desire the "rest" which He gives, but not His "yoke"— just as of old the multitudes sought Him for the loaves and fishes, yet had no heart for His searching teachings. People want the justification which the Gospel proclaims, but not the mortification of the old man which it enjoins. But this cannot be. In order to "come" to Christ, the sinner must turn from sin and all else that competes for his heart. The truth is that the vast majority of those now bearing His name love their worldly and fleshly lusts far more than they do Christ.

"Thus it is now with the carnal professors of the Gospel: because Christ answers not their expectation, they entertain prejudice against Him as represented in the Gospel, and are unwilling to come to Him. They want a Saviour that will let them live quietly in their sins, be indulgent to them in their fleshly courses, and yet bring them to heaven when they can live in sin no longer. But when the Gospel represents Christ as One who requires strictness and holiness in all of His followers, who calls for separation from the world in all that come to Him, who tells them they must suffer any evil rather than sin, and take up the cross if they will have Him for *their* Christ; when the Gospel offers One whom nothing will please but that holiness and strictness which the world derides; One whom persecutions and reproaches will attend all His followers; then prejudice seizes on their souls. Thus we see *why* so many will not come to Christ, and *who* they are" (D. Clarkson, 1680).

And "what shall the end be of them that *obey not* the Gospel of God?" (I Pet. 4:17). What *can* it be? What *must* be the portion of those who love darkness and hate the Light? Only one answer is possible. And Scripture does not leave us in ignorance thereof. "If they escaped not who refused Him that spake on earth, much more shall not we escape, if we turn away from Him that speaketh from Heaven" (Heb. 12:25). Escape they shall not. The Angel that hath a rainbow about His head, hath pillars of fire for His feet (Rev. 10:1) to consume them who refuse His peace. "He hath appointed a day, in the which He will judge the world in righteousness by that Man whom He hath ordained" (Acts 17:31). And in that Day He shall say, "But those mine enemies, which would not that I should reign over them, bring hither, and slay before me" (Luke 19:27).

Oh, my reader, if you value your soul at all, weigh thoroughly what has just been before you. Pass it not on to some one else, but take it home to thyself. Christ cannot be imposed upon, and soon it will be too late to undeceive yourself. "A diabolical life and a believing heart are contradictions. No man can with any reason lay claim to a faith in Christ who prefers the pleasures of the world before the sweetness of a Redeemer, that which is an offense to Him before that which is His delight. How can they believe in Christ that are carried down with the violent current of their own lusts, and regard not one tittle of His law? If faith be full of good works, then the lack of such clearly implies the absence of faith" (S. Charnock, 1680). May the Lord deign to add His blessing to these pages for His name's sake.

NOTES

NOTES

NOTES

NOTES

NOTES

NOTES

NOTES